QUASI-STELLAR OBJECTS

A Series of Books in Astronomy and Astrophysics

EDITORS: *Geoffrey Burbidge and Margaret Burbidge*

QUASI-STELLAR OBJECTS

Geoffrey Burbidge and Margaret Burbidge
UNIVERSITY OF CALIFORNIA, SAN DIEGO

 W. H. Freeman and Company
SAN FRANCISCO AND LONDON

PREFACE

Our knowledge of the universe is limited, and the wealth of natural phenomena on the universal scale that remain to be discovered by the passive method of observation is unparalleled in other fields of natural science. Every so often in astronomy observational discoveries burst upon us. The latest and most spectacular series of these has come through radio astronomy, which led first to the realization that explosive phenomena in stars, and hence remnants of supernovae, were important in our own galaxy; then to the discovery of radio galaxies; and most recently to the discovery of the quasi-stellar objects. Each of these observational phases has led, through rather simple theoretical arguments, to the conclusion that explosive phenomena on a very large scale are taking place in stars and galaxies.

Modern ideas about supernovae, which began with the detection of the first objects in external galaxies, have been much influenced by recent studies of the Crab Nebula and other remnants of galactic supernovae. Out of these studies has come the development of the old idea, first proposed in the 1930's, that the cosmic rays are produced by supernovae. Although it is clear that remnants of supernovae contain large amounts of high-energy particles, the way in which these particles were generated is not clear. It has been shown by Stirling Colgate and his collaborators that the actual explosion may generate a large flux of relativistic particles. Existing evidence suggests, however, that in the Crab Nebula particles are continuously being generated or accelerated, hundreds of years after the supernova exploded. This idea—that not only individual explosions in stars and galaxies are responsible for large releases of energy, but that activity goes on continuously—is an ever-present hint that we still understand very little of the real state of affairs.

With the discovery of the first radio galaxies and the realization by the mid-1950's that the synchrotron process is involved in them too, we became aware that very large amounts of energy must be present in them in the form of relativistic particles. Since 1956 the problem of explaining the origin of this energy and the mechanism by which it is released in this form has been attacked by many people, but no real understanding has been reached. Moreover, the way in which radio sources evolve in their characteristic double forms, and the origin of the magnetic fields, are still not understood. At the same time circumstantial evidence has accumulated that explosions frequently occur in galaxies.

In the midst of this ferment came the discovery of quasi-stellar radio sources—also through the methods of radio astronomy. As observations have accumulated it has become clearer and clearer that these are indeed a completely new class of object with no parallel in known astronomical phenomena. At first nearly everyone took the view that the very large redshifts in their spectra indicated that the objects were at cosmological distances, and on this basis their energetic properties have been a subject of intensive investigation. The idea that large masses are involved and that gravitational collapse might lead to very large releases of energy was proposed first to explain the occurrence of explosive events in radio galaxies. The work of Hoyle and Fowler on this came in 1963, just before the discovery of the first large redshifts of the quasi-stellar objects, and it looked as though the QSO's were the massive super-stars postulated by them. As we shall discuss in Chapter 18, however, it is now seen that this whole line of argument has its own difficulties, and at present the theoretical situation is not clear.

Because the QSO's vary in light and in radio flux over periods sometimes as short as days, and for other reasons, an alternative proposal has been made—that the objects are comparatively nearby although still outside our galaxy. Until recently it has been argued, almost without exception, that whatever the nature of the quasi-stellar objects, the redshifts are Doppler shifts. The reasons for this are discussed in Chapter 9. At the time of writing, however, there is a revival of interest in the idea that the redshifts may be gravitational in origin.

In view of the complexities and uncertainties in this field, one might ask whether it was a good idea to attempt to write a monograph at this time. Our first reason for doing this was a purely selfish one: we wished to collect together in a coherent fashion as much of the observational material as we could and see how it could be fitted together at this early stage. Having begun to do this in the spring of 1966 we thought that perhaps it might be worthwhile to add an account of the theoretical or semiempirical ideas on the nature of the QSO's together with our own critical evaluation of the state of affairs at present. Though the field is changing rapidly we thought that it might be useful to publish this account of things as they appear to us at the beginning of 1967. The book may have some interest in later years if only as a period piece written in the midst of new discovery and research. We are under no illusions that much of the discussion beyond the observational material will survive. The observations will remain to be added to. It will be seen from the discussion in the later chapters that there are so many conflicting ideas concerning theory and interpretation of the observations that at least 95 percent of them must indeed be wrong. But at present no one knows which 95 percent.

We have attempted to describe and interpret the ideas of many astronomers and physicists concerning what our 10-year-old daughter now describes as the crazy stellar objects. Among our friends who have made major contributions, and without whom the subject would not exist, are John Bahcall, W. A. Fowler, V. L. Ginzburg, F. Hoyle, Tom Kinman, Roger Lynds, Allan Sandage, Maarten Schmidt, and I. S. Shklovsky. They, and a host of others, have discovered, speculated, provoked, and argued with us about what is one of the most exciting topics in physics today. We are deeply grateful to all of them, and to many we have not mentioned by name, particularly the radio astronomers, who have been so generous in sending information in advance of publication. We are especially grateful to Dr. Roger Lynds of the Kitt Peak National Observatory, who has allowed us to reproduce some of his beautiful spectra. Finally, we wish to thank two people whose contributions have been indispensable—Mrs. Del Crowne, who prepared the diagrams and plates and helped greatly with the proofs and the index, and Mrs. Jean Fox, who typed the manuscript.

Geoffrey and Margaret Burbidge

La Jolla, California
February 1967

CONTENTS

QUASI-STELLAR OBJECTS

1

Introduction

One of the most remarkable observational discoveries of modern astronomy has been the identification of the quasi-stellar objects. These appear only as faint starlike images on photographic plates taken with the large telescopes, yet they are emitting enormous quantities of radio energy. The first name given to these strange astronomical objects was "quasi-stellar radio sources," shortened by some to "quasi-stellar sources," or "quasars." Then, as we shall see later, some starlike objects were found that are similar in all their optical properties to the quasi-stellar radio sources but do not emit any detectable radio energy. They have variously been described as quasi-stellar objects, blue stellar objects, quasi-stellar galaxies, and interlopers. To avoid confusion, we shall adopt the name "quasi-stellar objects" for all these objects, whether they are emitting radio energy or not.

Around 1950 the first reasonably accurate positions of radio sources were measured, and identifications began to be made with optically detected objects whose positions were known or could be accurately measured on photographic plates. During the last 10 or 15 years, radio astronomers have been compiling catalogues of increasing scope and accuracy. Since we shall be continually using the catalogue designations of these sources, it is appropriate here to describe the different numbering systems used.

Mills, Slee, and Hill in Australia prepared a catalogue of sources in the southern hemisphere, known as the MSH catalogue. The numbering system describes the position of the source: the first two numbers give the hour of its right ascension; this is followed first by a plus sign or a minus sign to denote the sign of its declination, and then by the tens digit of its declination in degrees. Finally, there is an italicized serial number arranged in order of increasing right ascension within the one-hour period. For example, MSH 14 − 12*1* denotes the 21st source in the 14-hour zone of right ascension, between −10° and −20° declination.

The radio astronomy group at Cambridge University prepared a series of catalogues, called 1C, 2C, 3C, 4C, and 5C. The 1C and 2C catalogues were superseded by the 3C, which is much more accurate, and there is a revised version of the 3C in which improvements to the 3C catalogue were made. In the 3C catalogue sources are merely numbered consecutively in order of increasing right ascension. Because most of the optical work on radio sources has been done in the northern hemisphere, 3C numbers are those most found in the literature. The newer Cambridge catalogues, the 4C and the 5C, go to the 3C catalogue were made. In the 3C catalogue, sources are than the 3C. Sources in the 4C catalogue have been arranged in lists in order of increasing right ascension, each list containing all sources observed in a 1° range of declination, with consecutive numbering within each list. Thus 4C 30.26 denotes the 26th source in the list covering declinations between 30° and 31°; it is identical with 3C 286.

Catalogues for both the northern and the southern hemisphere include sources that lie within a zone that extends into the other hemisphere, so there is some overlap. A catalogue of sources in the southern hemisphere has recently been compiled by Bolton and his colleagues in Australia. Their measurements were made at different frequencies from those used by Mills, Slee, and Hill, and they also included fainter sources. Because their work was done with the Parkes radio telescope, the catalogue is known as PKS, and the numbering gives the positions of the sources; the catalogue is arranged in order of increasing right ascension. The first two digits give the hour of the right ascension; the next two give the minutes of right ascension; and these are followed by the sign and the degrees of declination.

Lists of sources observed at the National Radio Astronomy Observatory (NRAO) and the Owens Valley Radio Observatory of the California Institute of Technology are both numbered in order of right ascension, with prefixes NRAO, and CTA or CTD (for the Owens Valley lists that contain QSO's). Sources discovered with the Arecibo radio telescope of the Cornell-Sydney Astronomy Center are numbered according to the system used in the Parkes catalogue, and are prefixed AO.

A catalogue is being prepared by the Italian radio astronomers at Bologna. The first part of this catalogue is denoted B1, and the numbering of sources follows the same scheme as that of the Parkes catalogue. Table 1.1 gives the frequencies used and the zones covered by these various catalogues, together with the lower limit of radio flux measured. The standard unit used in measuring radio fluxes—the "flux unit"—is 10^{-26} watts per square meter per cycle per second. The references in the literature are given at the end of this table.

In these various catalogues there are some radio sources whose positions are precisely determined, and many have been identified with optically detected objects visible on photographic plates. In fairly high galactic latitudes—well away from the equatorial plane of the galaxy—the sources are usually identified with external galaxies, some bright and some faint. Yet at some of the good radio positions, no obvious galaxy can be seen.

The first step in identifying such a radio source is to determine a very precise radio position. For sources that lie in the path traced by the moon during its passage across the sky, the method of lunar occultation—timing the instant at which the source disappears behind the edge of the moon and the instant at which it reappears—provides very accurate positions. This method has been used by Hazard and his colleagues, first in Australia and more recently at the Arecibo radio telescope in Puerto Rico. For sources that do not lie in the moon's path, observations with radio telescopes set up as interferometers can give positions that are not as accurate as those determined from occultation measurements but make identification feasible.

At a number of the good radio positions where no galaxy can be seen, there has been found a faint starlike object. The first to be discovered, by T. Matthews and A. Sandage at the Mount Wilson and Palomar Observatories and at the California Institute of Technology, was 3C 48, a stellar object of 16th magnitude; the announce-

Table 1.1

CATALOGUES OF RADIO SOURCES, WITH FREQUENCIES USED,
ZONES COVERED, AND LOWER FLUX LIMITS

Catalogue	Frequency (Mc/s)	Zone (declinations)	Lower Flux Limit $(10^{-26} Wm^{-2}(c/s)^{-1})$
MSH	85.5	$+10°$ to $-80°$	7
3C	159	$-22°$ to $+71°$	8
3C R	178	$-05°$ to $+90°$	9
PKS	$\begin{cases} 408 \\ 1410 \\ 2650 \end{cases}$	$+25°$ to $-90°$	$\begin{cases} 4 \\ 1 \\ 0.3 \end{cases}$
4C	178	$-07°$ to $+80°$	2
CTA	960	Approx. same as the 3C	3*
CTD	1421	$+24°$ to $+30°$	1.15
NRAO	$\begin{cases} 750 \\ 1400 \end{cases}$	Approx. same as the 3C	$\begin{cases} 0.5* \\ 0.4* \end{cases}$
Bl	408	to $+90°$	1

* Not complete to this flux level.

MSH Mills, B. Y., Slee, O. B., and Hill, E. R. 1958, Austr. J. Phys., **11**, 360.
———— 1960, Austr. J. Phys., **13**, 676.
———— 1961, Austr. J. Phys., **14**, 497.
3C Edge, D. O., Shakeshaft, J. R. McAdam, W. B., Baldwin, J. E., and Archer, S. 1959, Mem. Roy. Astr. Soc., **68**, 37.
3C R Bennett, A. S. 1962, Mem. Roy. Astr. Soc., **68**, 163.
PKS Bolton, J. G., Gardner, F. F., and Mackey, M. B. 1964, Austr. J. Phys., **17**, 340.
Price, R. M., and Milne, D. K. 1965, Austr. J. Phys., **18**, 329.
Day, G. A., Shimmins, A. J., Ekers, R. D., and Cole, D. J. 1966, Austr. J. Phys., **19**, 35.
Shimmins, A. J., Day, G. A., Ekers, R. D., and Cole, D. J. 1966, Austr. J. Phys., **19**, 837.
4C Pilkington, J. D. H., and Scott, P. F. 1965, Mem. Roy. Astr. Soc., **69**, 183.
Gower, J. F. R., Scott, P. F., and Wills, D. Mem. Roy. Astr. Soc., in press.
CTA Harris, D. E., and Roberts, J. A. 1960, Pub. Astr. Soc. Pacific, **72**, 237.
CTD Kellermann, K. I., and Read, R. B. 1965, Pub. Owens Valley Radio Obs., **1**, No. 2.
NRAO Pauliny-Toth, I. I. K., Wade, C. M., and Heeschen, D. S. 1966, Ap. J. Suppl., **13**, 65
Bl Braccesi, A., Ceccarelli, M., Fanti, R., Gelato, G., Giovannini, C., Harris, D., Rosatelli, C., Sinigaglia, G., and Volders, L.

ment of its stellar nature was made by Sandage, who reported the first optical observations at the 107th meeting of the American Astronomical Society in December 1960 (see *Sky and Telescope*, **21**, 148, 1961; see also Sandage, 1966e). Sandage, followed by a number of astronomers, both at Palomar and elsewhere, obtained spectra of 3C 48 and saw broad emission lines at wavelengths that did not correspond with features normally seen in the spectra of emission-line stars. Although the spectrum of the stellar object could not be understood, and consequently went unpublished, a few more QSO's were found and their brightnesses and colors measured; these will be described in Chapter 2.

With the measurement by the lunar occultation method of a precise position for the radio source 3C 273 (Hazard, Mackey, and Shimmins, 1963), the optical QSO 3C 273 was discovered. This was some three and a half magnitudes brighter than 3C 48, with a magnitude of 12.8, and it remains the brightest of the objects discovered so far. Schmidt (1963) then made a major breakthrough by identifying the broad emission lines that he measured in the spectrum of 3C 273 with lines in the Balmer series of hydrogen and a line of ionized magnesium at $\lambda_0 = 2798$ Å, shifted to longer wavelengths by a considerable factor. The shift—a *redshift* because it is toward longer wavelengths—is denoted by $z = \Delta\lambda/\lambda_0$, where $\Delta\lambda = \lambda - \lambda_0$, λ is the measured wavelength, and λ_0 is the laboratory wavelength. For 3C 273 Schmidt found $z = 0.158$; Hα ($\lambda_0 = 6563$ Å) was measured in the infrared with the same value of z by Oke (1963). Following this major development, Greenstein and Matthews (1963) were able to identify the spectroscopic features in 3C 48 and obtained a value of $z = 0.367$ for it. Between 1963 and 1966 a considerable number of QSO's were found through the radio positional identification method, and early in 1967 about 150 were known: these are listed in Table 1.2. This table gives the 1950 coordinates of the identified object (or a radio position if an optical position is not available); some objects have more accurately determined positions than others, and the accuracy is indicated by the number of figures given in each coordinate. The apparent visual magnitude m_v is listed next (approximate estimates from the Palomar Sky Survey prints are given in parentheses), followed by the redshift a, and the colors $B - V$ and $U - B$. The objects are listed in order of increasing right ascension α.

Early in 1965 Sandage and Véron, working on the identification problem, began to realize that a large population of QSO's that do not show detectable radio emission might be present (they were led to this conclusion by the accidental discovery of what Sandage called

Table 1.2

LIST OF QUASI-STELLAR OBJECTS

Object	α(1950)	δ(1950)	m_v	z	$B - V$	$U - B$
PHL 658	0ʰ 03ᵐ 25.4ˢ (radio)	+15° 53′ 10″	16.40	0.450	+0.11	−0.70
3C 2	0 03 48.70	−00 21 06.6	19.35	1.037	+0.79	−0.96
3C 9	0 17 49.83	+15 24 16.5	18.21	2.012	+0.23	−0.76
MSH 00 − 29	0 22 01	−29 45.5	(20)			
PHL 6638	0 44 35.3 (radio)	−07 22.0	17.72		+0.18	−0.69
PHL 923	0 56 31.7	−00 09 16	17.33	0.717	+0.20	−0.70
PKS 0056 − 17	0 56 36.8	−17 16 51	(17)	2.125		
PHL 938	0 58.2	+01 56	17.16	1.93	+0.32	−0.88
PKS 0106 + 01	1 06 04	+01 19.0	18.39	2.107	+0.15	−0.70
PKS 0114 + 07	1 14 49.7	+07 26.3	(18)			
AO 0118 + 03 (3C 39)	1 18 27.6	+03 28 19				
PKS 0119 − 04	1 19 55.8	−04 37 08	16.88	1.955	+0.46	−0.72
PKS 0122 − 00	1 22 55.5	−00 21 34	(16)	1.070		
3C 43	1 27 15.18	+23 22 52.0	(20.0)			
PHL 3375*	1 28.4	+07 28	18.02		+0.29	−0.51
PHL 1027*	1 30.5	+03 22	17.04		−0.03	−0.77
PHL 3424*	1 31.2	+05 32	18.25	1.847	+0.19	−0.90
3C 47	1 33 40.30	+20 42 16.0	18.1	0.425	+0.05	−0.65
PHL 1070*	1 34.8	+03 21	(17.6)			
3C 48	1 34 49.8	+32 54 20	16.2	0.367	+0.42	−0.58
PHL 1072*	1 35.2	+05 39	(18.3)			
PHL 1078	1 35 29.1 (radio)	−05 42.1	18.25	0.308	+0.04	−0.81
PHL 1093	1 37 22.9 (radio)	+01 16.3	17.07	0.260	+0.05	−1.02
PHL 1127*	1 41.5	+05 14	18.29	1.990	+0.14	−0.83
PHL 3740	1 44 14.9 (radio)	−05 54.2	18.61		+0.09	−0.65
PHL 1186*	1 47.6	+09 01	(18.6)			
PHL 1194*	1 48.7	+09 02	17.50	0.298	−0.07	−0.85
PHL 1222*	1 51.2	+04 48	17.63		+0.41	−0.78
PHL 1226*	1 51.8	+04 34	(18.2)			
3C 57	1 59 30.4	−11 47 00	16.40		+0.14	−0.73
PKS 0202 − 17	2 02 34.4	−17 15 37	(18)			
PHL 1305	2 26 21.6 (radio)	−03 54.3	16.96	2.065	+0.07	−0.82
PKS 0229 + 13	2 29 02.3	+13 09 42	(18)	2.07		
PHL 1377 = 4C − 4.6	2 32 36.4 (radio)	−04 16.9	16.46	1.436	+0.15	−0.89
PKS 0237 − 23	2 37 53.4	−23 22 05	16.63	2.223	+0.15	−0.61
PKS 0336 − 01	3 36 59.2	−01 56 19	18.41		+0.55	−0.82

* Object found in a selected field studied by Sandage and Luyten (1967).

Table 1.2, *continued*

LIST OF QUASI-STELLAR OBJECTS

Object	α(1950)			δ(1950)			m_v	z	$B - V$	$U - B$
3C 93	3^h	40^m	51.47^s	$+04°$	$48'$	$21.6''$	18.09		$+0.35$	-0.50
PKS 0347 + 13	3	47	14.0	$+13$	10	01	(19)			
MSH 03 − 19	3	49	09.5	-14	38	07	16.24	0.614	$+0.11$	-0.65
3C 94	3	50	04.1	-07	19	55	(17.5)	0.962		
PKS 0403 − 13	4	03	14.0	-13	16	16	(18)	0.571		
MSH 04 − 12	4	05	27.4	-12	19	34	(16)	0.574		
3C 119	4	29	07.84	$+41$	32	08.7	(>20.0)			
3C 138	5	18	16.5	$+16$	35	26	17.9	0.760	$+0.23$	-0.38
										(reddened).
3C 147	5	38	43.5	$+49$	49	43	16.9	0.545	$+0.35$	-0.59
PKS 0541 − 24	5	41	09.5	-24	22.7					
3C 172	6	59	04.5	$+25$	17	36	(17.2)			
3C 175	7	10	15.3	$+11$	51	30	(17.5)	0.768		
3C 175.1	7	11	14.3	$+14$	41	33	(18.0)			
3C 181	7	25	20.36	$+14$	43	47.2	18.92	1.382	$+0.43$	-1.02
PKS 0736 + 01	7	36	42.4	$+01$	43	57	(18)	0.191		
3C 186	7	40	56.67	$+38$	00	31.9	17.60	1.063	$+0.45$	-0.71
3C 190	7	58	44.1	$+14$	23	0	17.46		-0.20	-0.90
3C 191	8	02	03.78	$+10$	23	58.1	18.4	1.953	$+0.25$	-0.84
3C 196	8	09	59.4	$+48$	22	08	17.6	0.871	$+0.60$	-0.43
PKS 0812 + 02	8	12	47.2	$+02$	04	11	(17)	0.402		
PKS 0825 − 20	8	25	03.4	-20	16	31	18			
4C 37.24	8	27	55.0	$+37$	52	20	(18.2)	0.914		
3C 204	8	33	18.23	$+65$	24	05.9	18.21	1.112	$+0.55$	-0.99
3C 205	8	35	10.6	$+58$	04	46	(17.8)			
PKS 0837 − 12	8	37	27	-12	04.1		(17)	0.200		
3C 207	8	38	01.7	$+13$	23	05.4	18.15	0.684	$+0.43$	-0.42
3C 208	8	50	22.79	$+14$	03	58.3	17.42	1.110	$+0.34$	-1.00
PKS 0859 − 14	8	59	55	-14	03	37	(17.8)	1.327		
4C 22.22	9	01	56.5	$+22$	31	36	(19.0)			
3C 215	9	03	44.2	$+16$	58	16	18.27	0.411	$+0.21$	-0.66
3C 217	9	05	41.0	$+38$	00	27	18.50		$+0.25$	-0.86
3C 216	9	06	17.26	$+43$	05	59.0	18.48		$+0.49$	-0.60
PKS 0922 + 14	9	22	22.27	$+14$	57	26.2	17.96	0.895	$+0.54$	-0.52
4C 39.25	9	23	55.4	$+39$	15	24	(17.3)	0.699		
3C 230	9	49	25.5	$+00$	12	57	(17.5)			
3C 232 =										
Ton 469	9	54	31 (radio)	$+32$	37		15.78	0.534	$+0.10$	-0.68

Table 1.2, *continued*

LIST OF QUASI-STELLAR OBJECTS

Object		α(1950)			δ(1950)			m_v	z	$B - V$	$U - B$
AO 0952 + 17	9^h	52^m	11.92^s	+17°	57′	46.6″	(17.7)	1.471		
PKS 0957 + 00	9	57	43.84	+00	19	50.0	17.57	0.906	+0.47	−0.71
3C 239	10	08	37.5	+46	43	15	(17.5)			
3C 245	10	40	06.11	+12	19	15.1	17.25	1.029	+0.45	−0.83
PKS 1049 − 09	10	48	59.5	−09	02	12	16.79	0.344	+0.06	−0.49
3C 249.1	11	00	30.56	+77	15	08.1	15.72	0.311	−0.02	−0.77
3C 254	11	11	53.35	+40	53	42.0	17.98	0.734	+0.15	−0.49
PKS 1116 + 12	11	16	20.79	+12	51	06.3	19.25	2.118	+0.14	−0.76
PKS 1127 − 14	11	27	35.6	−14	32	57	16.90	1.187	+0.27	−0.70
3C 261	11	32	16.31	+30	22	1.0	18.24	0.614	+0.24	−0.56
PKS 1136 − 13	11	36	38.6	−13	34	09	(17)	0.55		
3C 263	11	37	09.38	+66	04	25.9	16.32	0.652	+0.18	−0.56
PKS 1148 − 00	11	48	10.2	−00	07	15	17.60	1.982	+0.17	−0.97
4C 31.38	11	53	44.4	+31	44	47	(19.4)	1.557		
3C 268.4	12	06	41.7	+43	56	05	18.42	1.400	+0.58	−0.69
PKS 1217 + 02	12	17	38.35	+02	20	20.9	16.53	0.240	+0.02	−0.87
3C 270.1	12	18	04.00	+33	59	50.0	18.61	1.519	+0.19	−0.61
4C 21.35	12	22	23.5	+21	39	27	(18.0)	0.434		
Ton 1530	12	22	57	+22	53		(16.8)	2.051		
3C 273	12	26	33.35	+02	19	42.0	12.8	0.158	+0.21	−0.85
PKS 1229 − 02	12	29	25.9	−02	07	31	16.75	0.388	+0.48	−0.66
PKS 1233 − 24	12	32	59.4	−24	55	46	(17)			
PKS 1237 − 10	12	37	07.3	−10	07	04	(18.2)			
3C 275.1	12	41	27.68	+16	39	18.7	19.00	0.557	+0.23	−0.43
BSO 1	12	46	29	+37	46	25	16.98	1.241	+0.31	−0.78
3C 277.1	12	50	15.31	+56	50	37.0	17.93	0.320	−0.17	−0.78
PKS 1252 + 11	12	52	07.86	+11	57	20.8	16.64	0.871	+0.35	−0.75
3C 279	12	53	35.94	−05	31	08.0	17.8	0.538	+0.26	−0.56
3C 280.1	12	58	14.15	+40	25	15.4	19.44	1.659	−0.13	−0.70
3C 281	13	05	22.52	+06	58	16.4	17.02		+0.13	−0.59
4C 22.38	13	24	29.9	+22	58	22	(18.9)			
PKS 1326 + 06	13	26	43	+06	56.4		(16)			
PKS 1327 − 21	13	27	23.2	−21	26	34	16.74	0.528	+0.10	−0.54
3C 287	13	28	16.12	+25	24	37.1	17.67	1.055	+0.63	−0.65
3C 286	13	28	49.74	+30	45	59.30	17.30	0.849	+0.22	−0.84
MSH 13 − 011	13	35	31.34	−06	11	57.4	17.68	0.625	+0.14	−0.66
3C 288.1	13	40	30.4	+60	36	55	18.12	0.961	+0.39	−0.82
PKS 1354 + 19	13	54	42.3	+19	33	41	16.02	0.720	+0.18	−0.55

Table 1.2, concluded

LIST OF QUASI-STELLAR OBJECTS

Object	α(1950)			δ(1950)			m_v	z	$B - V$	$U - B$
3C 298	14^h	16^m	38.59^s	+06°	42′	21″	16.79	1.439	+0.33	−0.70
4C 20.33	14	22	37.5	+20	13	49	(17.1)	0.871		
MSH 14 − 121	14	53	12.22	−10	56	39.9	17.37	0.940	+0.44	−0.76
PKS 1454 − 06	14	54	02.7	−06	05	45	18.0	1.249	+0.60	
3C 309.1	14	58	57.6	+71	52	19	16.78	0.904	+0 46	−0.77
PKS 1510 − 08	15	10	08.9	−08	54	48	16.52	0.361	+0.17	−0.74
PKS 1514 + 00	15	14	14.8	+00	26	01	(19)			
3C 323.1	15	45	31.2	+21	01	34	(15.8)	0.264		
MSH 16 + 03	16	03	39.5	+00	07	55	(18.0)			
Ton 256	16	12.0		+26	13		15.91	0.131	+0.57	−0.84
3C 334	16	18	07.40	+17	43	30.5	16.41	0.555	+0.12	−0.79
3C 336	16	22	32.45	+23	52	00.7	17.47	0.927	+0.44	−0.79
3C 345	16	41	17.70	+39	54	11.1	16−17.30	0.595	+0.29	−0.50
3C 351	17	04	03.58	+60	48	29.9	15.28	0.371	+0.13	−0.75
3C 380	18	28	13.38	+48	42	39.3	16.81	0.692	+0.24	−0.59
PKS 2115 − 30	21	15	11.1	−30	31	50	16.47		+0.49	−0.54
3C 432	21	20	25.64	+16	51	46.0	17.96	1.805	+0.22	−0.79
3C 435	21	26	37.6	+07	19	49	(19.5)			
PKS 2128 − 12	21	28	52.5	−12	20	19	15.98		+0.13	−0.67
PKS 2135 − 14	21	35	01.1	−14	46	27	15.53	0.200	+0.10	−0.83
PKS 2144 − 17	21	44	17.7	−17	54	05	(19.5)			
PKS 2145 + 06	21	45	35.9	+06	43	43	(17.5)			
PKS 2146 − 13	21	46	46.1	−13	18	24	(20)	1.800		
PKS 2154 − 18	21	54	12.5	−18	28.5		(16.5)			
PKS 2203 − 18	22	03	25.8	−18	50	16	(19)			
PKS 2216 − 03	22	16	16.3	−03	50	43	(17)	0.901		
3C 446	22	23	11.05	−05	12	17.0	18.39	1.403	+0.44	−0.90
PHL 5200	22	25	50.6	−05	30.6		(18.2)	1.981		
CTA 102	22	30	07.71	+11	28	22.8	17.32	1.037	+0.42	−0.79
3C 454	22	49	07.86	+18	32	46.6	18.40	1.757	+0.12	−0.95
3C 454.3	22	51	29.61	+15	52	53.6	16.10	0.859	+0.47	−0.66
PKS 2251 + 11	22	51	40.6	+11	20	39	15.82	0.323	+0.20	−0.84
4C 29.68 ≡										
CTD 141	23	25	41.3	+29	20	36	(17.3)	1.012		
PKS 2344 + 09	23	44	03.4	+09	14	04	15.97	0.677	+0.25	−0.60
PKS 2345 − 16	23	45	27.6	−16	47	50	(18)			
PKS 2354 + 14	23	54	44.7	+14	29	26	(18)	1.810		
PKS 2354 − 11	23	54	57.1	−11	42	23	(18)			

"interlopers," or blue stellar objects, on photographs that had been taken to identify objects associated with radio sources, but not at the radio positions). This work will be described in Chapter 2.

Schmidt (1964) has described the optical properties of the QSO's that make them unique:

1. Starlike objects identified with radio sources.

2. Variable light.

3. Large ultraviolet flux of radiation.

4. Broad emission lines in the spectra.

5. Large redshifts of the spectrum lines.

Bearing in mind the discoveries made since these criteria were established, we shall redefine the optical properties by modifying criteria 1 and 4. We replace 1 by

1a. Starlike objects *often* identified with radio sources.

This will take into account work discussed in Chapter 2 showing that there are objects that fulfill criteria 3 to 5 and may well fulfill 2 but are not detected as radio sources. Although few of these objects have so far been identified, they may exist in profusion. We replace 4 by

4a. Broad emission lines in the spectra, with absorption lines sometimes present.

This is to take account of the fact that there are now several QSO's known in whose spectra absorption lines have been measured and identified (see Chapter 3).

Probably related to the QSO's are objects that are not stellar but have variously been described as N-type galaxies (Matthews, Morgan, and Schmidt, 1964) and as blue compact galaxies (Zwicky, 1965). Some of these have fairly large redshifts, but not as large as those detected for the QSO's. Their spectra show some differences from those of the QSO's.

In the early chapters of this book we discuss the identification of QSO's, their line spectra and continuous energy distribution, their radio properties, and the time variations in the energy radiated by the QSO's. Next we give a brief account of attempts to measure proper motions of QSO's, followed by a discussion of their distribution in the sky.

After these mainly observational chapters, we consider the nature of the redshifts and give an account of the empirical models that have been proposed to explain the line spectra, the continuous energy distribution, and various correlations that have been found. The relation between properties of QSO's and the intergalactic medium is then discussed, as are the statistics of QSO's. In the final chapters of the book we deal with theories that have been put forward concerning the nature of the QSO's and their energy sources.

2

Identification of
Quasi-Stellar Objects

As we mentioned in the first chapter, the first radio source to be identified with a starlike object was 3C 48, and it was this identification that initiated the study of QSO's. As soon as the two 90-foot radio antennas working as an interferometer at the Owens Valley Radio Observatory were put into operation, a program was begun with the aim of determining precise positions of discrete radio sources. Although identifications of galaxies and remnants of supernovae in our galaxy had been possible before any very accurate radio positions were available, it was not possible to identify a source lying in an error rectangle of many minutes of arc with an inconspicuous optical object, such as a stellar image of 16th magnitude or fainter.

In 1960 the Owens Valley radio interferometer began producing accurate declination measurements of radio sources (Read, 1963). In previous surveys the errors in declination had been substantially larger than those in right ascension. There became available then some sources whose positions were known to an accuracy of about ±5″ in both coordinates. Some of these were found to have small radio angular diameters, which meant that they were of high radio surface brightness. Such sources were found by Maltby and Moffet (1962) with the two 90-foot antennas and by Allen, Anderson, Conway, Palmer, Reddish, and Ronson (1962) with the Jodrell Bank interferometer.

The identification of 3C 48 with the stellar object was made because there was no other object visible, on a plate taken with the 200-inch Palomar telescope, within the small error rectangle around

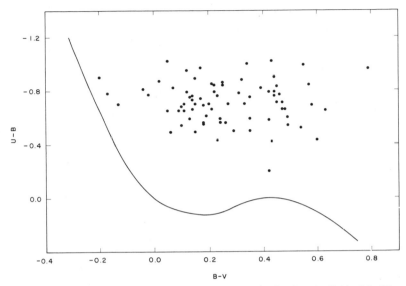

FIG. 2.1   *Two-color plot for all QSO's with measured colors in Table 1.2. The curve is the locus of normal unreddened galactic stars (highest temperature at upper left). The points are QSO's.*

the radio position. Further, 3C 48 was seen to be a not quite normal stellar object, because it had a faint wisp of nebulosity associated with it. Next, when Sandage measured the U, B, V colors of the object he found it to be unlike a normal main-sequence star. It has the values $B - V = 0.38$ and $U - B = -0.61$, which means that it emits a considerable excess of ultraviolet radiation, and lies well above the locus of main-sequence stars in Figure 2.1, up in the region where some white dwarfs, old novae, and related highly evolved stars lie. Finally, Sandage found that its spectrum showed broad emission features that did not correspond with those seen in the spectrum of any known galactic star.

It was the identification of 3C 273 in early 1963 that led to the next major advance. An accurate radio position was the key to the identification of 3C 273. Hazard, Mackey, and Shimmins (1963) measured its position by lunar occultation with the Parkes 210-foot radio telescope. As in 3C 48, the source has a small angular diameter and a high surface radio brightness. For this source the lunar occultation method yielded a position with an accuracy better than 1″, and showed that the radio source was double, with a separation of 19″.5, each component being less than 10″ in diameter. Hazard and his colleagues noted that the position of component B coincided with that of a stellar object of 13th magnitude. With the accurate radio position for the complex source, Schmidt (1963) definitely identified the stellar object noted by Hazard et al. (1963) as component B of the radio source, and noted that, like 3C 48, it had some nebulosity associated with it; but here, however, the nebulosity extended in the form of a faint jet, from component B toward component A, with component A lying at the end of the visible jet.

This object also proved to have U,B,V colors like those of 3C 48, and broad emission lines in its spectrum, which, as we shall see in Chapter 3, were identified by Schmidt.

Of the properties of 3C 48 and 3C 273 (small radio diameter, starlike object, excess of ultraviolet in the optical radiation, and peculiar emission-line spectrum) it is the excess of ultraviolet that has proved particularly valuable in identifying QSO's once accurate radio positions are available. Sources identified with stellar objects in the same period were 3C 196 and 3C 286 (Matthews and Sandage, 1963).* Like 3C 48 and 3C 273 these have small diameters and high radio surface brightnesses, and Sandage and Matthews noted that the only object lying within the error rectangle around the radio position was, in each case, a stellar object of 17th magnitude. A wisp of nebulosity is associated with the stellar object identified as 3C 196, but none has been found associated with 3C 286. The U,B,V colors were measured, and the stellar objects lie in the same region in which 3C 48 lies in the 2-color diagram.

---

* As is often true in a period of rapid discoveries, it is not possible to put the advances in chronological order by directly using the dates on references. Matthews and Sandage gave the fundamental optical identifications and data on 3C 48, 3C 196 and 3C 286 in the paper referred to, which was completed in 1962. At that time they believed, as did their colleagues, that these objects were likely to be galactic stars, and they analyzed their results on this assumption. The discovery of 3C 273 came while their paper was in press, and thus they added a note in proof concerning the extragalactic nature of these objects.

Griffin (1963) published a list of positions of optical objects found close to 42 radio sources with fairly small angular diameters and accurate radio positions. In addition to 3C 48, 3C 196, and 3C 286, this list included stellar objects at the positions of 3C 147 and 3C 298, which were later proved to be QSO's. No wisps of nebulosity were found around these objects, and in fact nebulosity is absent in the majority of QSO's now known and has not proved to be of great use in making identifications after the first few cases. The U,B,V colors of 3C 147 and 3C 298 were not measured at that time; Griffin's identifications were made solely on the basis of a starlike object being the only image seen within the error rectangle around an accurate radio position.

Hazard, Mackey, and Nicholson (1964) obtained very accurate radio positions of additional radio sources by the lunar occultation method, and suggested optical identifications for them; of these, 3C 245 and MSH $14 - 121$ were later proved, on the basis of photometry and spectroscopy, to be QSO's, as Hazard et al. (1964) had suggested, and 3C 39 (AO 0118 + 03) is also probably a QSO. Here again, accurate radio positions (in these cases, extremely accurate) were the sole basis for the identifications.

Because Sandage had discovered that unusual colors, that is, excesses of ultraviolet radiation, were characteristic of at least three QSO's, he determined to make use of this property in a search for new identifications. The revised version of the 3C catalogue (Bennett, 1962) had been published, and out of this list Clarke (1964) had chosen 88 sources of small angular diameter for the determination of radio positions of greater accuracy, using the 178 Mc/s interferometer at Cambridge. Ryle and Sandage (1964) made use of an optical search conducted by Longair (which they saw before publication in 1965) for objects in the fields of these 88 sources; Longair had found that starlike objects lay close to the radio positions of four of these sources.

Using the 100-inch Mt. Wilson telescope Sandage made two successive exposures on photographs taken on blue-sensitive emulsion, one through a blue filter and one through an ultraviolet filter, with the telescope displaced slightly between the two exposures. With the correct choice of exposure times, normal stars showed approximately equal images, but objects emitting an excess of ultraviolet could be easily distinguished on the plates by their relatively bright ultraviolet images. Such objects, found near radio positions, would very likely be QSO's.

By this method, Ryle and Sandage identified three new QSO's: 3C 9, 3C 216, and 3C 245. As we have already seen, 3C 245 was independently identified by Hazard et al. (1964). Accurate photometric measurements showed that all three objects had large negative values of $U - B$. Two of the objects, 3C 9 and 3C 245, were among those that Longair (1965) suggested might be QSO's on the basis of radio positions alone.

The next QSO to be identified was 3C 47 (Schmidt and Matthews, 1964), on the basis of an accurate radio position that coincided with an 18th-magnitude stellar object that appeared to be rather blue on comparison of the red and blue Palomar Sky Survey prints. It was confirmed as a QSO by its spectrum, which showed the characteristic, broad, redshifted emission lines; 3C 147, identified by Griffin (1963), was confirmed in the same way.

Adgie (1964) identified 3C 254 as a QSO using a radio position determined with the Royal Radar Establishment interferometer at Malvern. This radio position was more accurate than the earlier position determined at Owens Valley and enabled him to make use of Griffin's optically measured positions of objects in the fields of radio sources to pick the stellar object that coincided with the radio source.

We may take stock now of the kinds of measurements used in making identifications of QSO's:

1. Most important of all, an accurate radio position is needed. The most unequivocally accurate are those obtained from lunar occultations. Next in terms of accuracy are the positions obtained with the various radio interferometers that we have mentioned. To these we may now add the positions determined with the large steerable paraboloids at Parkes and the National Radio Astronomy Observatory. Several of the identifications described so far were made on the basis of a radio position alone.

2. Measurements of the radio brightness distribution are useful. The QSO's frequently have rather small radio angular diameters,

although the sources are sometimes resolved and found to be complex.

3. The peculiar U,B,V colors of QSO's enable them to be found by means of searches for objects with excess ultraviolet radiation. The best observations are direct photometric measurements, or those of the sort made by Ryle and Sandage, with double exposures through blue and ultraviolet filters. Failing such specially made observations, one can search the Palomar Sky Survey plates or prints for unusually blue stellar objects near radio positions. This method has now been extensively used, but it can lead to mistaken identifications, since a star that appears stronger on the blue print does not necessarily lie in the region of the two-color plot occupied by the QSO's—it might well be a normal high-temperature main-sequence star.

4. A spectrum taken of a suspected QSO will usually settle the question of its identification. The presence of broad emission lines that do not correspond to those seen at unredshifted wavelengths in hot evolved or main-sequence stars has always been proof that the object is a QSO. Sometimes, however, an object shows no spectral features at all (e.g., 3C 93), in which case its nature remains in doubt. The presence of spectral features seen in normal stars (e.g., absorption lines of ionized calcium, hydrogen absorption or emission lines) at unredshifted positions is taken as indicating that the suggested identification is wrong and the object is a galactic star. There are several radio sources for which identifications as QSO's have been suggested, but

Objects Once Identified in the Literature as Possible QSO's but Whose Spectra Have Since Shown Them to Be Galactic Stars (Collected from All Observers of QSO Spectra)

3C 36	3C 247	3C 435.1
PKS 0132 + 07	3C 289	PKS 2154 − 18
3C 68.2	PKS 1425 − 01	3C 437*
PKS 0251 + 18	3C 403*	3C 438*
Ton 883 (near 4C 34.27)	3C 411*	PKS 2338 − 16

* These objects are listed as possible QSO's by Wyndham (1965); in his later publication (Wyndham, 1966a) he has deleted them as possible QSO's.

when spectra were obtained, these were seen to be incorrect. We have listed (p. 17) all those we have been able to collect from various observers of spectra of QSO's.

5. Finally, we mention another type of measurement that may help in the identification of QSO's: a search for light variations. As will be discussed in Chapter 6, the optical radiation of QSO's is found characteristically to be variable. Consequently, if an observer is setting out to obtain the spectrum of a suggested QSO for which an apparent magnitude has been estimated from the Palomar Sky Atlas prints, and if he finds from visual inspection of the object in relation to neighboring stars that it is noticeably brighter or fainter than it is on the Sky Atlas, then he may feel fairly confident that the identification is good and that in obtaining a spectrum he will not be wasting his time.

To return to the lists of identifications that have been made: Sandage and Wyndham (1965) identified 11 more QSO's by means of positional agreement between a stellar object and a radio source together with either two-color photographic plates showing that the stellar object had an ultraviolet excess or the observation that the stellar object appeared stronger on the blue Palomar Atlas plate than on the red. Photoelectric U,B,V measurements for five objects confirmed that they lie in the region of the two-color plot occupied by the QSO's.

Later in 1965 the number of identified QSO's rapidly increased. Wyndham (1965) published the results of a search for optical identifications of 50 radio sources, several of which he suggested might be QSO's. Sandage, Véron, and Wyndham (1965) identified 21 new QSO's. A paper on the optical identification of all the sources in the revised 3C catalogue by Wyndham (1966a) suggested some new QSO identifications.

In 1965 and 1966, new catalogues of radio sources were becoming available, notably the Parkes catalogue, the Cambridge 4C catalogue, and the NRAO catalogue (Pauliny-Toth, Wade, and Heeschen, 1966), thus providing scope for many more identifications. The radio positions in the Parkes catalogue are accurate to about 1' in both coordinates, and Bolton and his colleagues have identified possible

QSO's by comparing the radio positions with the positions of nearby objects found on the Palomar Sky Survey prints to be blue and stellar. The results have been published in a series of papers by Bolton, Clarke, Sandage, and Véron (1965); Bolton, Clarke, and Ekers (1965); Ekers and Bolton (1965); Bolton and Ekers (1966a, 1966b, 1966c); and Clarke, Bolton, and Shimmins (1966). Between declinations $-20°$ and $+20°$ some 80 possible QSO's in the Parkes catalogue have been listed; optical confirmation by U,B,V photometry and spectroscopic observations has been made for more than half of these (Bolton, Clarke, Sandage, and Véron, 1965; Bolton, Shimmins, Ekers, Kinman, Lamla, and Wirtanen, 1966; Bolton and Kinman, 1966; Kinman, Bolton, Clarke, and Sandage, 1967).

Most of the identifications of Parkes radio sources with QSO's have been made by using the Palomar Sky Survey red and blue prints. Thus the zones covered by the catalogue have been searched only down to a declination of $-33°$, where the Palomar Atlas stops. Special plates were taken by Bolton with the 48-inch Palomar Schmidt telescope to extend the coverage to $-45°$, but because these plates were taken only in the red, only galaxies could be identified on them. It will be a lengthy job to photograph the southern radio source positions with existing telescopes in the southern hemisphere; two-color photographs should systematically be taken at all the radio positions.

The first two sections of the Cambridge 4C catalogue are now available (Pilkington and Scott, 1965; Gower, Scott, and Wills, 1966), and some lists of identifications of QSO's have been put out (Wyndham, 1966b; Scheuer and Wills, 1966; Wills, 1966). Of the eight identifications suggested by Wyndham, six have been confirmed spectroscopically.

Hazard, Gulkis, and Bray (1967) suggested that four very faint objects at the positions of weak radio sources of small angular diameter, which they had measured with the Arecibo radio telescope by means of lunar occultations, were QSO's. One of these, AO $0952 + 17$, has been confirmed and its redshift determined (AO stands for "Arecibo occultation").

New, highly accurate radio positions are becoming available, in addition to those obtained from measurements of lunar occultations, from work with the NRAO interferometer at Greenbank, the RRE interferometer at Malvern, and the one-mile interferometer of the Mullard RAO at Cambridge. Blue stellar objects lying within a few seconds of arc of positions as accurate as these have a high probability of being QSO's.

As can be seen from Table 1.2 the apparent magnitudes of the majority of QSO's so far identified lie in the range 16–19.

We turn now to the question of identifying radio-quiet QSO's (called variously blue stellar objects (BSO's), interlopers, and quasi-stellar galaxies by Sandage). We have described the method of identifying stellar objects at good radio positions by making two exposures on blue-sensitive emulsion, one through a blue and one through an ultraviolet filter. In applying this method Sandage, using the 100-inch Mt. Wilson telescope, and Lynds, using the 84-inch Kitt Peak telescope, both found that there were sometimes ultraviolet objects on their plates that did not lie close to the radio positions. When Sandage began taking photographs in ultraviolet and in blue light with the 48-inch Palomar Schmidt telescope, he found such objects turning up with a frequency of about three per square degree to a limiting magnitude $B \approx 18^m.5$. He realized that these objects were probably of the same type as those found in previous surveys made in high galactic latitudes by Humason, Zwicky, Luyten, Iriarte, Chavira, Haro, Feige, and others. The relevant references are listed by Sandage (1965): of particular importance is the list compiled by Haro and Luyten from photographs taken with the Palomar 48-inch Schmidt telescope; in this list the objects are given a number prefixed by PHL (for Palomar-Haro-Luyten). These earlier surveys had yielded a frequency of about four ultraviolet objects per square degree to a limiting magnitude $B \approx 19^m.0$.

Sandage constructed a 2-color plot for all the objects for which U,B,V photometry was available and divided the objects into two groups, those brighter and those fainter than $V = 14^m.50$. The brighter objects clearly lay mostly in the region occupied by the normal stars of luminosity classes III to V with temperatures of about 8000° and higher. Some lay in the region occupied by the metal-deficient stars belonging to the old halo population of our galaxy. Very few lay in the region occupied by the QSO's.

The situation was quite different for ultraviolet objects fainter than $V = 14^m.50$. Although some were clearly normal high-temperature or metal-deficient stars, the majority lay well above the normal sequence, right in the region occupied by the QSO's.

Sandage next looked at the frequency of such objects as a function of apparent magnitude. Suppose one plots log $N(m)$ against m, where m is the apparent magnitude and $N(m)$ is the number of objects brighter than magnitude m. For any uniform distribution of objects (or any mixture of objects of different brightnesses, provided that they are uniformly distributed) such a plot will give a straight line of slope 0.6. This comes about because the number N of objects brighter than apparent luminosity L varies as $N \propto L^{-3/2}$ or log $N = k - \frac{3}{2}$ log L. Converting luminosity L to magnitude m, we get

$$\log N = k + 0.6 \log m.$$

Sandage had seen from the 2-color diagram for objects brighter than magnitude 14.5 that most of these were galactic stars. Galactic stars are not distributed uniformly; their space density decreases away from the galactic plane. Consequently, one would expect the plot of log $N(m)$ against m here to have a slope less than 0.6, and Sandage found that indeed this was so. But at about $m = 15$ the slope changed abruptly, not to a value of 0.6 but to a value of 0.383. Sandage deduced that he was encountering a different type of object here; in fact, he concluded that the majority of the objects fainter than 15th magnitude were extragalactic, and had such large redshifts that cosmological effects must account for the slope being almost 0.4 rather than 0.6. Thus very large redshifts ($z > 1$) would be expected for all of these objects.

Spectra of six objects were taken to check the hypothesis. One turned out to be a galactic star; two had continuous spectra with no visible emission or absorption features, and their nature remained in doubt; and three proved to be extragalactic. One of the last group can actually be seen on the Palomar Sky Survey prints to have a measurable diameter and is thus not a QSO; its spectrum showed a rather small redshift. But the other two had definitely stellar images, and the spectrum of one of these was indistinguishable from the spectra of radio QSO's and had a large redshift; this was called BSO 1, and it is included in Tables 1.2 and 3.1. The other had a similar spectrum and a smaller redshift; it is Ton 256 (Ton = Tonanzintla) and is also included in Tables 1.2 and 3.1.

The conclusion then drawn by Sandage was that virtually all high-latitude blue stellar objects fainter than 15th magnitude are radio-quiet QSO's.* This meant that, with a frequency of four per square degree, these objects should be 500 times more numerous, spatially, than the QSO's identified with radio sources. The validity of this conclusion hinges on Sandage's interpretation of the plot of log $N(m)$ againt m; alternative interpretations were given almost immediately by Kinman (1965) and by Lynds and Villere (1965).

We must conclude from the break in slope of the plot of log $N(m)$ against m that the fainter objects are a different population from the brighter ones. But Kinman found from more recent determinations of the density of horizontal-branch stars in the halo of our galaxy as a function of distance from the plane, and from better estimates of the frequency of white dwarfs, that he could represent the observed plot of log $N(m)$ against m quite well by a combination of these. Lynds and Villere reached essentially the same conclusion. Thus the bulk of the objects in question are probably galactic stars —white dwarfs, evolved hot subdwarfs, and halo stars of the horizontal-branch type. This conclusion was supported by a random sampling done by Kinman of spectra of 12 stars of about 16th magnitude; all were found to be galactic stars.

Sandage (1965) certainly provoked controversy by the announcement that he had discovered in the so-called quasi-stellar galaxies "a major new constituent of the universe." In fact this statement went too far, because (a) as we have just described, there are considerable uncertainties associated with his claim that the objects were as common as his estimate indicated, and (b) others who had

---

* The term "radio-quiet" used by Sandage is a comparative one. All he meant was that up to that time no radio source had been detected at that position. However, such QSO's may be radio sources at lower power levels than have been covered in the surveys to date, or they may be radio sources emitting only at high frequencies, at which surveys have not been made. Already several attempts have been made to check whether some of these objects are in fact weak radio emitters.

earlier investigated the existence of ultraviolet stellar objects at high galactic latitudes had realized that some might be extragalactic. The surveys have isolated objects with strong ultraviolet excesses. Undoubtedly a large number of them are high-latitude galactic stars. To establish that an object is extragalactic it is necessary to obtain a spectrum that shows a redshift. A weaker criterion that has been used is to find that an object is not truly stellar, which would suggest that it is a very small galaxy.

One of the first of these to be discovered was HZ 46 (Humason and Zwicky, 1947). The object had a small redshift ($z = 0.045$), and Humason and Zwicky remarked in their paper that it was probably a galaxy with a foreground star, which suggests that they were uncertain of its nature. A number of other extragalactic objects were reported by Haro (1956) and by Zwicky (1965 and previous references given there). However, many of these objects for which spectra have been obtained by Sandage, Zwicky, Arp (1965), and others, have small redshifts in comparison with those of the QSO's in general. Therefore, if we accept the conventional explanation of these redshifts, the objects either have normal galactic luminosities, though they are highly condensed, or have much lower luminosities. At such small luminosity distances they cannot have great cosmological significance. Only a comparatively small number of these have so far been shown to have large redshifts, $z > 1$. They are BSO 1 (Sandage, 1965), PHL 938 (Kinman, 1966), Ton 1530 (Hiltner, Cowley, and Schild, 1966), and PHL 1127 and PHL 3424 (Sandage and Luyten, 1967). Some of them may be subsequently detected as weak radio sources. If it turns out that the redshifts of the QSO's are not distance indicators, then it may be that all of these objects (radio-emitting QSO's, QSO's detected by the optical method with both large and small redshifts, and compact objects which are not quite stellar in appearance) have the same physical origin and rather similar luminosities. But if the redshifts are interpreted in the conventional way, then these objects have a large dispersion in luminosity. At present it is misleading to describe any of them as galaxies unless unambiguous evidence for the presence of stars can be produced. This is rarely if ever the case except for a few objects described by Zwicky in which stellar absorption lines are seen.

Sandage and Luyten (1967) have isolated a larger sample of such objects in a selected field of 40 square degrees; they used colors and zero proper motion as criteria for selecting possible QSO's. Spectrograms were obtained for 27 of the objects thus selected, and ten of these candidates were confirmed as QSO's, although redshifts have so far been determined for only three of them. Van den Bergh (1966) has also prepared a list of faint blue objects emitting excess ultraviolet radiation, and some show light variations.

At present it is difficult to estimate the true frequency of QSO's among the fainter blue stellar objects in the high-latitude surveys. Kinman concluded that it was 20 percent or less of Sandage's estimate. Sandage and Luyten, from the sample field that they studied, estimated a frequency of 0.4 objects per square degree down to photographic magnitude 18, and between one and three objects per square degree down to a limiting magnitude of 19.7. The radio-quiet QSO's brighter than 18th magnitude would then be 100 times more frequent than those that are radio sources in the 3C R catalogue, and the total number of QSO's brighter than 19.7 magnitude, over the whole sky, would be about 100,000.

3

Line Spectra of Quasi-Stellar Objects

The first spectrogram of 3C 48 was obtained in 1960 by Sandage. Early spectroscopic work was carried out by Greenstein, Münch, and others on this object. For a number of years Schmidt had been obtaining spectra of radio galaxies. Following his major discovery concerning 3C 273 in the early part of 1963 he was largely responsible for all of the spectroscopic observations of QSO's until 1964, when others entered the field. At that time E. M. Burbidge began to observe spectra of QSO's at the Lick Observatory, and she and T. D. Kinman are continuing this work there. About the same time C. R. Lynds and his colleagues began to observe QSO's with an image tube spectrograph at the Kitt Peak National Observatory (Lynds, Stockton, and Livingston, 1965). Subsequently V. C. Rubin and K. Ford obtained spectra with an image tube spectrograph, first at the Lowell Observatory and later with the 84-inch Kitt Peak telescope. Recently W. A. Hiltner and his colleagues obtained spectra with an image tube spectrograph on the 82-inch McDonald telescope. Dibai and Pronik (1964) obtained spectra of 3C 273, and from 1965 on QSO's were observed with an image tube spectrograph at the Sternberg Crimean station (Dibai and Yesipov, 1967a,b). Infrared spectra of 3C 273 have been obtained at Haute Provence by Andrillat and Andrillat (1964), and L. Divan (1965) also obtained spectra of 3C 273. At the time of writing we estimate that spectra of some 120 QSO's have been observed, and 100 redshifts, all those known as of February 1967, are given in Table 3.1. Although in the early days it was thought that because of the faintness of these objects they were the preserve of the very largest telescopes, the development of the image tube spectrographs used with more modest apertures (∼80 inches) has led to major contributions, particularly from the Kitt Peak observers. An image tube spectrograph has very recently come into operation at the Lick Observatory (Burbidge and Kinman, 1966), and an image tube spectrograph will soon be available at Palomar; consequently, more spectra of even fainter objects (> 19^m) are to be expected.

Appended to Table 3.1, the list of all of the redshifts so far measured, are the references from which it has been compiled, given in chronological order.

LINE IDENTIFICATIONS

The identification of four broad emission lines in the spectrum of brightest QSO, 3C 273, as the Balmer lines Hβ–Hε with a redshift $z = 0.158$ provided the breakthrough in understanding the line spectra of these objects by demonstrating that considerable redshifts are present (Schmidt, 1963). From the redshift given by the Balmer lines, Schmidt identified a broad emission feature as a blend of the Mg II doublet λλ 2796, 2803, which had hitherto been seen only in solar spectra taken outside the Earth's atmosphere. Oke (1963) detected Hα in 3C 273.

The λ 2798 feature was then identified in 3C 48, and this together with several other emission lines, gave a larger redshift for this object (Greenstein and Matthews, 1963). A detailed analysis of 3C 48 and 3C 273 was then made by Greenstein and Schmidt (1964); Table 3.2 gives the features detected in their spectra.

The identification of 17th- and 18th-magnitude stellar objects with radio sources (Table 1.2), in conjunction with the redshifts found for 3C 273 and 3C 48, and later for 3C 47 and 3C 147 by Schmidt and Matthews (1964), suggested that objects with really large redshifts, greater than $z = 1$, might be found (Burbidge, 1964). In the spectra of these objects the ultraviolet region normally inaccessible from ground-based instruments, and therefore at that time unobserved except in the sun, could be expected to be shifted into the visible region, posing a considerable problem in identifying the lines.

It is clear from the list of lines in Table 3.2, which are all *emission*

Table 3.1

QUASI-STELLAR OBJECTS WITH REDSHIFTS

Object	z	m_v	$B - V$	$U - B$
Ton 256	0.131	15.91	+0.57	−0.84
3C 273	0.158	12.8	+0.21	−0.85
PKS 0736 + 01	0.191	(18)		
PKS 0837 − 12	0.200			
PKS 2135 − 14	0.200	15.53	+0.10	−0.83
PKS 1217 + 02	0.240	16.53	+0.02	−0.87
PHL 1093	0.260	17.07	+0.05	−1.02
3C 323.1	0.264	(15.8)		
PHL 1194	0.298 ?	17.50	−0.07	−0.85
PHL 1078	0.308	18.25	+0.04	−0.81
3C 249.1	0.311	15.72	−0.02	−0.77
3C 277.1	0.320	17.93	−0.17	−0.78
PKS 2251 + 11	0.323	15.82	+0.20	−0.84
PKS 1049 − 09	0.344	16.79	+0.06	−0.49
PKS 1510 − 08	0.361	16.52	+0.17	−0.74
3C 48	0.367	16.2	+0.42	−0.58
3C 351	0.371	15.28	+0.13	−0.75
PKS 1229 − 02	0.388	16.75	+0.48	−0.66
PKS 0812 + 02	0.402	(17)		
3C 215	0.411	18.27	+0.21	−0.66
3C 47	0.425	18.1	+0.05	−0.65
4C 21.35	0.434	(18.0)		
PHL 658	0.450	16.40	+0.11	−0.70
PKS 1327 − 21	0.528	16.74	+0.10	−0.54
3C 232	0.534	15.78	+0.10	−0.68
3C 279	0.538	17.8	+0.26	−0.56
3C 147	0.545	16.9	+0.35	−0.59
PKS 1136 − 13	0.554	(17)		
3C 334	0.555	16.41	+0.12	−0.79
3C 275.1	0.557	19.00	+0.23	−0.43
MSH 04 − 12	0.567	(16)		
PKS 0403 − 13	0.574	(18)		
3C 345	0.595	16.8	+0.29	−0.50
MSH 03 − 19	0.614	16.24	+0.11	−0.65
3C 261	0.614	18.24	+0.24	−0.56
MSH 13 − 011	0.625	17.68	+0.14	−0.66

Table 3.1, continued

QUASI-STELLAR OBJECTS WITH REDSHIFTS

Object	z	m_v	$B - V$	$U - B$
3C 263	0.652	16.32	+0.18	−0.56
PKS 2344 + 09	0.677	15.97	+0.25	−0.60
3C 57	0.68	16.40	+0.14	−0.73
3C 207	0.684	18.15	+0.43	−0.42
3C 380	0.692	16.81	+0.24	−0.59
4C 39.25	0.699	(17.3)		
PHL 923	0.717	17.33	+0.20	−0.70
PKS 1354 + 19	0.720	16.02	+0.18	−0.55
3C 254	0.734	17.98	+0.15	−0.49
3C 138	0.760	17.9	+0.23	−0.38
3C 175	0.768	(17.5)		
3C 286	0.849	17.30	+0.22	−0.82
3C 454.3	0.859	16.10	+0.47	−0.66
PKS 1252 + 11	0.871	16.64	+0.35	−0.75
4C 20.33	0.871	(17.1)		
3C 196	0.871	17.6	+0.60	−0.43
PKS 0922 + 14	0.895	17.96	+0.54	−0.52
PKS 2216 − 03	0.901 ?	(17)		
3C 309.1	0.904	16.78	+0.46	−0.77
PKS 0957 + 00	0.906	17.57	+0.47	−0.71
4C 37.24	0.914	(18.2)		
3C 336	0.927	17.47	+0.44	−0.79
MSH 14 − 12l	0.940	17.37	+0.44	−0.76
3C 288.1	0.961	18.12	+0.39	−0.82
3C 94	0.962	(17.5)		
4C 29.68 = CTD 141	1.012	(17.3)		
3C 245	1.029	17.25	+0.45	−0.83
CTA 102	1.037	17.32	+0.42	−0.79
3C 2	1.037	19.35	+0.79	−0.96
3C 287	1.055	17.67	+0.63	−0.65
3C 186	1.063	17.60	+0.45	−0.71
PKS 0122 − 00	1.070	(16)		
3C 208	1.110	17.42	+0.34	−1.00
3C 204	1.112	18.21	+0.55	−0.99
PKS 1127 − 14	1.187	16.90	+0.27	−0.70
BSO 1	1.241	16.98	+0.31	−0.78

Table 3.1, concluded

QUASI-STELLAR OBJECTS WITH REDSHIFTS

Object	z	m_v	$B - V$	$U - B$
PKS 1454 − 06	1.249	18.0	+0.60	
PKS 0859 − 14	1.327	(17.8)		
3C 181	1.382	18.92	+0.43	−1.02
3C 268.4	1.400	18.42	+0.58	−0.69
3C 446	1.403	18.4	+0.44	−0.90
PHL 1377	1.436	16.46	+0.15	−0.89
3C 298	1.439	16.79	+0.33	−0.70
AO 0952 + 17	1.472	(17.7)		
3C 270.1	1.519	18.61	+0.19	−0.61
4C 31.38	1.557	(19.4)		
3C 280.1	1.659	19.44	−0.13	−0.70
3C 454	1.757	18.40	+0.12	−0.95
PKS 2146 − 13	1.800	(20)		
3C 432	1.805	17.96	+0.22	−0.79
PKS 2354 + 14	1.810	(18)		
PHL 3424	1.847	18.25	+0.19	−0.90
PHL 938	1.93	17.16	+0.32	−0.88
3C 191	1.953	18.4	+0.25	−0.84
PKS 0119 − 04	1.955	16.88	+0.46	−0.72
PHL 5200	1.98	(18.2)		
PKS 1148 − 00	1.982	17.60	+0.17	−0.97
PHL 1127	1.990	18.29	+0.14	−0.83
3C 9	2.012	18.21	+0.23	−0.76
Ton 1530	2.051	(16.8)		
PHL 1305	2.064	16.96	+0.07	−0.82
PKS 0229 + 13	2.07	(18)		
PKS 0106 + 01	2.107	18.39	+0.15	−0.70
PKS 1116 + 12	2.118	19.25	+0.14	−0.76
PKS 0056 − 17	2.125	(17)		
PKS 0237 − 23	2.223	16.63	+0.15	−0.61

Sources: The redshifts given in this Table were taken from Schmidt (1963, 1965, 1966, 1967), Schmidt and Matthews (1964), Burbidge (1965a,b, 1966), Burbidge, Lynds, and Burbidge (1966), Burbidge and Rosenberg (1965), Burbidge and Kinman (1966), Lynds, Stockton, and Livingston (1965), Lynds and Stockton (1966), Stockton and Lynds (1966), Lynds, Hill, Heere, and Stockton (1966), Kinman (1966), Greenstein and Matthews (1964), Sandage (1965), Ford and Rubin (1966), Hiltner, Cowley and Schild (1966), Lynds (1967a,b), Kinman and Burbidge (1967), Sandage and Luyten (1967), Dibai and Yesipov (1967b).

Table 3.2

Identification	Rest Wavelength (Å)	Equivalent Widths (Å)	
		3C 273	3C 48
[O III]	5007	24	Present
Hβ	4861	86	28
Hγ	4340	Present	Present
Hδ	4102	Present	—
Hε	3970	Present	—
[Ne III]	3869	—	Present
[O II]	3727	—	12
[Ne V]	3426	—	6
[Ne V]	3346	—	
[Ne V]	2975	—	Present
Mg II	2798	11	10

lines, permitted and forbidden, and characteristically very broad, that these are the sort of features to be expected in hot gaseous nebulae with physical conditions similar to those of planetary nebulae; that is, with an electron temperature of order 10^4 °K. They are also the kind of emission lines found in the spectra of radio galaxies like Cygnus A and in those of nuclei of Seyfert galaxies. Osterbrock (1963) had prepared a list of emission lines to be expected in the ultraviolet spectra of planetary nebulae, with computed relative intensities, and this was clearly just what was needed in looking for line identifications in QSO's. Schmidt (1965) compiled a search list of emission lines (partly from Osterbrock's work) with which he identified emission features in five more QSO's, all of which proved to have very large redshifts, going up to $z = 2.012$ for 3C 9, in whose spectra Lyman α was seen for the first time, as a strong emission feature. Table 3.3 gives a search list similar to Schmidt's, but including more of Osterbrock's lines as well as Osterbrock's newly calculated wavelengths of [Mg V] and [Mg VII] lines.

The four strongest emission lines in the wavelength range ex-

Table 3.3

SEARCH LIST OF LINES FOR IDENTIFICATION
OF SPECTRAL FEATURES OF QUASI-STELLAR OBJECTS

Ion	$\lambda(\text{Å})$	Ion	$\lambda(\text{Å})$
N II	1085	[Mg VII]	2512
Si II	1194	[Mg VII]	2632
Si III	1206	[Mg V]	2786
Ly-α	1216	Mg II	2798
N V	1240	[Ar IV]	2854
Si II	1263	[Ar IV]	2869
C II	1335	[Mg V]	2931
Si IV	1394–1403	[Ne V]	2973
[O IV]	1406	O III	3133
N IV]	1488	He II	3203
C IV	1549	[Ne V]	3346
[Ne V]	1575	[Ne V]	3426
[Ne IV]	1602	[O II]	3727
He II	1640	[Ne III]	3869
O III]	1663	Hζ	3889
[N III]	1750	[Ne III], Hϵ	3968
Si II	1808–1817	Hδ	4102
C III]	1909	Hγ	4340
[O III]	2321	[O III]	4363
[C II]	2326	Hβ	4861
[Ne IV]	2424	[O III]	4959
[O II]	2470	[O III]	5007

tending from about 5000 A toward shorter wavelengths are Ly-α, C IV λ1549, C III] λ1909, and Mg II λ2798. The line C III] λ1909 is partially forbidden, but the other three lines are all resonance transitions involving the ground level of the ion in question. If a spectrum shows only two emission lines, the ratio of whose wavelengths agrees with any of the ratios of rest wavelengths from these four lines, then it is relatively certain that they are the correct identifications. Although one generally finds other pairs of rest wavelengths giving the same ratio to within the observational errors, the absence of lines that should be present can be used to rule them out of consideration.

For example, one might find a possible pair involving one of the [Ne V] lines, or a Balmer line, but such identifications would not be acceptable if a stronger [Ne V] line, or a lower Balmer line, were definitely absent from the spectrum.

It is in this way—by identifying two or more of the lines with features previously found or expected in the spectra of QSO's—that the redshifts listed in Table 3.1 were determined. Table 3.4 gives details of the emission features detected in the spectra of 60 of the objects, collected from the published data and from some observations by C. R. Lynds that were published in an earlier version of this table by Burbidge, Burbidge, Hoyle, and Lynds (1966). Plates 1 to 4 show spectra of several QSO's, with a range of redshifts and intensities in the emission lines.

The nomenclature used in Table 3.4 is as follows: line strengths are given first for each entry, with W = weak, M = medium, S = strong, v = very; widths are given second after a comma, with w = wide (40–100 Å), m = medium (20–30 Å), n = narrow (10–15 Å); for many lines, actual widths have been estimated. Asterisks indicate that a line has been measured but no information on its width or strength is available.

The table has been divided into two parts, objects with $z < 1$ being in the first part and those with $z > 1$ in the second part. For $z < 1$, lines with rest wavelengths shorter than O III] $\lambda 1663$ are not shifted into the observable range. Similarly, for $z > 1$, lines of long wavelengths are redshifted beyond the region normally studied. Since the lines [Ne V] $\lambda 3346$, [Ne III] $\lambda 3968$, [O III] $\lambda 4959$ are weaker members of doublets, the stronger lines of which are included in the table, they add no new information and therefore are not included.

ABSORPTION LINES

Absorption lines have now been found in the spectra of a number of QSO's; until recently it was thought that the frequency of such objects was very small. The first QSO investigated, 3C 48, shows a sharp absorption feature at 3892 Å (Greenstein and Schmidt, 1964) which was unidentified. Since then a few objects have been found to show single absorption features. In 1966 the first QSO with a rich absorption-line spectrum, 3C 191, was discovered by Burbidge, Lynds, and Burbidge (1966), and Stockton and Lynds (1966), and in 1966–1967 a number of objects containing several absorption lines were found. The wavelengths of these absorption lines, together with the line-identifications that have been made, are given in Table 3.5. It will be seen from this table that all of the objects with enough absorption lines for an absorption-line redshift to be determined have $z > 1.9$, and comparison with Table 3.1 shows that seven out of the fourteen QSO's with $z_{em} > 1.9$ have absorption lines. But of the remaining 86 QSO's in Table 3.1 only eight show absorption lines, and in nearly all of these only a single line is found. Of the absorption-line objects with $z > 1.9$, only one is a 3C object, three are Parkes objects, and three are Palomar-Haro-Luyten objects. Thus at present the admittedly poor statistics suggest that the presence of absorption lines is strongly correlated with large redshift; furthermore, absorption lines appear more frequently in objects that are not powerful radio emitters (and in many cases are not known to be radio sources). We now discuss the QSO's with several absorption lines individually.

3C 191. In this QSO the absorption lines are sharp, and most of them arise from the ground states of the relevant ions. The lines were identified by Lynds, Stockton, and ourselves by using Osterbrock's tables of expected *emission* lines in gaseous nebulae, and they include Ly-α and C IV λ1549. Table 3.5 lists all the identified lines in 3C 191 in the left column; a "P" below any QSO means that the line opposite was measured in its spectrum. Not all of the absorption lines were identified in 3C 191, but the redshift was very well determined from the 16 identified lines, and since this redshift was nearly the same as that derived from the usual few emission lines, any lingering doubts about the validity of large redshifts from spectra in which only two emission lines (e.g., Ly-α and C IV λ1549) were visible have been dispelled. Two unidentified lines at 3408 Å and 3971 Å in 3C 191, measured on both Kitt Peak and Lick spectra, would have rest wavelengths at 1156.6 and 1347.7 Å.

One of the line-identifications of Lynds, Stockton, and ourselves, NV λ1240.1, was questioned by Bahcall (1966b). He suggested that this line might be due instead to a blend of Mg II $\lambda\lambda$1239.9, 1240.4.

Table 3.4, part 1 ($z < 1$)

LINES SEEN IN QSO'S AND THEIR ESTIMATED STRENGTHS AND WIDTHS

Object	C III] 1909	Mg II 2798	[Ar IV] 2854 2869	[Mg V] 2931	[Ne V] 2974	O III 3133	He II 3204
3C 273[1]		*					
1217 + 02		W, ~20 Å			W, 30 Å	*	*
3C 249.1		W, 40 Å					
3C 277.1		M, <10 Å					
1510 − 08[2]		S, w					
3C 48		S, w			W, w		
3C 351							
3C 215[3]		S, 20 Å			$W, >m$		
3C 47[4]		*, 20 Å					
4C 21.35		S, 60 Å					
1327 − 21		S, 80 Å			W		
3C 279		S, w	M, w	W			
3C 147[5]						*	
3C 334[6]		S, 30 Å		W	W	W	W
3C 275.1		S, 20 A				*	*
3C 345[7]		S, w	W, w	*	W		*
MSH 03 − 19		M, 80 Å					
3C 261		S, 100 Å	W				
MSH 13 − 011		M, w					
3C 263[8]		*	*		*		
3C 380[9]		vS, 30 Å	M, 30 Å				
4C 39.25	M	M, 30 Å	M	*			
1354 + 19[10]		S					
3C 254	*	*					
3C 138	S, 25 Å	S, 40 Å					
3C 286	*	W, 80 Å					
1252 + 11	W	S	W, n		*	*	
4C 20.33	M, 40 Å	M, 40 Å					
3C 196	W, 40 Å	*					
0922 + 14[11]	vW, w	M, 60 Å			*		
3C 309.1[12]	S, m	vS, 60 Å					
0957 + 00[13]	S, 40 Å	M, 60 Å					
3C 336	W, 60 Å	W, 40 Å					
MSH 14 − 121	M, 60 Å	M, 60 Å				W	

1. Balmer lines Hα (vS,w), Hδ, Hϵ also seen.
2. Weak, fairly broad absorption in shortward wing of Mg II λ2798.
3. Hγ, [O III] λ4363 blended. Additional line seen at 2830 A (He I?).
4. Hγ, [O III] λ4363 blended.
5. Mg II λ2798 not seen.
6. Weak Hδ also seen. Hγ, [O III] λ4363 blended.
7. Mg II λ2798 complex and variable.

[Ne V] 3426	[O II] 3727	[Ne III] 3869	Hγ 4340	[O III] 4363	Hβ 4861	[O III] 5007
	?		M, w		vS, w	M, m
W, 20 Å	W, 20 Å	M, 20 Å	M, 30 Å	M, 30 Å	S, 30 Å	S, 10 Å
vW, n	vW, w	W, 20 Å	W, 40 Å		W, 40 Å	M, <10 Å
W, <10 Å	M, <10 Å					
W, w					W, w	
M, 30 Å	>M, n	M, n	S, w		S, vw	>Hβ
W	W, n	*			>W, 25 Å	M, vn
W, >m	W, ?n	W	*	*	M, 25 Å	>M, n
*, 20 Å	W	*, 20 Å	*	*		*, 20 Å
W, n			W, w		M, 100 Å	
W	W			M		
M, 20 Å	W, w	M, w	*			
*	*, 30 Å	*				
W			W	W		
	W, n					
W		W	*			
W, 80 Å						
	M, n	W, n				
		W, w				
	*					
W, 20 Å	W, 20 Å	W, 20 Å	*			
W						
W, n		W, n				
*	*	*				
	M, 20 Å					
W						
W	M, 25 Å					
*	vW, ?n					
M, n						

8. Ca II absorption seen by Ford and Rubin (1966).
9. Hydrogen lines seen; weak.
10. Hδ also measured.
11. C II] λ2326 possibly present.
12. C II] λ2326 (W,w) also measured.
13. Mg II λ2798 complex.

Table 3.4, part 2 (z > 1)

LINES SEEN IN QSO'S, AND THEIR ESTIMATED STRENGTHS AND WIDTHS

Object	Ly-α 1216	Si IV 1393 1402 [O IV] 1406	C IV 1549	He II 1640	O III] 1663	C III] 1909	Mg II 2798
4C 29.68 (≡ CTD 141)						M, m	W, w
3C 245						*	*
CTA 102						*	*
3C 287		*				*	*
3C 186[1]						M, 25 Å	W, 40 A
3C 208[2]			M			M	M
3C 204			W			M	
1127 − 14						S, w	S, w
BSO 1[3]		*				W	
1454 − 06						M, w	M, 70 A
0859 − 14			S, w	W, n		M, w	
3C 181			M			M	
3C 446			S, w			M, m	
3C 298[4]			W	W, w		M	M
0952 + 18			S, w	W, w	W, w	W, w	
3C 270.1[5]		W	S, w			M	
4C 31.38			S, 50 Å	M, w			
3C 280.1[6]	S, 80 Å	M, 40 Å	vS, ?	M, 20 Å		W, 20 Å	
3C 454	S		S	W	?	W	
3C 432	S		S			?vW	
3C 191[7]	S, w		S, w	W		W	
PHL 938[8]	S, w	W, w	S, w				
1148 − 00[9]		M	vS	M	M	M	
3C 9	S, w		S, w				
0106 + 01	S, 70 Å	W, w	M, w			W, m	
1116 + 12[10]	S, 30 Å	?	S, 30 Å	W		vW	

1. Very weak [Ne V] λ3426 also seen.
2. C II] λ2326 also measured; weak.
3. Self-absorption in C IV λ1549.
4. Absorption dominates in C IV λ1549.
5. Deep absorption in shortward wing of C IV λ1549.
6. Both Si IV λ1394 and [O IV] λ1406 emission lines seen; emission lines of C II λ1335 and N IV] λ1438 definitely present; Si II emission lines possibly present.
7. Numerous narrow absorption lines seen, C IV 1549 being the strongest. Only emission lines are listed here.
8. Self-absorption in shortward wing of Ly-α and C IV 1549.
9. C II] λ2326 also measured.
10. Absorption in shortward wing of Ly-α. Absorption at 1150 Å. Weak emission from N II λ1085.

Table 3.5

IDENTIFIED ABSORPTION LINES IN QUASI-STELLAR OBJECTS WITH SEVERAL LINES

Absorption Lines	3C 191 $Z_{abs} = 1.947$	PHL 938 $Z_{abs} = 1.91$	PKS 1116 + 12 $Z_{abs} = 1.947$	PHL 5200 $Z_{abs} = 1.90\text{--}1.98$	PKS 0237 − 23 $Z_{abs} = 1.95$	PKS 0237 − 23 $Z_{abs} = 2.20$	PKS 0119 − 04 $Z_{abs} = 1.965$
C III λ1175.7	P				P?		P?
Si II λ1194.1	P				P?		
Si III λ1206.5	P	P?				P	P
Ly-α λ1215.7	P	P	P			P	P
S II λ1231.8	P					P	
N V λλ1238.8, 1242.8			P?	P	P	P	P
S II λ1256.1	P				P	P	
Si II λ1260.7	P				P		
Si II λ1265.0	P				P		
C II λ1335.3	F				P	P	
Si IV λ1393.7	F				P	P	P
Si IV λ1402.7	F				P	P	P
Si II λ1526.7	F						
Si II λ1533.4	F						
C IV λ1549.1	P	P	P	P	P		P

This is not very likely, however, for two reasons. First, the spectrum of 3C 191 with the highest dispersion, taken by Stockton at Kitt Peak, resolves this feature into its two fine-structure components, and they agree in wavelengths with the NV tabular wavelengths. The pair of Mg II lines are too close in wavelength to be resolved in this way. Second, the Mg II lines are the second member of the principal series in Mg II, and the transition probability can be only one or two percent of that of Mg II $\lambda 2798$. Sharp absorption components have not been seen in Mg II $\lambda 2798$ in any QSO's. Unfortunately, Mg II $\lambda 2798$ falls in the infrared in 3C 191, at 8254 Å, and therefore has not been examined.

PHL 938. Kinman found narrow and possibly double absorption components on the short-wavelength side of both the Ly-α and C IV $\lambda 1549$ emission lines in PHL 938, which is a radio-quiet QSO. If the absorption line near Ly-α is really double, then it might consist of Si III $\lambda 1206.5$ and Ly-α (see, however, Plate 11).

PKS 1116 + 12. A strong absorption component appears in the short-wavelength wing of Ly-α in a spectrum of the QSO PKS 1116 + 12 taken by Lynds and Stockton (1966). It is about 26 Å from the center of the Ly-α emission, which corresponds to about $8\frac{1}{2}$ Å in the rest wavelength frame, and it is most probably due to Ly-α. Schmidt (1966), however, made no mention of any Ly-α absorption in the wing of the emission line in this QSO. Moreover, Bahcall, Peterson, and Schmidt (1966) spent considerable effort in a search for absorption lines that might be due to an intergalactic medium in the spectrum of PKS 1116 + 12; one such line was found 200 Å on the short-wavelength side from the center of the redshifted Ly-α emission line, and this line (somewhat broad) may also be seen on the spectrum reproduced by Lynds and Stockton (although, of course, its identification as Ly-α is hypothetical). But, of a second feature at a corresponding shortward shift from the C IV $\lambda 1549$ emission observed by Bahcall and his colleagues, there is not a sign on the published Kitt Peak spectrum. Bahcall, Peterson, and Schmidt measured one other line at 3648 Å, which might be NV $\lambda 1240$. We believe that the possibility of *variable absorption components* should be borne in mind. If such absorption components do indeed come and go over a short period of time, they clearly must be due to gas connected with the object itself, and not to gas in an intergalactic medium.

PHL 5200. This QSO was identified as the radio source 4C − 5.93 by Scheuer and Wills (1966), and its spectrum was photographed by Lynds (1967a). The spectrum is like that of no QSO hitherto observed: at first glance it resembles that of a supernova. There are three wide absorption bands, each next to emission features that adjoin them on their long-wavelength sides, and the boundary between the emission and absorption features is extremely sharp. The emission lines actually show three separate (though closely spaced) redshifts. Lynds suggested that the very broad absorption lines were produced in an expanding shell of gas around the central energy source, with a large velocity gradient in this shell and a big average difference in velocity from that of the main set of emission lines, while one explanation for the two additional sets of emission lines was that they might be produced by the dissipation of shock waves passing through the envelope. One other absorption feature, this time a narrow one, was measured by Lynds at 3886 Å, and was identified by him as OI λ1304.

PKS 0237 − 23. The second QSO discovered to have a large number of narrow absorption lines in its spectrum was PKS 0237 − 23, a radio source that was unusual in having a strongly curved radio spectrum, suggesting that the radio source is very small (we discuss radio spectra and their significance in Chapter 5). Arp, Bolton, and Kinman (1967) found that this QSO had the largest emission-line redshift yet measured, $z = 2.223$, and this was confirmed by E. M. Burbidge (1967). Since six of the emission lines characteristically found in spectra of QSO's were present, this redshift was firmly established. The rich absorption-line spectrum, however, was considerably difficult to interpret. Arp, Bolton, and Kinman proposed a set of line identifications that gave a redshift of 2.20, fairly close to the emission-line redshift, but most of these identifications were not convincing. Whereas some of the lines they suggested, like Ly-α and

Si III $\lambda1206.5$, were normally expected features, others, like As I, Co II, and P II, would have required the absorbing gas to have a very unusual composition, and even some of the more common elements that were suggested, such as Ti III, Cr III, Mn II and Mn III, were not convincing because, for example, only parts of some spectroscopic multiplets appeared to be present. Moreover, there was a considerable spread in the redshifts given by the individual lines.

E. M. Burbidge (1967) suggested another set of identifications, with a redshift very different from that derived from the emission lines, namely $z = 1.95$. Although no unusual elements were suggested, these identifications were not altogether satisfactory because several lines were left unexplained and some of the relative intensities of the identified ones did not check with those in, for example, 3C 191.

Greenstein and Schmidt (1967) subsequently concluded that *both* redshifts were present—a surprise indeed, for the difference between them is large. With the two redshifts, many of the difficulties in identification were removed. Some remained, however; for example, Ti III had to be retained as an identification for some quite strong lines in the system $z = 2.20$ (although Greenstein and Schmidt discarded the other identifications of heavier elements by Arp et al.), and the problem of incomplete multiplets remains. Moreover, several quite strong lines are still unidentified—in particular, lines at 3790, 3838, 4025, 4148, 4386, and 4455 Å. It would not surprise us if still other redshifts are eventually found to be present in this most puzzling object.

PKS 0119 − 04. In the five QSO's discussed above, the absorption lines all occur on the short-wavelength side of the centers of the emission lines, sometimes very close (as in 3C 191) and sometimes separated by a large amount (as in PKS 1116 + 12 and PKS 0237 − 23). But Kinman and Burbidge (1967) found absorption lines on the other side of the emission lines in the spectrum of PKS 0119 − 04. One might account for a shift to a shorter wavelength as a Doppler shift produced in an expanding shell of gas, driven off the QSO by, for example, an explosive event or radiation pressure, but a shift to a longer wavelength would then have to be due to gas falling into the central object. We return to these problems of interpretation of the redshifts in Chapter 9.

Aside from the direction of the wavelength shift in PKS 0119 − 04, its spectrum posed none of the problems that were present for PKS 0237 − 23, since the absorption lines in PKS 0119 − 04 were all those expected theoretically and found in 3C 191.

Plates 5 to 12 show some of the spectra described above.

QSO's with single absorption lines. Apart from the QSO's whose spectra have enough lines for a redshift to be obtained, there are several more with only one line or a dubious line. We already mentioned 3C 48, in which a possible line at 3892 Å was noted by Greenstein and Schmidt. The first recorded observation of an absorption line that was undoubtedly present was in the radio quiet QSO, BSO 1; Sandage (1965) noted that on Schmidt's spectrogram of this object the broad emission of C IV λ1549 was bisected by a sharp absorption. Ford and Rubin (1966) found redshifted Ca II H and K absorption lines (which are, of course, resonance absorptions from the ground state) in their spectra of 3C 263 and PKS 1217 + 02 (only the K line was seen here); the redshifts of these lines agreed with those obtained from the emission lines. Lynds, however, did not see these absorption lines on the Kitt Peak spectra of the same objects. Absorption components in the C IV λ1549 line are present in 3C 270.1 (Schmidt, 1966) and 3C 298 (Lynds et al., 1966).

Burbidge and Kinman (1966) saw a weak hazy absorption component on the short-wavelength side of a broad emission due to Mg II λ2798 in the spectrum of PKS 1510 − 08; this is the only object known to us at present for which an absorption component has been seen in this line (it is, of course, a resonance ground-level transition).

Single absorption lines have also been seen in the wings of emission lines in the spectra of other QSO's photographed by Burbidge and Kinman at Lick Observatory. In PHL 1377, the absorption is on the short-wavelength side of the emission, while in PKS 0056 − 17 it is on the long-wavelength side, as it is in PKS 0119 − 04. Finally, there are three QSO's found by optical methods

Table 3.6

QUASI-STELLAR OBJECTS WITH ONLY ONE OR TWO
ABSORPTION LINES IN THEIR SPECTRA

Object	Measured Wavelength (Å)	Suggested Identification
3C 48	3892	—
BSO 1	3473	C IV λ1549
3C 270.1	3870	C IV λ1549
3C 298	3780	C IV λ1549
PKS 1217 + 02	4882	Ca II λ3934
3C 263	6516, 6568	Ca II λλ3934, 3968
PKS 1510 − 08	3780	Mg II λ2798
PHL 1127	3590	Ly-α λ1216
PHL 1194	3590	—
PHL 1222	3590	—
PHL 1377	3747	C IV λ1549
PKS 0056 − 17	4850	C IV λ1549

by Sandage and Luyten (1967); each of these has an absorption line at 3590 Å. These may all be Ly-α. All these measurements of one or two lines are collected together in Table 3.6.

A remarkable result is shown in Table 3.7. The absorption-line redshifts for all but one of the objects with $z_{em} > 1.9$ are very close to 1.95. If we also include the objects in which there is only one line and which often have $z_{em} < 1.9$, we find that for nearly all cases the absorption-line redshift is either 1.95 or is very close to the emission-line redshift of the object. This effect was first discovered by G. Burbidge (1967b), who found a large number of coincidences in wavelength of absorption lines in the QSO's 3C 191, PKS 0237 − 23, PKS 1116 + 12, PHL 5200, and PHL 938. Several objects have been added to the list since then. In addition it was found that the blue stellar object HZ 29 has a large number of coincidences in wavelengths of absorption lines with 3C 191 and PKS 0237 − 23 (Burbidge, Burbidge, and Hoyle, 1967). This object is not included in the table, though it may be a quasi-stellar object with $z = 1.95$. Alternatively it may be a galactic object in which the same physical

Table 3.7

ABSORPTION-LINE REDSHIFTS IN QUASI-STELLAR OBJECTS

Object	z_{abs}	z_{em}
3C 191	1.947	1.953
PKS 0237 − 23	1.95, 2.20	2.223
PKS 1116 + 12	1.947	2.118
PHL 5200	1.90–1.98	1.98
PHL 938	1.91	1.93
PKS 0119 − 04	1.965	1.955
Ton 1530	1.94	2.051
Objects with one line		
PHL 1127	1.95	1.99
PHL 1194	1.95	(0.298)
PHL 1222	1.95	
PKS 0056 − 17	2.131	2.1
3C 270.1	1.498	1.519
3C 298	1.439	1.439
PHL 1377	1.419	1.436
BSO 1	1.241	1.241
3C 263	(0.655)	0.652
PKS 1510 − 08	0.351	0.361
3C 48	?	0.367
PKS 1217 + 02	0.242	0.240

process is taking place as that which gives rise to the redshift of 1.95 in the QSO's. Some of the lines in this object were identified with neutral helium lines at zero redshift by Greenstein and Matthews (1957), so that the situation here is somewhat confused.

For the QSO's with only one absorption line, the results are ambiguous. In a number of cases the single line might be a line redshifted by the same amount as the emission lines, or, if it coincides with one of the lines in 3C 191 or PKS 0237 − 23, it might have a redshift of 1.95. In Table 3.7 we have given the redshifts obtained from the assumed line-identifications listed in Table 3.6.

These results suggest very strongly that in many of the QSO's there is a standard absorbing region that gives a redshift of 1.95.

Unless it can be shown that this region is not intrinsic to the QSO's, this result has an important bearing on our present beliefs concerning the nature of the redshifts, and the possibilities are discussed in Chapter 9.

If this standard redshift is not intrinsic to the QSO's, then the absorption must arise somewhere in the light path between the object and the observer. What are the possibilities? Interstellar absorption in our own galaxy cannot be the answer, because then the same features would be present in the spectra of stars and galaxies, and they are not. Absorption in a local but extragalactic cloud of gas that is moving away from us at a velocity just less than $0.8c$ can also be ruled out because these absorption lines do not appear in the spectra of galaxies.

Could we be observing the QSO's through an absorbing cloud that is cosmological in origin? This would mean that at an epoch corresponding to a redshift of 1.95 the intergalactic gas must have been absorbing for a short time. There are two objections to this hypothesis. First, we saw in Table 3.5 and in the account of the absorption lines seen in the spectra of 3C 191, PKS 0237 − 23, and PKS 0119 − 04, that in several ions the absorptions arise from a ground state that has fine structure levels in it. This means that the excited levels of the ground state are populated by the ions. Bahcall and Salpeter (1966), however, showed that these excited levels, although they lie above the zero level by only a small fraction of an electron volt, would not be populated at all in the very low density gas and very dilute radiation field of the intergalactic medium. A second, and more direct, objection to the absorption being produced in cosmological gas clouds is that in one QSO, PKS 0119 − 04, the redshift of the absorption lines is *greater* than that of the emission lines.

Thus we must conclude that this standard redshift is intrinsic to the objects. This is entirely unreasonable if the redshifts of the QSO's are due to the expansion of the universe. If the QSO's are comparatively local objects moving at relativistic speeds, then they must be moving at the same speed. This also appears to be unlikely, but we shall discuss this type of model in Chapter 14. Thus we are led finally to the conclusion that this standard redshift may not be a Doppler

C III
1909

Mg II
2799

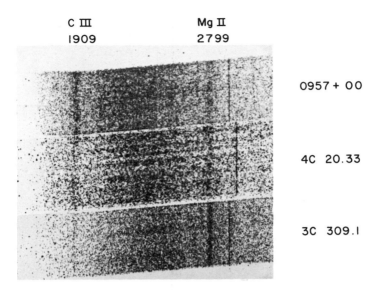

0957 + 00

4C 20.33

3C 309.1

PLATE 1. *Spectra of three QSO's with redshifts near 0.9, photographed by Lynds with the image-tube spectrograph at the Kitt Peak National Observatory. The spectra have been aligned at the emission lines of C III and Mg II, and show very marked differences in the intensity ratio of these lines. The sharp emission line to the right of Mg II λ2798 is the night-sky line [O I] λ5577.*

3889

4471

5016

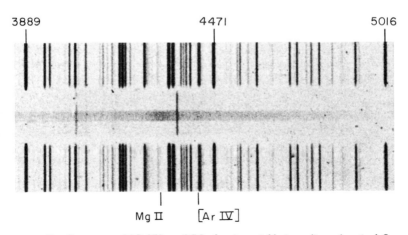

Mg II   [Ar IV]

PLATE 2. *Spectrum of 3C 279, a QSO that is variable in radio and optical flux and has z = 0.538, showing Mg II and [Ar IV] features, photographed at Lick Observatory. This was the first QSO in which [Ar IV] was detected. Wavelengths of 3 lines in comparison spectrum are marked. Narrow emission lines across whole window are Hg lines from city lights.*

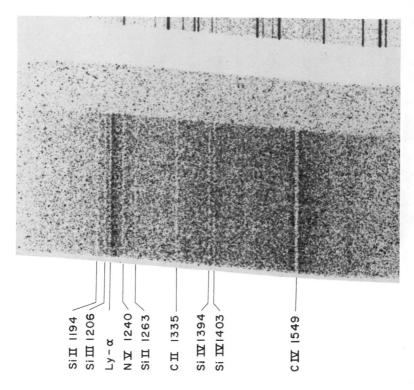

Si II 1194
Si III 1206
Ly–α
N V 1240
Si II 1263
C II 1335
Si IV 1394
Si IV 1403
C IV 1549

PLATE 7. *Spectrum of 3C 191, first QSO to show many absorption lines ($z =$ 1.947), photographed by Stockton and Lynds at Kitt Peak National Observatory. Note the narrowness of the absorption lines, in comparison with the broad underlying emission features at Ly-α and C IV λ1549.*

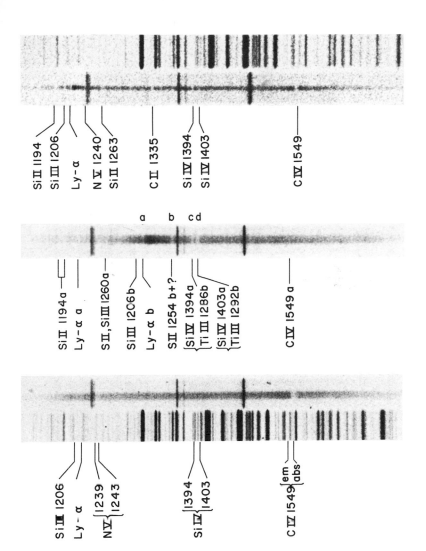

PLATE 8. *Spectra of three QSO's with absorption lines, photographed at Lick Observatory. (Top) 3C 191. (Middle) PKS 0237 − 23 (with two sets of absorption lines at different redshifts, but note that identifications are tentative). (Bottom) PKS 0119 − 04. Narrow lines across whole window in all spectra are Hg lines from city lights. Features marked a, b, c, d in middle spectrum may be seen under higher resolution in Plate 9.*

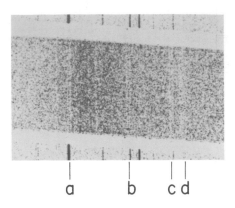

PLATE 9. *Spectrum of PKS 0237 − 23 photographed at relatively high dispersion by Lynds at Kitt Peak National Observatory. Note resolution of absorption lines a, b, c, d (see Plate 8) into narrow components.*

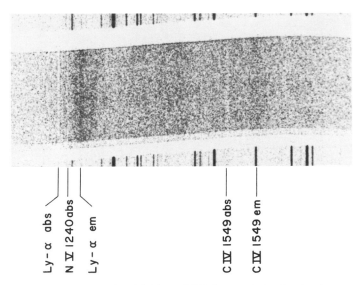

PLATE 10. *Spectrum of Ton 1530 (z = 2.051 from emission lines), photographed by Lynds at Kitt Peak National Observatory. Absorption lines are relatively narrow and have z = 1.94. Other absorption lines can be seen besides those marked.*

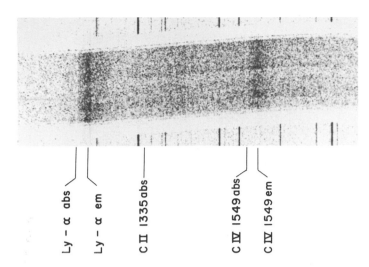

Ly – α abs   Ly – α em   C II 1335 abs   C IV 1549 abs   C IV 1549 em

PLATE 11. *Spectrum of PHL 938 (z = 1.94), photographed by Lynds at Kitt Peak National Observatory. Note the very strong broad emission lines of Ly-α and C IV λ1549, and the very narrow absorption lines on their short-wavelength side.*

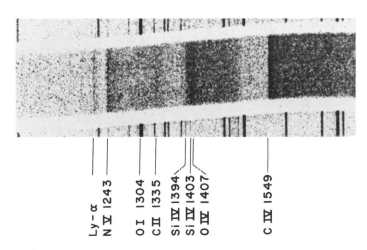

Ly – α   N V 1243   O I 1304   C II 1335   Si IV 1394   Si IV 1403   O IV 1407   C IV 1549

PLATE 12. *Spectrum of PHL 5200 (z = 1.98), photographed by Lynds at Kitt Peak National Observatory. Note very broad absorption features alongside broad emissions, and sharp boundary between them. Fairly narrow emission components of Si IV λλ1394, 1403, and C IV λ1549 at two other lesser redshifts are visible within the corresponding absorption bands.*

shift, but is perhaps a gravitational shift. It is then natural to suppose that the redshifts of the QSO's are gravitational in origin and that values up to $\sim$2.2 are possible, but that $z = 1.95$ is an important standard value. The nature of the redshifts will be discussed in detail in Chapter 9.

We have gone into considerable detail in describing the absorption lines in the spectra of QSO's, because these may in the end provide more clues for solving the problem of the nature of the QSO's than do the emission lines. Apart from the preliminary results just described, if absorption lines are ever detected that can be shown to arise in the intergalactic medium, much information of importance to cosmology may be obtained. This will be discussed in Chapter 12.

IONS SEEN IN THE SPECTRA OF QSO'S; ABUNDANCES OF THE ELEMENTS

It is clear from the preceding account of lines identified in the spectra of QSO's, and in particular from an examination of Tables 3.1, 3.4, and 3.5, that the spectral lines found in these objects come from ions with a wide range of ionization potential, in the light elements that are most abundant in the sun and stars of the solar neighborhood. The elements H, He, C, N, O, Ne, Mg, Si, S, and Ar are all represented.

Of the elements heavier than Ar, only Fe has been shown with certainty to be present, and this only in the spectrum of 3C 273, the one QSO that stands out from the others as being unusual in having much the brightest apparent magnitude. Wampler and Oke (1967) made careful measurements with the scanning photoelectric spectrophotometers at Lick and Palomar, and derived accurate wavelengths and intensities of some weak bands in the spectrum at 5200–5400 Å and 5950–6200 Å, whose presence had been suspected earlier by Greenstein and Schmidt. Wampler and Oke showed that the only reasonable identifications for these features were groups of Fe II lines—*permitted* lines—that appeared in the spectrum of Nova Herculis 1934 when it was near maximum light. They searched for the corresponding forbidden lines of [Fe II] that appear in the spectrum of the nebulous star η Carinae, but found that these were definitely not present in 3C 273. The absence of [Fe II] lines from spectra in which Fe II lines are clearly present sets lower limits to the electron density; we return to this point in Chapter 10.

Aside from Fe, the only other heavier element that has been tentatively identified in the spectrum of a QSO is Ti III, in the absorption-line spectrum of PKS 0237 − 23, and here, as we pointed out, the identification is not unequivocal. The identifications of P, Cr, Mn, Co, and As suggested by Arp and his colleagues for lines in the spectrum of PKS 0237 − 23 are very doubtful.

When Wampler and Oke found Fe II in the spectrum of 3C 273, they suggested another interesting identification, that of the Na I D lines, for an emission feature observed near 6835 Å. Sodium has a very low first ionization potential, and one would expect there to be practically no neutral sodium in the strong radiation field of a QSO. If this finding is confirmed, it will have to be taken into account in constructing possible models for the QSO's (see Chapter 10).

From O to Ar, the elements that are seen (with the exception of weak Na I in 3C 273) are those with 4-structure nuclei, which lie above the adjacent elements in the abundance distribution for the solar neighborhood. The relatively high abundances of the 4-structure nuclei in the "normal" abundance table is well understood in terms of the usual theory of nucleosynthesis in stars (Burbidge, Burbidge, Fowler, and Hoyle, 1957). Because the original search list of spectral lines, from which line-identifications were made, was compiled from Osterbrock's work on the expected ultraviolet spectrum of planetary nebulae, in which normal abundances were assumed, it is clear that the relative strengths of the spectral lines are consistent with a distribution of abundances of the elements in QSO's that are entirely normal—that is to say, similar to the relative abundances of the elements in normal stars near the sun. Even the Fe II emission lines seen by Wampler and Oke in the spectrum of 3C 273 can be produced by a normal abundance of iron, so long as these lines arise in the same region as does the Mg II emission at $\lambda 2798$; this has to be a region in which the ultraviolet flux is not too great, so that the proportion of doubly ionized Fe and Mg does not rise too high.

In view of the extraordinary properties of the QSO's, this is a very surprising result; Shklovsky (1964) was the first to draw attention to this. Osterbrock and Parker (1966) then calculated the relative emission-line strengths to be expected from a hot gas with normal abundances of the elements and, with one exception, found very good agreement with the observations. The exception is He; they predicted that the line of He II $\lambda 1640$ should be of comparable intensity with C IV $\lambda 1549$, whereas it is actually weaker in all spectra in which it appears, and in the spectra of some QSO's it has not been seen. Osterbrock and Parker suggested that compared with hydrogen and the heavier elements, helium might be less abundant in QSO's than in the normal abundance distribution.

There is a possible escape from this conclusion, however, which was pointed out by Burbidge, Burbidge, Hoyle, and Lynds (1966). Osterbrock and Parker did not calculate an ionization equilibrium for QSO's, but *assumed* a distribution among the various ionization stages which seemed reasonable. They took He as being 50 percent doubly ionized. This might not be a valid assumption; if the level of ionization is dominated by the properties of H and He, as is suggested in one of the empirical models discussed in Chapter 10, then there might well be less doubly ionized He than was assumed. It is not possible to be more definite than this without calculating the ionization equilibrium of QSO's.

WIDTHS OF THE SPECTRAL LINES

The first spectrograms obtained of 3C 48 and 3C 273 showed that the emission lines were very broad, some 20–30 Å. Even broader lines were found later in spectra of other QSO's, with measured widths sometimes as great as 100 Å. Table 3.4 gives either a descriptive or a numerical estimate of line widths for most of the objects that are listed there. These are the *observed* widths; to obtain widths as emitted in the rest frame at the source, the observed widths should be divided by $(1 + z)$.

Some QSO's, however, show quite narrow emission lines, and sometimes a range of line widths is found in one object. Characteristically, the resonance lines Ly-α, C IV $\lambda 1549$, and Mg II $\lambda 2798$ are the broadest, and the forbidden lines are narrowest. In one interesting QSO, PKS 1217 + 02, Lynds found that the forbidden lines of [O III] at λ4959 and λ5007 are much narrower than [O III] λ4363, which has a higher excitation for the upper level of the transition. Such effects suggest stratification in the region producing the spectral lines, and we shall consider them in more detail in Chapter 10 when we discuss the causes of line broadening and empirical models.

The absorption lines, when present, are usually very much narrower than the emission lines, again suggesting stratification. In 3C 191, with its large number of absorption lines, Stockton's spectrum obtained at Kitt Peak shows that the lines that are not blended have about the same width as the weaker comparison lines, or about 8 Å between half-intensity points. This sets an upper limit of about 3 Å to their width at the source, when we correct for the redshift of 1.95. The absorption features in the spectrum of PHL 5200, however, are about 100 to 150 Å wide.

4

Continuous Energy Distribution

THE OBSERVATIONS

The most precise way of measuring the intensity of the continuum radiation as a function of frequency—the continuous energy distribution—is to use spectrum scanners with fairly narrow band-passes. This, however, is a very time-consuming task, and relatively few objects have been measured in this way, by Oke (1965, 1966), by Field, Solomon, and Wampler (1966), and by Wampler (1967). Measurements made with wide band-pass filters, such as U, B, V measurements, give much less detailed information, and integrate the effect of the spectrum lines into the continuum radiation, but they can be made much more easily for faint objects, and require less telescope time. Matthews and Sandage (1963), Ryle and Sandage (1964), Sandage (1965), Sandage and Wyndham (1965), Sandage and Véron (1965), Sandage, Véron, and Wyndham (1965), Bolton, Clarke, Sandage, and Véron (1966), Bolton, Shimmins, Ekers, Kinman, Lamla, and Wirtanen (1966), Bolton and Kinman (1966), Sandage (1966a), and Kinman, Bolton, Clarke, and Sandage (1967) have made U, B, V measurements, and their data are given in Tables 1.2 and 3.1, where the identifications and redshifts are given.

In order to compare scanner measurements of objects with different redshifts, the observed absolute-energy distribution has to be shifted back to the wavelength in a system at rest with respect to the observer. If f_ν is the observed flux per unit frequency interval at the observed frequency, then the total radiated energy F_ν per unit frequency interval at the rest frequency is given by

$$F_\nu = \frac{4\pi c^2}{H_0^2} f_\nu \frac{z^2}{(1 + z)} \text{ erg sec}^{-1} \text{ (c/s)}^{-1} \tag{4.1}$$

for a cosmology with $q_0 = +1$. For $q_0 = 0$ a further factor, $(1 + \frac{1}{2}z)^2$, multiplies the right-hand side of equation (4.1). For local objects moving at relativistic speeds, c^2z^2/H_0^2 should be replaced by (distance)$^{-2}$.* Fluxes of seven QSO's measured with a scanner by Oke (1966) and corrected by equation (4.1) to a reference frame at rest with respect to the observer are shown in Figure 4.1.

For 3C 273 the observations have been extended into the infrared by Johnson (1964) and by Johnson and Low (1965), and both 3C 273 and 3C 279 have been measured in the millimeter region by Low (1965) and by Epstein (1965). Figure 4.2 shows a composite spectrum of 3C 273 based on these data, adapted from a plot by Stein (1966).

In a plot of $(U - B)$ against $(B - V)$, the main-sequence stars lie in a narrow well-defined band, as shown in Figure 2.1. The QSO's, however, lie in a region well above the main-sequence stars; this comes about because the QSO's emit much more strongly in the ultraviolet than normal stars with the same $(B - V)$ colors. It is for this reason that the search method described in Chapter 2, for picking out objects with excess ultraviolet radiation, is so useful and simple a method of discovering optical QSO's.

THE CONTINUOUS ENERGY DISTRIBUTION COMPARED WITH THERMAL EMISSION

The form of the continuous energy distribution is of considerable theoretical interest. We saw in Chapter 3 that the line spectra indicate that the electron temperatures are of the order of 10^4 °K, and when the line spectra are examined in more detail (Chapter 10), we find

---

* H_0 is the present value of the Hubble constant, and measures the rate of expansion of the universe, and q_0 is the present value of the deceleration parameter, a measure of the rate at which the expansion is slowing down. If R_0 is the present radius of the universe, and $\ddot{R}_0$ the value of the second derivative of R with respect to time, then $q_0 = -\ddot{R}_0/R_0H_0^2$.

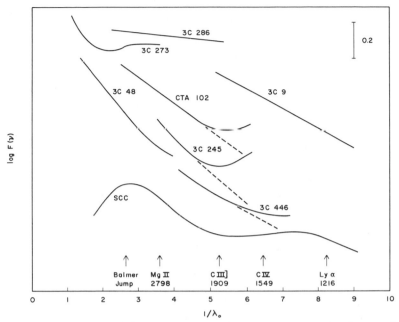

FIG. 4.1 *Results of Oke's measurements of continuous energy distribution of 7 QSO's. The energy flux as a function of frequency ν is $F(\nu)$; $\log F(\nu)$ is plotted against the reciprocal of the rest wavelength λ_0. The curves have been displaced vertically by arbitrary amounts; the scale of the ordinate is indicated in the upper right corner of the diagram. The broken lines in CTA 102, 3C 245, and 3C 446 are the suggested true continuum plots if the turn-ups of these three curves are due to a residual effect of emission lines. The curve SCC is Sandage's computed average curve, which includes the effect of emission lines.*

that the temperatures are probably 20,000°–30,000 °K. For all the QSO's for which scanner observations have been made it is clear that continuous radiation from a plasma at this comparatively low temperature does not explain the observations. The reasons for this are that (1) the Balmer jump would be a very prominent feature, and this is not so in the QSO's so far studied, and (2) the general shape of the continuum computed for these temperatures does not agree with the observations. Oke compared the observed energy distribution of 3C 273 first with that from a low-temperature ($T_e \simeq 14,000°$)

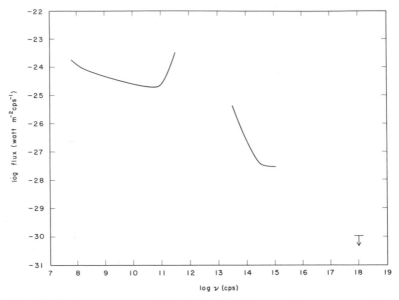

FIG. 4.2   *Continuous energy distribution in 3C 273 over radio, microwave, infrared, and optical frequency regions. The arrow at log ν = 18 represents the measured upper limit to x-ray flux. [After Stein (1966).]*

plasma and then with that from a high-temperature (160,000°) plasma, and found that neither was entirely satisfactory (see also Divan, 1965). Figure 4.3, taken from a paper by Hoyle, Burbidge, and Sargent (1966), shows the energy distribution of 3C 273 as far as the near infrared, and it is clear that the observed continuous energy distribution does not accord with any model in which the radiation is emitted thermally from a hot gas. The very marked increase in the flux in the near and far infrared must be due to radiation emitted by a nonthermal process. There are only two processes that appear to be possible in this situation. They are synchrotron emission and emission by the inverse Compton process. If either process is occurring a flux of high-energy electrons must be present; for synchrotron emission a magnetic field must be present, and for the inverse Compton process we must invoke the presence of an intense radiation field of low-energy quanta. We shall return to this question

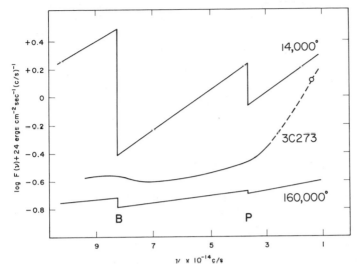

FIG. 4.3 *Continuous energy distribution in 3C 273 in optical and near infrared, together with the computed form of the hydrogen emission spectrum at two temperatures. The curves have been displaced vertically by arbitrary amounts.* [*After Hoyle, Burbidge, and Sargent (1966).*]

in Chapter 11. In other QSO's (see Oke, 1966) it is conceivable that the continuum could arise from a very hot gas ($T \sim 10^5$–5×10^5 degrees).

RELATION BETWEEN CONTINUOUS ENERGY DISTRIBUTION AND THE COLORS $(U - B)$, $(B - V)$

We have already mentioned that the U,B,V measurements necessarily include the flux radiated in any emission lines occurring in the band-pass of the filter together with the pure continuum radiation admitted through each filter. Yet, aside from this complication, the U,B,V measurements clearly provide the ingredients of a rough integral equation from which the original energy distribution $F(\nu)$, very much blurred by the breadth of the U,B,V band-passes, can be recovered.

This is so because the $(B - V)$ and $(U - B)$ colors are related to the first derivatives of the energy distribution function. This was realized by McCrea (1966) and by Kardashev and Komberg (1966), and they set out to derive $F(v)$ from the U,B,V measurements. Sandage (1966a) made a more detailed study using more extensive data.

The zero points of the U,B,V magnitude scales, calibrated by means of stars of known energy distribution, give

$$U - B = 2.5 \log \frac{F_B(v)}{F_U(v)} - 0.910,$$

$$B - V = 2.5 \log \frac{F_V(v)}{F_B(v)} + 0.091,$$

(4.2)

where the fluxes are expressed per unit frequency interval, according to Matthews and Sandage (1963) and Sandage (1966a). Here the mean effective frequencies of the U,B,V bands are 8.36×10^{14} c/s, 6.84×10^{14} c/s, and 5.45×10^{14} c/s, respectively, from $\bar{\lambda}_U = 3593$ Å, $\bar{\lambda}_B = 4408$ Å, and $\bar{\lambda}_V = 5515$ Å. Using equations (4.2) and these effective frequencies, and correcting the frequencies to zero redshift for any object of known z, one will then have the flux ratios at these frequencies, and consequently an approximate $F(v)$.

The converse of the problem of recovering the energy distribution of a source from measurements of $(U - B)$ and $(B - V)$ is to predict the colors for given energy distributions. The colors can easily be computed because the transmission functions $S(v)$, or $S(\lambda)$, of the U,B,V systems are known. We have

$$U - B = 2.5 \log \frac{\int_0^\infty S_B(v)F(v)\,dv}{\int_0^\infty S_U(v)F(v)\,dv},$$

(4.3)

and a similar equation for $B - V$; the limits for the integrals can be replaced by the upper and lower frequency cutoffs of the U,B,V filters.

In the first work on the colors of QSO's, Matthews and Sandage (1963) showed that the colors computed from energy distributions with both an exponential dependence and with power-law dependences on frequency, when plotted in the $(U - B)$, $(B - V)$ diagram, do indeed fall in the region occupied by the QSO's. This is also the region crossed by the line forming the locus of black bodies of various temperatures in this diagram (as well as the region occupied by white dwarfs, ex-novae, and other hot dwarf stars at late evolutionary stages).

We conclude, then, that continuous energy distributions of the form

$$F(\nu) \propto \nu^{-n} \qquad (4.4)$$

or

$$F(\nu) \propto e^{-\nu/\nu_0} \qquad (4.5)$$

will account for the general range of the $(U - B)$ and $(B - V)$ colors that are observed for QSO's.

OBSERVED CORRELATIONS BETWEEN COLORS AND REDSHIFTS OF QSO'S

When one examines the colors of QSO's of known redshift, some very interesting correlations become apparent. McCrea (1966) was the first to point out the existence of the correlations, and Kardashev and Komberg (1966) and Barnes (1966) independently discussed them. Figures 4.4 and 4.5 show plots of $(B - V)$ and $(U - B)$ against z for all the objects currently available. While there is considerable scatter, the systematic nature of the plots is apparent.

McCrea realized that a relationship between colors and redshift must be due to the intrinsic form of the energy distribution emitted by the objects. When $F(\nu)$ is recovered from the U,B,V measurements by the method described in the preceding section, then the QSO's divide into two distinct groups, one in which $F(\nu)$ is concave to the ν axis or not noticeably curved, and one in which $F(\nu)$ is convex to the ν axis. Of the QSO's with redshifts available at the time of McCrea's work, all those in the "concave" group were found to have $z \leq 0.7$, with an average $z = 0.5$, and all in the "convex" group had $z > 0.8$, with an average $z = 1.0$.

The correlation becomes even more striking if one plots $Q = (U - B) - (B - V)$ against z, as is shown by Figure 4.6. The scatter is less than in the plots of $(U - B)$ and $(B - V)$ alone.

Kardashev and Komberg (1966) arrived independently at the

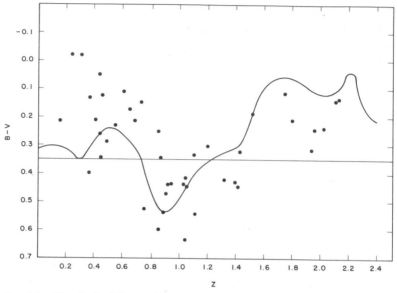

FIG. 4.4   *Magnitude difference B − V against redshift z for QSO's in Table 3.1. The curve is computed from a continuous energy distribution spectrum of form F(ν) ∝ ν⁻¹ plus emission lines with adopted rest-frame intensities given in Table 4.2. The horizontal line represents the continuum F(ν) ∝ ν⁻¹ without any emission lines.* [*After Burbidge and Strittmatter (1966).*]

conclusion that the colors give information on the energy distribution being received through the U,B,V filters. Sandage (1966a), using more extensive photometric data, assumed that there is an intrinsic $F(\nu)$ distribution, similar for all QSO's whatever their redshift, and set out to derive this from the measured $(U − B)$ and $(B − V)$ in the way we have described. With an $F(\nu)$ that has some structure in it—changes of slope, maxima and minima—one samples different parts of such a curve in looking at QSO's with different redshifts through the U,B,V filters with fixed band-passes.

Let us return for a moment to the simple functions given by equations (4.4) and (4.5) for $F(\nu)$. It is clear that, although these both reproduce quite well the general region of the $(U − B)$, $(B − V)$ plot in which the QSO's lie, neither function can account for the observed

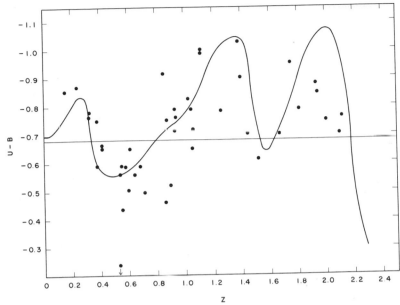

FIG. 4.5 *Magnitude difference* $U - B$ *against redshift z for QSO's in Table 3.1 (see legend of Fig. 4.4 for details).*

correlations of colors with redshifts. If $F(\nu)$ is given by equation (4.4), the slope of the continuum at a given frequency is clearly independent of redshift for any value of n, and hence the observed $(B - V)$, $(U - B)$ colors would be independent of redshift. If $F(\nu)$ is given by equation (4.5), then the slope of $F(\nu)$ increases linearly with $(1 + z)$. Thus if all QSO's had the same intrinsic energy distribution of this form with the same value of ν_0, there would be a systematic steepening of the observed slope of the continuum with increasing redshift of the objects, but this could not account for the rather complicated dependence of $(U - B)$, $(B - V)$, and Q on z.

The actual form of the $F(\nu)$ curve that Sandage derived by piecing together the results for 43 QSO's whose colors he had measured is shown in Figure 4.1 along with Oke's spectral scans of

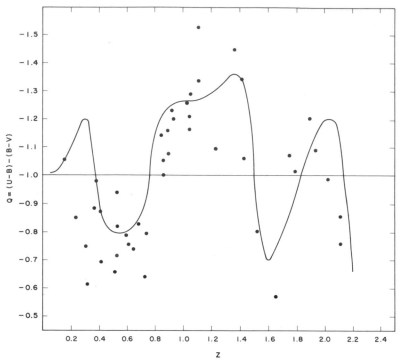

FIG. 4.6   *Color difference $Q = (U - B) - (B - V)$ against redshift z for QSO's in Table 3.1 (see legend of Fig. 4.4 for details).*

seven objects. This curve has a maximum near $\lambda_0 = 2800$ A and a depression near $\lambda_0 = 2100$ Å, and in fact it does not reproduce at all well the observed $F(\nu)$ curves.

EFFECTS OF THE EMISSION LINES
ON THE OBSERVED COLORS

The broad band-passes of the U,B,V filters admit the energy radiated by redshifted emission lines that fall within the appropriate ranges, and these will contaminate the continuum radiation selected by these measurements. In the scanner measurements, however, the intensities of the emission lines have been measured, and their effects have wherever possible been removed from the continua. The intensities of the emission lines in six of the objects, expressed as equivalent widths, are given in Table 4.1 (Oke, 1966). These equivalent widths are quite large, and it is clear that their contaminating effect on the U,B,V measures will be appreciable. Further, the observed equivalent width of a line increases linearly with $(1 + z)$ from its rest frame value, so that the effect of the lines on the colors will be most important at large redshifts. Strittmatter and Burbidge (1967) therefore suggested that the observed correlations between the colors and redshifts are due to the effect of the emission lines, and that Sandage's average composite $F(\nu)$ curve recovered from the color measurements is in fact the result of the superposition of a true continuum distribution of simple form, such as that given by equation (4.4) or equation (4.5), and emission lines blurred and broadened to a great extent by the large acceptance band-widths of the U,B,V filters. The composite curve has indeed a maximum near $\lambda_0 = 2800$ Å, and the strong Mg II line is at $\lambda_0 = 2798$ Å. Further, the depression near $\lambda_0 = 2100$ Å can be related to the occurrence of the C III] line at 1909 Å.

If the intrinsic continuous spectra are of the form given by equation (4.4) or equation (4.5), they should appear as straight lines in Figure 4.1. Certainly none of the scanner measurements show any sign of a maximum at 2800 Å. The plots for CTA 102, 3C 245, and 3C 446 do, however, turn upward at the high-frequency end, but this occurs at positions, in the observer's frame, whose wavelengths are near the ultraviolet atmospheric cutoff, where extinction corrections are notoriously difficult to make. Further, the emission features of C IV $\lambda1549$ and C III] $\lambda1909$ occur in this region in the energy distributions of both CTA 102 and 3C 245, while in 3C 446 there are emission features of Si IV $\lambda1398$ and [O IV] $\lambda1406$, as well as the strong C IV $\lambda1549$ near the high-frequency end of the observed spectrum, and these may not have been fully taken into account.

It therefore seems plausible that the continuous energy distributions of these three sources could be represented by the broken lines in Figure 4.1. The continuous energy distributions of all the QSO's except 3C 286 would then have closely similar slopes; none would show any marked change in gradient (excluding the Balmer

Table 4.1

EMISSION-LINE INTENSITIES (IN EQUIVALENT WIDTH UNITS)
MEASURED BY OKE FOR SIX QUASI-STELLAR OBJECTS

Object and Line (λ_0)	Equivalent Width (Å)	Object and Line (λ_0)	Equivalent Width (Å)
3C 48		CTA 102	
2798	15	1909	82
4861	110	2798	112
5007	264	4101	(98)
3C 286		5007	(144)
1909	10	3C 446	
2798	15	1550	230
4861	86	1640	50
5007	250	1909	20
3C 245		3C 9	
1909	18	1216	460
		1550	98

discontinuity in 3C 273), and the observed distribution for 3C 9, which straddles the region of interest, and for which subtraction of emission line contributions may most accurately be effected, would then follow the general rule. Indeed, with the exception of 3C 286, all the observed continua could be represented by functions of the form given by equation (4.4) or equation (4.5), with $n \approx 1$ or $\nu_0 \approx 3 \times 10^{14}$ c/s, respectively.

COMPUTATION OF COLORS AS FUNCTION OF REDSHIFT FOR SIMPLE POWER-LAW $F(\nu)$ PLUS EMISSION LINES

Strittmatter and Burbidge's hypothesis, then, is that the average composite $F(\nu)$ curve derived from the colors represents the true continuum distribution together with the emission lines. This can be tested by computing the variation of $(U - B)$, $(B - V)$, and Q with z for an adopted $F(\nu)$ and adopted strengths for the emission lines.

A continuum of the form $F(\nu) \propto \nu^{-1}$ is taken, because this

Table 4.2

ADOPTED EMISSION-LINE INTENSITIES (IN EQUIVALENT WIDTH UNITS)

Line (λ_0)	Equivalent Width (Å)
Ly-α1216	175
C IV λ1549	124
C III] 1909	13
Mg II 2798	94
[Ne V] 3426	16
[O II] 3727	16
Hγ 4340	26

choice gives satisfactory mean colors of $(U - B) = -0.68$ and $(B - V) = 0.35$. The average equivalent widths, in the rest frame, that are adopted for the emission lines are listed in Table 4.2; they are based on Oke's measurements, given in Table 4.1, and on eye-estimates made by Burbidge, Burbidge, Hoyle, and Lynds (1966) of the line intensities in many QSO's. The line intensities will then vary as $(1 + z)$, and it is a simple matter to compute $(U - B)$ and $(B - V)$ for any redshift.

The curves in Figures 4.4, 4.5, and 4.6 show the results of the computation. Clearly they represent quite well the observed run of $(U - B)$, $(B - V)$, and Q as a function of z, but there is considerable scatter in the observed points about the computed line. We now consider causes of this scatter.

The quantity $Q = (U - B) - (B - V)$ is independent of both the redshift and the slope of the continuum—that is, n or ν_0 in the two possible expressions for $F(\nu)$. Thus in plotting Q against z, most of the scatter due to fluctuations in the slope of the continuum is removed if the latter can actually be represented by equations (4.4) or (4.5). This explains why the scatter in the plot of Q against z is much less than that in the corresponding plots of $(U - B)$ and $(B - V)$. The remaining scatter in the plot of Q may be attributed to differences in line strengths among the QSO's. The much larger scatter in the plots of $(U - B)$ and $(B - V)$, however, is primarily due to the effect of variations in the slope of the continuum (n or ν_0) among the QSO's.

The computed curve in Figure 4.6 lies slightly above the observed points in the region around $z = 0.8$, where the strongest influence is due to the Mg II line at $\lambda 2798$. The suggestion is that the Mg II lines in the sample are systematically stronger for $z < 0.8$ than for $z > 0.8$; this effect has also been suggested from visual inspection of the spectra.

Finally, let us consider whether it might be possible to predict redshifts from the photometric data. Clearly the use of $(U - B)$ or $(B - V)$ colors is precluded by the considerable scatter in the observed correlations. The color difference, Q, is somewhat better suited to this purpose, but since it is many-valued its utility is doubtful, except in QSO's with only one line and hence several possible z's.

THE K-CORRECTION FOR QSO'S

For any class of distant objects, such as the normal or radio galaxies, that may be used for tests of various cosmological theories, the measured apparent magnitudes have to be corrected for the so-called K-effect (Humason, Mayall, and Sandage, 1956). The nature of this effect is as follows. A galaxy has a certain integrated continuous energy distribution $F(\lambda)$ as a function of wavelength λ, which is the result of summing the contributions from all the classes of stars (in their correct relative numbers) that make up the galaxy. For nearby galaxies $F(\lambda)$ can be determined observationally. The V magnitude of the galaxy, a measured quantity, is given by the integral of the intrinsic $F(\lambda)$ times the transmission function of the V filter. For a distant galaxy with a moderately large redshift, the V filter admits a range of wavelengths different from that admitted for a galaxy at rest with respect to the observer; that is, the two wavelength ranges come from different parts of the $F(\lambda)$ distribution as emitted in the reference frame of the observer. Consequently, in comparing apparent magnitudes of distant and nearby galaxies, a correction has to be applied to the distant ones to take account of this effect. The magnitude of the K-effect has been calculated for elliptical galaxies by Sandage (1966d). We have

$$m_{\text{observed}} = m_{\text{true}} + K, \qquad (4.6)$$

and, with the strong depression of $F(\lambda)$ on going toward shorter wavelengths in elliptical galaxies, K is positive and the observed magnitudes are too faint.

Similarly, if the QSO's are at cosmological distances and one wants to compare apparent magnitudes for objects with a large range of distances, it is necessary to compute the change of apparent magnitude due to redshifting the energy distribution as emitted at the source through the fixed measuring bands of the U,B,V system.

The K-term can be divided into two parts. First, there is a bandwidth correction due to the compression of a bandwidth $d\nu_0$ at ν_0 to the redshifted $d\nu_z = d\nu_0/(1+z)$ at redshift z. This term is negative and is $-2.5 \log(1+z)$. Second, there is a term due to the actual form of the curve of $F(\nu)$ vs ν, so that a different region of $F(\nu)$ is observed in the measuring band for objects with different z. This term is $2.5 \log F_0(\nu)/F_z(\nu)$. If $F(\nu)$ decreases with increasing ν, as the observations and equations (4.4) and (4.5) show, this term is positive. For $F(\nu) \propto \nu^{-n}$, a redshifted object has $\nu_z = \nu_0/(1+z)$, so that the observed flux is that corresponding to $(1+z)^n$ times the observed frequency, and $F_z(\nu) = F_0(\nu)/(1+z)$. Thus the observed magnitude of the object is too faint and K is positive. For $F(\nu) \propto \nu^{-1.00}$ this term is $2.5 \log(1+z)$ and just cancels the bandwidth correction.

The true K-correction must include the effect of the lines as well as the effect of the continuum; it is therefore appropriate to use Sandage's average composite curve to determine it. Table 4.3 gives values of K computed by Sandage (1966a) and normalized to a redshift $z = 1.0$, which falls in the middle range of the observational data. A positive value of K means that the magnitude of the redshifted source (i.e., the observed magnitude) is too faint compared with what it would have been at a redshift $z = 1.0$. Therefore K is to be subtracted, with its tabulated sign, from observed magnitudes to obtain corrected values. This is in the same sense as that used in deriving K-corrections for elliptical galaxies (e.g., Sandage, 1965), and in the same sense as given in equation (4.6). It should be noted, however, that Sandage (1966a) defines the K-correction for QSO's as having the *opposite* sign from that for galaxies, so that the signs are all reversed from what we give in Table 4.3. He clearly states the sign of the correction in the text and in the footnote to his paper, and so there should be no confusion.

Table 4.3

SANDAGE'S COMPUTED K-CORRECTIONS FOR
QUASI-STELLAR OBJECTS, NORMALIZED TO $z = 1.0$

z	K_V	K_B	K_U	$K_B - K_V$	$K_U - K_B$
0.0	(+1.00)	(+0.35)	(+0.05)	(−0.65)	(−0.30)
0.2	+0.57	0.00	−0.09	−0.57	−0.09
0.4	+0.22	−0.13	−0.03	−0.35	+0.10
0.6	+0.09	−0.13	−0.05	−0.22	+0.18
0.8	−0.01	−0.06	+0.08	−0.05	+0.14
1.0	0.00	0.00	0.00	0.00	0.00
1.2	+0.06	+0.02	−0.10	−0.04	−0.12
1.4	+0.11	+0.01	−0.22	−0.10	−0.23
1.6	+0.14	−0.12	−0.30	−0.26	−0.18
1.8	+0.14	−0.21	−0.36	−0.35	−0.15
2.0	+0.10	−0.31	−0.35	−0.41	−0.04
2.2	+0.03	−0.38	−0.29	−0.41	+0.09
2.4	−0.03	−0.42		−0.39	
2.6	−0.13	−0.42		−0.29	
2.8	−0.19	−0.38		−0.19	
3.0	−0.23	−0.33		−0.10	

The magnitude corrections are very small except near $z = 0$, because the average composite curve is fairly close to $F(\lambda) \propto \lambda^{-1.0}$ except for the longer wavelengths, and here it is probable that the composite curve adopted by Sandage departs from the true energy distribution.

For values of $z > 2.2$ K_U has not been computed, because for $z > 2.5$ the Lyman limit at rest wavelength 916 Å comes into the measuring band of the U filter, and we do not know what is the flux of continuous radiation in QSO's below this wavelength. Maybe very little radiation with $\lambda < 916$ Å escapes from the objects; if this were so K_U would become large and positive and the QSO's would no longer be distinguishable as objects that are relatively bright in the ultraviolet. Thus if we attempt to find QSO's only by looking for objects with large ultraviolet excesses we *may* discriminate against objects with z greater than about 2.5.

5

Radio Emission from Quasi-Stellar Objects

The majority of quasi-stellar objects were first identified through their property of emitting radio energy. Within the range of frequencies at which the radio surveys have been conducted, they exhibit a wide range of flux levels, as do the radio galaxies. We give the radio fluxes for the identified QSO's in Table 5.1. If we assume that they are at the distances indicated by their redshifts, then, because the redshifts are large compared with those of the radio galaxies, many of them are emitting at the power levels of the strongest radio emitters, in the range 10^{43}–10^{45} erg/sec.

The distribution of radio brightness for most of the objects in Table 5.1 has not been determined. Investigation shows, however, that a number of radio sources identified as QSO's show structures similar to those found for radio galaxies (Moffet, 1966); that is, they are often double, with large separations between the two components. Examples of QSO's with large separations between radio components are 3C 47 (Schmidt and Matthews, 1964), MSH 14 − 12*1* (Burbidge, 1965a) and 3C 9 (Schmidt, 1965). If the objects are at cosmological distances, with $q_0 = 1$, the separations between the two components for these three QSO's are: 207 kpc for 3C 47, 133 kpc for MSH 14 − 12*1*, and 130 kpc for 3C 9. If the objects are local ($d = 10$ Mpc), the corresponding separations are: 3.4 kpc for 3C 47, 1.8 kpc for MSH 14 − 12*1*, and 1.9 kpc for 3C 9.

In addition, many QSO's have at least one radio component with a diameter corresponding, at a cosmological distance, to a size that is comparable to those found for radio galaxies in general

Table 5.1

RADIO FLUXES, S, FROM QUASI-STELLAR OBJECTS (S in Flux Units)

Object	S_{2650}	S_{1410}	S_{408}	S_{178}	$S_{85.5}$	Spectral Index	Remarks
PHL 658 =							
4C 15.01				4.3			
3C 2	2.3	4.0	8.3	15.0		−0.7	
3C 9	1.2	2.1	6.6	15.0		−0.9	
MSH 00 − 29	1.6	3.3	8.2		33	(−0.9)	
PHL 6638				3.1			
PHL 923 =							
4C − 0.06				5.3			
PKS 0056 − 17	0.9	1.7	5.5		29	−1.0	
PHL 938							radio quiet
PKS 0106 + 01	0.9	1.4	3.5			−0.7	
PKS 0014 + 07	0.8	1.6	3.0			−1.1	
AO 0118 + 03 =							
3C 39	0.6	1.2	5.0		16	−1.1	
PKS 0119 − 04	1.0	1.3	2.2			−0.4	
PKS 0122 − 00	1.4	1.5	1.5			−0.1	
3C 43				11.5			
PHL 3375							radio quiet
PHL 1027							radio quiet
PHL 3424							radio quiet
3C 47				26.4			
PHL 1070							radio quiet
3C 48				47			
PHL 1072							radio quiet
PHL 1078 =							
4C − 5.06				2.2			
PHL 1093 =							
4C 1.04				3.8			
PHL 1127							radio quiet
PHL 3740 =							
4C − 5.07				6.6			
PHL 1186							radio quiet
PHL 1194							radio quiet
PHL 1222							radio quiet
PHL 1226							radio quiet

Table 5.1, *continued*

RADIO FLUXES, *S*, FROM QUASI-STELLAR OBJECTS (*S* in Flux Units)

Object	S_{2650}	S_{1410}	S_{408}	S_{178}	$S_{85.5}$	Spectral Index	Remarks
3C 57	2.0	2.9	6.5		14	−0.6	
PKS 0202 − 17	1.3	1.2	1.1			+0.1	
PHL 1305 =							
4C − 3.07				3.2			
PKS 0229 + 13	1.4	1.2		2.3		+0.2	
PHL 1377 =							
4C − 4.06				6.1			
PKS 0237 − 23						curved	5 f.u. at 610 Mc/s
PKS 0336 − 01	2.2	1.5	3.5			curved	
3C 93	1.6	2.5	8.1	9.5	35	−0.9	
PKS 0347 + 13	< 0.2	0.5	2.8			−1.4	
MSH 03 − 19	1.4	2.9	11.6		44	−0.9	
3C 94	1.5	3.1	9.9		25	−0.8	
PKS 0403 − 13	3.0	3.3	8.7			−0.5	
MSH 04 − 12 =							
0405 − 12	2.5	2.8	9.3		31	curved	
3C 119				15.0			
3C 138	7.1	9.3	17.5	18.5		−0.4	
3C 147				58			
PKS 0541 − 24	0.6	1.1	2.9		13	−0.9	
3C 172				14.0			
3C 175	1.3	2.7	8.6	16.0		−1.0	
3C 175.1	1.1	2.0	5.2	11.5		−0.9	
3C 181	1.1	2.1	6.3	13.0		−0.9	
PKS 0736 + 01	2.0	2.9	2.9			−0.4	
3C 186				13.5			
3C 190	1.2	2.7	9.5	11.0		−1.0	
3C 191	0.8	2.0	7.7	10.5		−1.1	
3C 196				59			
PKS 0812 + 02	1.0	2.0	6.0			−0.9	
PKS 0825 − 20	2.1	3.7	11.7		26	−0	
4C 37.24				8.5			
3C 204				9.5			
3C 205				12.5			

Table 5.1, continued

RADIO FLUXES, S, FROM QUASI-STELLAR OBJECTS (S in Flux Units)

Object	S_{2650}	S_{1410}	S_{408}	S_{178}	$S_{85.5}$	Spectral Index	Remarks
3C 207	1.8	2.6	7.3	10.0		−0.7	
3C 208	1.2	2.6	$(10.0)^+$	16.0		−1.0	+incl. 3C 208.1
PKS 0859 − 14		3.5				−0.6	
4C 22.22				5.1			
3C 215	0.9	1.4	4.6	10.0		−0.9	
3C 216				18.5			
3C 217				12.0			
PKS 0922 + 14	0.4	0.7	2.8			−1.0	
4C 39.25				5.4			
3C 230	1.5	$(3.2)^+$	$(12.0)^+$	21		−1.0	+incl. 0950 + 00
3C 232 = Ton 469				8.5^+			+at 159 Mc/s
AO 0952 + 17			1.5^+				+at 430 Mc/s
PKS 0957 + 00	0.6	1.0	3.1			−0.9	
3C 239				12.0			
3C 245	2.0	3.0	7.6	9.5		−0.7	
PKS 1049 − 09	1.2	1.7	5.8		9	−0.7	
3C 249.1				11.5			
3C 254				19.0			
PKS 1116 + 12	1.6	1.9	5.5			−0.6	
PKS 1127 − 14	6.5	6.2	5.0			+0.2	
3C 261				7.5			
3C 263				13.0			
PKS 1136 − 13	2.8	4.1	12.8		44	−0.8	
PKS 1148 − 00	2.6	2.9	3.5			−0.1	
4C 31.38				7.5			
3C 268.4				9.0			
PKS 1217 + 02	0.5	0.8	1.7			−0.9	
3C 270.1				12 0			
4C 21.35				6.6			
Ton 1530							radio quiet
3C 273	37.3	41.2	55.1	67	167	−0.1	
PKS 1229 − 02	1.5	1.7	4.6			−0.5	
PKS 1233 − 24	1.4	2.3	6.4		28	−0.9	
PKS 1237 − 10	1.2	1.8	1.6			−0.6	

Table 5.1, continued

RADIO FLUXES, S, FROM QUASI-STELLAR OBJECTS (S in Flux Units)

Object	S_{2650}	S_{1410}	S_{408}	S_{178}	$S_{85.5}$	Spectral Index	Remarks
3C 275.1	1.6	2.9	9.4	16.0		−0.9	
BSO 1							radio quiet
3C 277.1				12.0			
PKS 1252 + 11	1.1	1.2	(2.8)⁺			−0.1	⁺incl. 1250 + 11
3C 279		6.3	15	20	37		
3C 280.1			5.5	11.0			
3C 281 = NRAO 419		1.0	5.4		22	−1.1	
4C 22.38				5.2			
PKS 1326 + 06	<0.2	<0.5	2.0				
PKS 1327 − 21	1.3	2.0	5.4			−0.8	
3C 287				15			
3C 286				21			
MSH 13 − 011	1.9	3.2	10.1		35	−0.8	
3C 288.1				9.5			
PKS 1354 + 19	1.5	2.3	6.0			−0.7	
3C 298	2.7	6.2	24.4	44		−1.1	
4C 20.33				7.4			
MSH 14 − 121	2.5	3.7	10.2		41	−0.7	
PKS 1454 − 06	0.9	1.2			16	−0.8	
3C 309.1				17.0			
PKS 1510 − 08	3.0	3.0	3.0			0.0	
PKS 1514 + 00	1.8	2.5	4.4		16	−0.6	
3C 323.1				9.0			
MSH 16 + 03	1.4	2.2	7.9		35	−0.9	
Ton 256							radio quiet
3C 334	1.1	2.2	6.3	10.0		−0.9	
3C 336				13.5			
3C 345				10.0			
3C 351				11.0			
3C 380				57			
PKS 2115 − 30	1.5	2.4	5.7		15	−0.7	
3C 432	0.7	1.7	8.0	11.5		−1.2	
3C 435	1.1	2.4	6.6	9.5		−0.9	

Table 5.1, concluded

RADIO FLUXES, S, FROM QUASI-STELLAR OBJECTS (S in Flux Units)

Object	S_{2650}	S_{1410}	S_{408}	S_{178}	$S_{85.5}$	Spectral Index	Remarks
PKS 2128 − 12	2.2	1.8	1.5			+0.2	
PKS 2135 − 14	2.0	3.0	10.0		33	−0.8	
PKS 2144 − 17	0.6	1.4	1.9			−1.2	
PKS 2145 + 06	3.1	3.0	3.4			curved	
PKS 2146 − 13	0.9	1.5	5.6		13	−0.9	
PKS 2154 − 18	0.9	3.6	8.8		25	curved	
PKS 2203 − 18	4.9	6.2	7.8		16	−0.3	
PKS 2216 − 03	1.0	0.9	2.8		18	curved	
3C 446	4.4	6.0	10.3	17	30	−0.5	
PHL 5200 = 4C − 5.93				3.2			
CTA 102	5.3	6.7	7.1	5.1		curved	
3C 454	1.2	2.4	4.6	9.0		−0.8	
3C 454.3	10.0	12.8	15.8	15.0		−0.2	
PKS 2251 + 11	0.9	1.6	3.7			−0.8	
4C 29.68 = CTD 141				6.7			
PKS 2344 + 09	1.4	2.1	2.7			−0.5	
PKS 2345 − 16	1.3	1.2	2.5			−0.2	
PKS 2354 + 14	0.5	1.4	3.7			−1.1	
PKS 2354 − 11	1.7	1.8	2.9			−0.2	

Sources: Fluxes have been taken from the Parkes, 3C revised, 4C, and MSH catalogues (referred to in Chapter 1). Some entries are from the compilation by W. E. Howard and S. P. Maran (Ap. J. Suppl., **10**, 1965). Spectral indices where given are from the Parkes catalogue. No attempt has been made to give fluxes for all of the frequencies at which they have been measured.

(Moffet, 1966) and is ~50 kpc. If the objects are at cosmological distances then the large sizes and the high power levels mean that the energy content of the sources in relativistic particles and magnetic flux have the minimum values of ~10^{60} ergs (Burbidge and Burbidge, 1965). However, although some QSO's have radio properties that render them indistinguishable from the radio galaxies, recent investigations have shown that, in contradistinction to most radio galaxies, many of the QSO's have at least one exceedingly small radio component that may or may not be the only component.

The suggestion that some of the radio sources would have very small angular diameters came first from attempts to interpret their radio spectra. It is well known that the radio sources have spectra of the form $P(\nu) \propto \nu^{\alpha}$, where α is an index with a median value near -0.7 (Conway, Kellermann, and Long, 1963). For a fraction of the sources examined the spectra show a pronounced curvature, getting flatter toward longer wavelengths. These sources have small sizes and large brightness temperatures. Many of them have a maximum in their spectra, and the flux appears to decrease at longer wavelengths. To explain this property LeRoux (1961), Slish (1963), and Williams (1963) proposed that the curvature of the low-frequency part of the spectrum is probably due to synchrotron self-absorption.

If we use the absorption coefficient of synchrotron radiation and apply it to a uniform circular source, the spectrum has the form

$$S_{\nu} = 2.0 \times 10^{-44} F(\alpha)\theta^2 B^{-1/2}\nu^{5/2}[1 - e^{-\tau(\nu)}], \tag{5.1}$$

where S_{ν} is the flux density $(Wm^{-2}(c/s)^{-1})$, $\tau(\nu)$ is the optical depth, θ is the angular diameter in seconds of arc, B is the magnetic field, and $F(\alpha)$ is a function of the spectral index. Dent and Haddock (1966) have obtained the following empirical expression for $F(\alpha)$:

$$F(\alpha) = (0.249 + 0.026\alpha)(0.331 - \alpha),$$

which is accurate to better than 1% for a range in α from 0 to -2.

From (5.1) it is easily shown that

$$\theta^2 = 8.9 \times 10^{21} F(\alpha)^{-1/2}\nu^{-5/4}S(\nu_1)^{1/2}B^{1/4} \tag{5.2}$$

where ν_1 is the frequency at which $\tau(\nu) = 1$, and $S(\nu_1)$ is the flux density at ν_1. Thus if the radio spectrum is known, so that it is possible to estimate the frequency at which synchrotron self-absorption sets in, the angular size can be calculated as a function of the magnetic field strength. For example, for the quasi-stellar sources 3C 48, 3C 119, 3C 147, 3C 298, CTA 21, and CTA 102, Williams obtained maximum angular diameters of $0\rlap{.}''4$, $0\rlap{.}''3$, $0\rlap{.}''2$, $0\rlap{.}''6$, $0\rlap{.}''01$, $0\rlap{.}''11$, respectively, using assumed values of $B = 10^{-4}$ gauss.

Thermal absorption due to a shell of ionized gas surrounding the source may also occur, and one can calculate an "emission measure" $\int N_e^2 \, ds$, where s is measured in parsec. To give the angular sizes as above, values of this emission measure have to be in the range 3000 to 5000, and for CTA 102 and CTA 21, they are 20,000 and 34,000, respectively.

We consider next the methods that are being used to investigate the structure of the sources of small angular size. These are:

1. Long-base-line interferometry, which is being carried out extensively in England by the Jodrell Bank group, working now in conjunction with the radio astronomers at Malvern (Allen et al., 1962; Anderson, Donaldson, Palmer, and Ronson, 1965; Barber, Donaldson, Miley, and Smith, 1966; Adgie et al., 1965). These groups are now working with effective baselines of up to 604,000 wavelengths at a frequency of 1422 Mc/s. The NRAO astronomers at Greenbank, West Virginia, have also carried out similar work (Clark and Hogg, 1966).

2. The method of lunar occultations (Hazard, Mackey, and Shimmins, 1963; von Hoerner, 1966; Hazard, Gulkis, and Bray, 1966).

3. The method of using the irregularities in the interplanetary plasma that cause sources of small diameter to scintillate (Hewish, Scott, and Wills, 1964; Cohen, 1965).

Detailed studies have been carried out, particularly for 3C 273 (Hazard, Mackey, and Shimmins, 1963; von Hoerner, 1966; Hazard et al., 1966), and a considerable number of sources have been studied using long-base-line interferometry. We discuss first the results achieved by this method.

The QSO's 3C 279, 3C 345, and 3C 380 have been shown to have sizes $<0\rlap{.}''1$ by the observations at 1422 Mc/s of Barber et al. (1966). These objects all show evidence for large fluxes at high frequencies (Dent and Haddock, 1966), and 3C 279 and 3C 345 are known to show time variations in flux in the high-frequency range (Chapter 6). It should also be mentioned here that 3C 84, which is not a QSO, but a radio galaxy (NGC 1275), also shows the same characteristics and is variable in flux at frequencies above 3000 Mc/s. This source is known to be at a distance of about 50 Mpc, and at this distance

$0''\!.1 = 25$ pc. The variable nature of the high-frequency component suggests that it has a dimension ≤ 1 light-year or $\leq 0''\!.001$. A number of other QSO's have been studied by the interferometer technique at 408 Mc/s, and the certainly identified QSO's 3C 286, 3C 147, 3C 48, 3C 273, 3C 287, CTA 21, CTA 102, 3C 119, 3C 138, 3C 279, 3C 345, and 3C 380 all have significant fluxes coming from sizes $\leq 0''\!.5$.

The method of lunar occultations is being used to determine positions of sources and structural characteristics by a number of groups, notably by Hazard, and also by von Hoerner; they have worked extensively on 3C 273. Hazard, Mackey, and Shimmins (1963) were the first to show that this object was double, with a separation of $19''\!.6$, and that the two components had very different spectra. Component A had a value of α of about -0.9, whereas component B, which is associated with the optical object and agrees in position with it to about $0''\!.1$, had a spectral index with $\alpha \sim 0$. Both components are elongated along the line joining them. It appears now from the work of von Hoerner that the structure of both components depends strongly on frequency. Component B is a single strong component about $2''$ wide at 2695 Mc/s; at 735 Mc/s it shows a halo about $6''$ long and a core $\leq 1''$ in diameter, which emits 30% of the flux. The core is less pronounced at 405 Mc/s, but at the lower frequencies B shows a deep minimum at the center. Component A seems to have a central dip at 2695 Mc; at 735 Mc it has a halo about $10''$ long and a core $< 1''$ in diameter (with 30% of flux) at the lower frequencies. Component A has a length to half power points of about $4''$, but shows a faint, very flat extension about $23''$ long. According to this more recent work the spectrum of A is a straight line with $\alpha = -0.68 \pm 0.08$. The spectrum of B is a straight line only above 400 Mc/s, with $\alpha = +0.25 \pm 0.08$; it cuts off toward lower frequencies. Each component is then divided into an outer part and a central part $4''\!.8$ long. The central spectrum of A is still straight with $\alpha = -0.82 \pm 0.22$, whereas the low-frequency cutoff for the center of B is very steep. The two outer halos are very similar and give $\alpha = -0.45 \pm 0.20$. Such a complex structure has so far been found only in 3C 273, but it may be expected to be generally present.

Method (3) has been used to show that the angular sizes of the QSO's 3C 48, 3C 119, 3C 138, and 3C 147 have components that lie in the size range 0″.3 to 0″.8 (Hewish, Scott, and Wills, 1964). Scintillation measurements have now been carried out at Arecibo (Cohen, Gundermann, Hardebeck, Harris, Salpeter, and Sharp, 1966; Cohen, Gundermann, Hardebeck, and Sharp, 1967) for a considerable number of sources. In addition, according to Bolton (1966) a considerable amount of scintillation data has been obtained by Ekers with the 210-foot Parks radio telescope. The Arecibo observations set very small limiting diameters to the sources that show a high percentage of scintillation—for example, 3C 279.

To return to the method of long-base-line interferometry, some results by Palmer and his colleagues (1967) became available while this book was going to press. Their results for those objects that are certainly identified as QSO's, or have been suggested as possible QSO's, and for two radio galaxies, are given in Table 5.2.

Table 5.2

LIMITS TO SIZES OF SOME SOURCES OF SMALL RADIO DIAMETER

Object	Angular Size (seconds of arc)	Object	Angular Size (seconds of arc)
CTA 21	<0.05	3C 279	<0.025
3C 84 (RG)	<0.025	3C 287	<0.05
PKS 0403 − 13	≲0.05	3C 286	<0.05
3C 119	<0.05	3C 309.1	≲0.05
PKS 0430 + 05 (RG)	≲0.05	PKS 1510 − 08	≲0.05
3C 138	Double; <0.2	3C 345	<0.05
3C 147	Double; <0.2	3C 380	<0.05
PKS 0834 − 20	≲0.05	PKS 2145 + 06	≲0.05
PKS 1055 + 01	≲0.05	PKS 2203 − 18	≲0.05
PKS 1127 − 14	≲0.05	3C 446	≲0.05
PKS 1148 − 00	≲0.05	CTA 102	<0.05
PKS 1245 − 19	≲0.05	3C 454.3	<0.025

6

Variations in the Flux
Emitted by Quasi-Stellar Objects

OPTICAL VARIABILITY

Following the identification of the first QSO, 3C 48, Smith and Hoffleit (1961) looked back on old plates of the Harvard plate collection to attempt to determine whether 3C 48 was variable in light. They concluded that there was no detectable variation within the rather large margin of error ($\sim0^{m}\!.3$) that resulted from the poor quality of the old plate material. However, the first observations using accurate photoelectric methods (Matthews and Sandage, 1963) show that 3C 48 varies in optical flux. The extent of the variations is $\sim0^{m}\!.4$ over a period of ~13 months. In addition to this Matthews and Sandage reported that a variation of about $0^{m}\!.04$ had been measured in a period of 15 minutes in October 1961, and they concluded that night-to-night variations, as well as variations over periods of months, were real. This detection of short-period variations was made before the redshifts were discovered, and appears to have been overlooked in the subsequent discussion of the significance of variations.

Following the discovery of 3C 273, Smith and Hoffleit (1963) and Sharov and Efremov (1963) attempted to measure the light curve of this object using the old plate collections, which date back about 70 years at the Harvard and Pulkova Observatories. They found that its light varied by a factor of 2 over periods of years, and that "flashes"—variations of shorter duration (months or weeks) may have occurred. Smith and Hoffleit suggested that a characteristic period of about 13 years could be detected in the observations, but this result remains in doubt. Although many spectra of this object have been taken since 1963, none of them show any evidence for spectroscopic variation.

With the identification of considerable numbers of QSO's the opportunity to look closely into the question of variability is at hand, provided that the objects are followed closely with adequate equipment. The spectroscopic observers have noted that in several cases eye estimates of the magnitudes of the QSO's they were observing varied markedly from the magnitudes estimated at the time of identification. However, such observations only indicate that there are changes of about 0^m5 or greater over periods measured in months or years. For more accurate measurements of variation we are dependent largely on the work of Sandage and of Kinman and his colleagues. Sandage has found (Sandage, 1964; Sandage, Véron, and Wyndham, 1965; Sandage, 1966c) the following variations:

3C 47: $\Delta B = 0^m20$, based on observations on 2 nights in 9 months.

3C 48: $\Delta B = 0^m30$, based on observations on 16 nights over 4 years (Sandage, 1964). More recently (Sandage, 1966c) the flux emitted by this object has remained fairly constant.

3C 196: $\Delta B = 0^m27$, based on observations on 9 nights over 45 months. The object has gradually brightened, and there was a sudden increase in December 1963.

3C 216: $\Delta B = 0^m37$, observed on 3 nights in 14 months.

3C 273: The most recent observations (1965, 1966) show that the object has not varied by more than $\Delta B \sim 0^m4$, though larger variations were detected in the past.

3C 454.3: $B = 15^m7$ in August 1954, 16^m75 in September 1965, and 16^m55 in October 1965.

3C 43: $B \sim 19^m0$ in 1954 and $B = 20^m5$ in 1965 (based on two plates taken 11 years apart).

3C 2: $B \geq 21^m1$ September 1954, $\sim 20^m5$ September 1960, $\sim 19^m5$ August 1963, and $\sim 19^m5$ November 1964.

In 3C 2 some significant color changes have been indicated.

We see from these results that, although the QSO's have only been observed intermittently, variations have frequently been observed, and it seems probable that optical variability is a common property of these objects.

More detailed investigations have been made of 3C 345 and

3C 446. Goldsmith and Kinman (1965) observed 3C 345 fairly continuously over a period of ∼100 days in the interval June–September 1965. They found that the object increased in brightness by about $0\overset{m}{.}4$ in a period of ∼20 days and then decreased more slowly, but showed smaller variations over periods of less than a week until early October 1965. A single observation of this object was made later in October by Sandage (1966a), who found that it had brightened again by about one magnitude. Thus for this object it has been established that large variations occur over periods of weeks or days. During the period June–September 1965 it was observed spectroscopically (Burbidge and Burbidge, 1966), and the structure of Mg II λ2798 was seen to change (see Plate 3). Observations of 3C 345 are being continued at Lick Observatory by Kinman and his colleagues; the object was still varying markedly in early 1967.

When spectra of 3C 446 were being obtained in 1964 and 1965, that object had an apparent magnitude of about $18\overset{m}{.}4$ (Burbidge, 1965b; Schmidt, 1966). However, it brightened by $3\overset{m}{.}2$ sometime between October 1965 and June 24, 1966, when Sandage (1966b) observed its brightness to be about $15\overset{m}{.}2$. In the period July–September 1966 it was studied in detail (Sandage, Westphal, and Strittmatter, 1966; Kinman, Lamla, and Wirtanen, 1966). In about 10 days in late July it decreased in brightness by about two magnitudes, but by early August its brightness was increasing rapidly again. From the middle of August until late September it was bright, near 16^m, but varied on several occasions by $0\overset{m}{.}5$ to $0\overset{m}{.}8$ within a day or so. These are the largest short-period variations yet observed in a quasi-stellar object. Kinman et al. (1966) showed also that the continuous radiation shows a high degree (∼10%) of linear polarization. During July 1966, when 3C 446 was very bright, Sandage obtained spectra of the object and found that the lines appeared to be extremely weak, as compared with their strengths in the spectra taken when the object was much fainter. Sandage et al. showed that this could be explained by supposing that the intrinsic line strengths have remained constant and that this apparent weakness is due entirely to the increased continuum emission corresponding to the increase of brightness of about 3 magnitudes.

As will be discussed in Chapter 11, the condition that a large change in flux takes place in a time τ sets a limit to the size of the region R such that $R \leq c\tau$. This condition can only be relaxed if the matter that is giving rise to the radiation is itself moving at relativistic speed (see Chapter 11). Thus the importance of the flux variations is that they set limits to the sizes of the objects, and for 3C 446, this limit is now about one light-day. The fact that the line-producing region did not change during the period of variations of 3C 446 shows that this region is much larger than the source giving rise to the continuum. For 3C 345, however, no significant apparent changes in line strength occurred during a period when the continuum was changing in strength; thus it may be that the line-producing region and the continuum-producing region are comparable in size, though the uncertainties are greater because the total change in brightness was smaller for 3C 345 than it was for 3C 446.

RADIO VARIABILITY

Early in 1965 Sholomitsky (1965) announced that CTA 102 was showing rapid cyclic variations at radio frequencies near 1000 Mc/s with a period of about 100 days. Since this result was announced several groups have attempted to verify it. For example, Maltby and Moffet (1965a) checked their records of observation of this object during or immediately before and after the period observed by Sholomitsky and at frequencies close to his observing frequency. No confirmation of this result has been obtained by them or by any other group, and thus it is not generally accepted at the time of writing. However, Dent (1965) announced that he had found a secular variation in 3C 273B at a frequency of 8000 Mc/s that indicated that the object was increasing in brightness by about 17% per year. He also had weaker evidence for variation in 3C 279 and 3C 345. Maltby and Moffet (1965b) then investigated 3C 273B at a number of frequencies and showed that there appeared to be a secular increase in flux at frequencies down to about 970 Mc/s, below which no significant variation was observed.

More recently a number of radio astronomical groups have been looking into the question of variability in radio flux at high frequencies in a number of QSO's. Kellermann and Pauliny-Toth (1966) have looked at variations of a number of QSO's at frequencies of 750 Mc/s and 1360 Mc/s, using observations made in 1962 and 1963, and in 1965 and 1966. They have combined them with other observations made at higher frequencies—2700 Mc/s, 5000 Mc/s and 15,000 Mc/s at NRAO and at other observatories—to find additional variations. The QSO 3C 279, for which Dent (1965) first reported variation, shows very striking variations, and its flux has been increasing very sharply. These workers have also confirmed the variations found by Dent for 3C 273, and find that the sources 3C 345, 3C 418, and 3C 454.3 are variable. In addition, 3C 84, which is a source in the nucleus of the Seyfert galaxy NGC 1275, has also been shown to vary. Variation was first shown to exist for this source by Dent (1966) at 8000 Mc/s. Other variable radio sources are NRAO 190, for which there is no optical identification, and 3C 120, which is a radio galaxy.

3C 273 is the only quasi-stellar object that has been investigated in the millimeter wavelength range (Chapter 4), and Epstein and his collaborators (Epstein, 1965; Epstein, Oliver, and Schorn, 1966) have shown that significant changes in the flux at 3.4 mm are taking place over periods of months or weeks.

So far, radio variations have not been found to take place over such short periods as those found for optical variations. In all cases in which restrictions can be placed on the size of the object by using the simple condition $R \leq c\tau$, the maximum permissible values of R are smaller than the minimum sizes derived from the radio interferometry or scintillation techniques discussed in Chapter 5. By those techniques angular sizes $\leq 0''.1$ can be deduced for some objects. If the QSO's are at cosmological distances, then $1''$ is about 1–3 kpc, so that $0''.1$ is about 100–300 pc. If the objects are local, so that, for example, their distances are 1–10 Mpc, then $0''.1$ corresponds to about 0.5–5 pc. However, the condition $R < c\tau$ leads to values of R for the optical or millimeter radiation regions less than or equal to 10^{-1}–10^{-6} pc. We shall discuss the restrictions on the models of QSO's derived by using these results in Chapter 11.

7

Proper Motions

If the QSO's were really local objects, within, let us say, a few hundred parsecs of the sun, as had to be considered in the original discussion by Greenstein and Schmidt (1964) on whether they could be collapsed stellar objects with large gravitational redshifts, then we might have expected that proper motions would be detectable.

Jeffreys (1964) made a study of the proper motion of 3C 273, using 14 plates covering the period 1887–1963. The plate material was not homogeneous, since it came from Harvard and Van Vleck observatories and from the Astrographic Catalogue, but an attempt was made to reduce the systematic errors involved in such a proper motion determination by using a large number of reference stars. The absolute proper motion was found to be:

$$\mu_\alpha = +0\rlap{.}''0009 \pm 0\rlap{.}''0025/\text{yr},$$

$$\mu_\delta = -0\rlap{.}''0012 \pm 0\rlap{.}''0025/\text{yr}.$$

Because of the position of 3C 273, in a direction approximately at right angles to the direction of the sun's peculiar motion, Jeffreys concluded that the object was likely to be more distant than 2000 pc (unless it were traveling parallel to the sun at the same speed). Its high galactic latitude would then mean that, if it belonged to our galaxy, it might well have a different galactocentric velocity from that of the sun, which should in turn lead to a detectable proper motion unless it were at an even greater distance, effectively outside the galaxy.

Luyten and Smith (1966) made a study of 12 QSO's, using plates taken with the Palomar 48-inch Schmidt telescope and eight comparison stars per object in most cases. For 3C 273 and 3C 48, old Harvard plates were used in addition, and essentially the same result was found for all 12 objects—that the relative proper motions were of the same order of magnitude as the estimated mean errors. The proper motion measured for 3C 273 did not agree with that measured by Jeffreys. The twelve objects were averaged in three groups, and the mean proper motions were found to be the inverses of the expected parallactic motions of the comparison stars, as would be expected if the QSO's had zero absolute proper motion. Luyten and Smith concluded that since the QSO's are essentially stationary objects with stellar images, they are ideal objects to use in determining the corrections from relative to absolute proper motions.

It is of some interest to ask whether the proper motions of the QSO's would be detectable if they were comparatively local objects moving at relativistic speeds at distances of a few megaparsecs from the galaxy (Chapter 11). We have calculated proper motions for the QSO's for which Luyten and Smith (1966) have attempted to measure

Table 7.1

COMPARISON OF MEASURED WITH CALCULATED PROPER MOTIONS
(Check whether QSO's moving at relativistic speeds at a distance of 10 Mpc would have detectable proper motions.)

Object	z	μ, calculated (seconds of arc per year)	μ, measured (seconds of arc per year)
3C 9	2.012	0.005	0.021 ± 0.015
3C 48	0.367	0.002	0.011 ± 0.005
3C 191	1.946	0.005	0.034 ± 0.020
3C 196	0.872	0.003	0.025 ± 0.015
3C 207	0.683	0.003	0.013 ± 0.018
3C 215	0.411	0.002	0.023 ± 0.020
3C 249.1	0.311	0.002	0.003 ± 0.014
3C 273	0.158	0.001	0.009 ± 0.005
3C 280.1	1.659	0.005	0.021 ± 0.021
3C 286	0.849	0.003	0.011 ± 0.010

proper motions. To do this we have assumed that the QSO's are all at the same distance, 10 Mpc, and that they have transverse velocities equal to their recessional velocities, which have been calculated from the redshifts. The results are shown in Table 7.1, where these calculated proper motions are compared with those measured by Luyten and Smith, converted to absolute proper motions, which are quoted in the table with their errors. It is clear that proper motions as small as those calculated could not be detected from the data. However, if the objects were much closer—at distances of ~ 1 Mpc or less—they would have proper motions large enough to be measurable. Thus if the objects are moving at relativistic speeds they must be at distances greater than a few Mpc. If the redshifts have nothing to do with velocity, then the objects could, of course, be much closer than 1 Mpc and show no detectable proper motion.

8

The Distribution of Quasi-Stellar Objects

With only about 150 QSO's positively identified, little information is to be gained by looking at the distribution of these objects in the sky. Plots of their distribution will at the present time reflect the areas over which searches for identifications have been conducted. Thus, for example, we do not know to what degree the distribution of QSO's is isotropic. The work of the Cambridge radio astronomers has shown that the data are compatible with the view that there is a fairly high degree of isotropy for the radio sources as a whole. In the large-scale surveys, however, complete identifications and division into the two categories of quasi-stellar objects and radio galaxies have not been made, and it is premature to claim, as does Longair (1966), that the results obtained so far suggest that the QSO's are at cosmological distances. For example, if they are ejected from or are otherwise associated with a variety of galaxies—a possibility that will be discussed later in this chapter and in Chapters 9 and 15—then we may expect to see a local cloud of QSO's associated with the nearer galaxies (or with our own galaxy) that will tend to be the brighter objects and may show some anisotropy in their distribution, but the fainter QSO's, which will be the majority, may be associated with a wider sample of galaxies, including more distant ones. These will imitate the distribution of this larger sample of galaxies, that is, an isotropic distribution will result.

Apart from this it is of some interest to ask whether the identified QSO's are distributed in such a way as to suggest that they may have some physical relationship with extragalactic systems. The evidence bearing on such relationships comes from different sources and should be considered no more than preliminary.

THE RELATION BETWEEN QUASI-STELLAR OBJECTS AND CLUSTERS OF GALAXIES

If the objects are at cosmological distances they are approximately 3^m brighter than the brightest galaxies in clusters. For the galaxies, however, there will be an appreciable K-correction, which will not apply to the QSO's (Chapter 4); for a redshift of $z = 0.5$, the correction amounts to nearly 2^m (Sandage and Miller, 1966). Consequently if a QSO lies in a cluster it will appear approximately five magnitudes brighter than the brightest galaxies in the cluster for redshifts near 0.5. For example, 3C 295, a radio galaxy with a redshift of $z = 0.46$ (Minkowski, 1960), lies in a cluster, and the brightest galaxy in this cluster, apart from 3C 295 itself, has a magnitude of $20^m.9$, which is in agreement with the argument given above. The majority of identifications of QSO's have been made with the 48-inch Palomar Survey plates, the normal limit of which is $20^m.0$ (visual). A preliminary conclusion is, therefore, that clusters would be identified on these plates only if the QSO's were brighter than 15^m. Only 3C 273 is brighter than this, and certainly no cluster is associated with it. It is known, however, that there is only a weak correlation of redshift with apparent magnitude, and from Table 3.1 we see that there are twenty-three QSO's now known besides 3C 273 with redshifts of $z < 0.5$, and of these, seven have magnitudes brighter than 16^m and thirteen have magnitudes brighter than 17^m. Moreover, 3C 232 has a redshift of $z > 0.5$, but is brighter than 16^m. In these cases the K-correction for galaxies in the cluster, if such were present, would be less than $1^m.9$. We might expect, therefore, that the difference between the apparent brightness of the QSO and that of the cluster galaxies would often be less than 4 magnitudes, so that galaxies would be detectable. But none have been seen.

Plates reaching 1–2 magnitudes fainter than Sky Survey plates have been taken of the fields around a number of QSO's, and inspection of these plates shows no galaxies. For 3C 48 Sandage and Miller

(1966) have used a special emulsion with which they were able to reach apparent magnitude $24^m.5$ (blue), and no galaxies were found.

Recently Sandage found that 3C 268.4 appeared to lie in a cluster. However, the redshift of this object is 1.40, and for such a redshift galaxies would be much fainter than the limit reached ($\sim 22^m$ in that case). Consequently, if the redshift is a Doppler shift it must be concluded that 3C 268.4 is either a background object (if the QSO's are at cosmological distances) or a foreground object (if the QSO's are local). If the redshifts of the QSO's are gravitational shifts (see Chapter 9) we might expect in a case such as that of 3C 268.4 to see a QSO with a large (gravitational) redshift physically associated with a group of galaxies that have much smaller (Doppler) redshifts. If this were so we could determine the distance of the QSO by measuring the redshift of the cluster. This is probably the only method available for estimating absolute brightnesses of QSO's if the line shifts are gravitational in origin.

Provided that the redshifts are Doppler shifts the preliminary conclusion is that QSO's are not associated with faint cluster galaxies. But much more work is needed to make this result conclusive.

ARE QUASI-STELLAR OBJECTS ASSOCIATED WITH INDIVIDUAL BRIGHT GALAXIES?

If it could be established that QSO's are associated with a particular kind of galaxy, then we would have to conclude that some genetic relationship existed between them. If such a conclusion were reached, it would establish that the QSO's are local objects. Evidence bearing on this possibility has recently been presented by Arp (1966a,b). He compared the positions of radio sources in the 3C catalogue with the positions of the objects included in his Atlas of Peculiar Galaxies (Arp, 1966c) and concluded that peculiar galaxies lie closer to the radio sources than would be expected if the radio sources were distributed at random with respect to the peculiar galaxies. He noticed that radio sources with similar flux densities tend to form pairs separated by 2°–6° on the sky and stated that there was a tendency for a certain class of peculiar galaxy to fall approximately on the line joining the pair. These peculiar galaxies are often elliptical galaxies that, he believes, show evidence for structures that may have been ejected from (or may be falling into) them.

There is evidence that more than two radio sources are associated with some of these peculiar galaxies. Among these there are some in which the radio sources involved have previously been identified with optical objects, either fainter galaxies or QSO's. Thus Arp has deduced that galaxies themselves are ejected from peculiar galaxies, as are QSO's. If we accept the view that the radio sources are associated with peculiar galaxies, how certain is it that the optical identifications of some of these radio sources with galaxies are correct? The identifications of the QSO's cannot be questioned. If the identifications of galaxies with radio sources are spurious, it will nearly always be the case that the measured redshifts of the "radio galaxies," as background objects, will be greater than the redshift of the peculiar galaxy. This, then, would be a perfectly good explanation for non-velocity shifts in the radio galaxies that Arp discussed.

If the original identifications are good, as is very likely, the question of the nature of radio galaxies must be investigated intensively and, of course, the large redshifts must be accounted for.

The way in which Arp has deduced that other galaxies and sometimes galaxies in general—for example, the Virgo cluster—have been ejected from a given peculiar galaxy is still rather obscure. It seems that he has often selected a certain system because he sees in it some optical peculiarities that suggest explosion, and as a result he believes very strongly that he can explain the distributions of many of the bright nearby galaxies in terms of ejection leading to some spiral or ring-shaped distribution. As far as we can see there is really no physical evidence presented for this aspect of the phenomenon.

It is appropriate to say something about the physical properties of the peculiar galaxies that Arp believes are the sources of ejection. Careful study of the spectroscopic observations of these objects shows that in none of them is it possible to deduce from the velocity distribution in the gas that there are large differences of velocity that might be interpreted as evidence for explosive phenomena. In fact the only objects for which such evidence has been found are radio galaxies, such as M82 and NGC 1275, which are not discussed by Arp.

Thus none of the evidence so far presented shows that *galaxies* with *no* known associated radio sources are ejected from other peculiar galaxies. The evidence does tend to show, however, that radio sources may be ejected from peculiar galaxies, and that sometimes these radio sources have been optically identified without ambiguity with stellar objects (the radio-galaxy phenomenon may be related).

Unless all of the evidence presented by Arp can be shown to be spurious then we must conclude that the QSO's do not lie at cosmological distances. At present many workers are skeptical of the data, in part because they have not seen the material in detail. Intensive work on this aspect of the QSO's is underway at present, and the recent investigation of Wagoner (1967a) is of great interest. He has carried out analyses of the two-dimensional distribution of radio sources and of their distribution relative to peculiar galaxies. The method used consists essentially of computing the angular distances from each object in a given class to both the first and second nearest neighbors in the same class or in another class. The resulting distribution of distances is then compared with that expected if the objects were randomly distributed on the sky. Objects that lie in regions of possible galactic obscuration and those close to the declination limits of the radio catalogues have been excluded.

Wagoner first considered the relationship between Arp's peculiar galaxies and revised 3C radio sources. He found that there is an excess of small separations and a lack of large separations as compared to a random distribution. In fact, the mean separation is 3.6 standard deviations less than that expected from a random distribution for the nearest neighbors, and 3.0 standard deviations less for the second nearest neighbors. It appears that the effect is strongest for the spiral galaxies, numbers 1–101, and the elliptical galaxies, 102–145, as compared to the other classes in the catalogue of Arp (1966c). There are sharp drops in frequency at separations of 4° and 6°. Next, a very interesting fact emerges if one looks at the types of radio sources involved. Most of the deviation from randomness appears to be due to the identified sources, the quasi-stellar objects and the radio galaxies, rather than to the unidentified sources.

This analysis has not been more quantitative than this for the following reason. Because the Arp Atlas of Peculiar Galaxies was not compiled in a systematic way, certain areas of the sky contain an anomalously large number of galaxies. However, since the radio source catalogue was compiled uniformly, clumping alone would not be expected to introduce large spurious effects, as indicated by the fact that a rotation of the distribution of all peculiar galaxies by 12 hours in right ascension resulted in distributions whose means were within one standard deviation of those expected. A more serious source of artificial associations can arise through less obvious selection effects, such as the possibility that some peculiar galaxies were included in the catalogue because they were in an intensively investigated area surrounding a radio source.

For these reasons Wagoner carried out a similar analysis using Vorontsov-Vel'yaminov's Catalogue of Interacting Galaxies. This was compiled in 1959 in a more uniform manner from Sky Survey prints. Roughly half of this catalogue is included in Arp's Atlas. From this, rather similar results were obtained. The observed mean distances to nearest and second nearest neighbors are both 2.9 standard deviations less than the expected means. Rotation of the distribution of the interacting galaxies by 1, 2, and 12 hours in right ascension yields distributions of nearest neighbors whose means differed from the expected value by less than 0.7 standard deviations, and yields means for the second-nearest neighbors that differed by less than 1.7 standard deviations. The types of interacting galaxies most responsible for this apparent correlation have not been investigated. However, the dependence on the type of radio source was studied by Wagoner. As is the situation with the galaxies in Arp's Atlas, it is the identified sources that are correlated most strongly; the nearest neighbors that are QSO's are 2.0 standard deviations closer than expected, and those that are radio galaxies are 1.9 standard deviations closer. The unidentified sources are 1.2 standard deviations closer. Thus Wagoner's results show that there is some evidence for a *statistical* association of certain types of peculiar galaxies and radio sources. He also looked into the distribution of the radio sources themselves in the 4C catalogue and in the Parkes catalogue, and found evidence for nonrandom distributions. These results, however, may be due to unknown selection effects and should not be given great weight at present.

The theoretical implication of Arp's hypothesis will be discussed in Chapters 9 and 15.

CORRELATION BETWEEN POSITION AND REDSHIFT OF QSO'S

Strittmatter, Faulkner, and Walmsley (1966) have investigated the distribution of the magnitudes of the redshifts over the sky. They have divided the QSO's into four groups: Group I with $z > 1.5$, Group II with $1.5 > z > 1.0$, Group III with $1.0 > z > 0.5$, and Group IV with $0.5 > z > 0$. When they carried out this analysis 67 redshifts were available. They included 11 QSO's that fall into Group I, and found that with the exception of 3C 191 all the objects in this group divided into two very compact and almost antipodal groups (in galactic coordinates). The objects in Group II are more widely spread in the northern galactic hemisphere, though still in about the same position as those of Group I, whereas the members of this group that are in the south are almost coincident with those of Group I. The members of Groups III and IV are more widely spread over the sky. There are redshifts for 101 QSO's listed in Table 3.1 (all those known at the end of March 1967). Of the additional objects whose redshifts were not available to Strittmatter, Faulkner, and Walmsley, seven lie in Group I and two in Group II. The additional objects in both groups all lie in the regions delineated by the original analysis. The complete distribution is plotted in Figure 8.1.

Selection effects that may affect this result have been discussed by Strittmatter et al. and by Penston and Robinson (1967). There is obviously a strong observational bias in favor of certain regions of the sky both in the radio measurements and in the optical identifications and observations. The objects do not form a uniform group, since they are made up largely of objects identified as radio sources from the 3C catalogue and the Parkes catalogue, and those identified by the optical method (Haro-Luyten objects). Only two of the objects

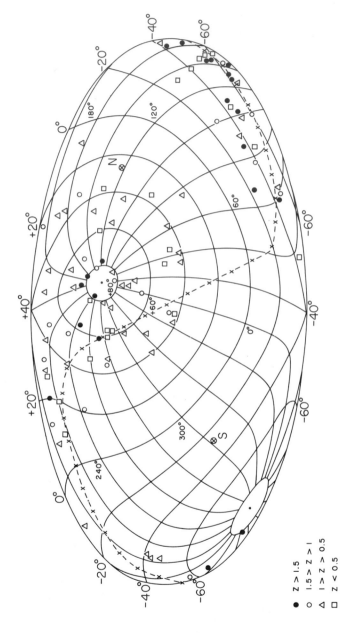

FIG. 8.1 *Redshifts of the 100 QSO's given in Table 3.1 plotted as a function of position in the sky in galactic coordinates. Different symbols are used for the four ranges of redshift, as indicated in the key. The direction of the Earth's north and south poles are denoted by N and S, and the broken line represents the projection of the Earth's equator on the sky.*

● z > 1.5
○ 1.5 > z > 1
△ 1 > z > 0.5
□ z < 0.5

in Group I, 3C 9 and 3C 191, are from the 3C catalogue. There is no obvious reason, however, why selection of this kind should give rise to a correlation of redshift with position for the identified objects. Since there is some tendency for the QSO's with large redshifts to appear fainter, it might be supposed that obscuration near the galactic plane would favor their detection at high galactic latitudes, and thus account for the tendency of the Group I objects to cluster near the polar caps. There are three objections to this. First, most of the Group I objects are more than one magnitude brighter than the optical limit of observation; second, if galactic absorption were important the objects in Groups II to IV should appear brighter at the poles than nearer the equator, and this is not so; and third, the Group I objects are not distributed uniformly about the pole. In the first two or three years of observation the observers, hoping to obtain large redshifts, tended to concentrate on the fainter objects. This might have a bearing on the second objection. By 1966, however, it had been realized that, because the relation between apparent magnitude and redshift shows great scatter, little was to be gained by concentrating on fainter objects, so there is little observational bias at present on this account. The one possible selection effect that remains to be discussed is that the observers have tended to neglect certain parts of the sky as compared with others because of weather conditions, or due to personal observing habits. Penston and Robinson have suggested that such factors may be involved. This effect would be most marked if one observer, working with one telescope in one geographical location, had been responsible for most of the data. For example, Sandage has been responsible for the bulk of the U,B,V photometry of the QSO's so far, and if the sample for which redshifts had been obtained were restricted solely to objects for which he had *previously* obtained U,B,V photometry, then the distribution might depend on his personal observing habits. But the observations have not proceeded in this way, and there are many instances in which redshifts of the QSO's have been obtained before U,B,V photometry was carried out, or at least before it was known that colors had been measured. The redshifts have mostly been measured at Kitt Peak, Lick, and Palomar, and it may be asked whether the weather patterns in Arizona and Northern and Southern California have led to a discrimination against certain areas of the sky. But the weather patterns are not the same in each of these places, and since the objects have been measured over several observing seasons there is no effect here. The same arguments apply when we consider the observers' habits. Penston and Robinson seriously suggested that perhaps selection effects were to be expected because the observers tended to be absent (at conferences) during the summer observing season! This is simply not true.

Of course, there is a region of the sky south of declination $-30°$ that has not been investigated at all, since there are no facilities for obtaining spectra of QSO's in the southern hemisphere. We must also allow for the fact that the equatorial regions of the galaxy are inaccessible because of obscuration. If we take account of all of these effects, it appears that, on the basis of the present data, the anisotropy is likely to be a real effect. The objects in Group I occupy less than about 10 percent of the sky. Future observations may still invalidate this result but we shall discuss possible explanations now on the assumption that the effect may be real.

The most obvious interpretation is that the QSO's are not at cosmological distances but are objects associated with our galaxy. Alternatively, we can suppose that they are not cosmological, but still not of galactic origin. In this case the concentrations near the poles of the galaxy must be due to chance. This is an entirely reasonable possibility, since the Coma cluster of galaxies and part of the Virgo cluster lie near the north galactic pole, and others, such as the Pegasus cluster, lie near the south pole. These clusters are at distances within the range that might encompass local but extragalactic QSO's —that is, 10–100 Mpc.

If the objects lie at cosmological distances, then the anisotropy of QSO's would require either that the universe is anisotropic beyond $z \simeq 1$, or that it is inhomogeneous on the same scale. The first of these suggestions is in conflict with the generally accepted view that present observations are compatible with complete isotropy of the universe. (This argument is based on the conclusion that the radio sources in the 4C catalogue are distributed isotropically, and on isotropy of the microwave background radiation, which is commonly thought to have a cosmological origin. It should be mentioned in passing that in our view neither of the arguments is wholly secure.) Rees and Sciama (1967) have attempted to explain the anisotropy by supposing that large-scale inhomogeneities (of a scale ~1500 Mpc) are present. They argue that QSO's may be more frequent in the higher-density regions. There is some question, however, whether such large-scale inhomogeneities are compatible with the isotropy of the background microwave radiation to the degree observed (~0.3 %).

If the anisotropy of the redshifts is still maintained as the number increases, the most likely explanation in our view would be that the QSO's are not at cosmological distances. But if compelling evidence from other directions suggests that they must be at cosmological distances, then large-scale anisotropy or inhomogeneity in the universe must be seriously considered.

SIMILARITIES IN PAIRS OF RADIO SOURCES

There is some evidence concerning the similarity of pairs of radio sources. Moffet (1965) has shown that the radio sources 3C 343 and 3C 343.1 have very similar power levels and very similar radio spectra, though they are separated by 29'. They are both exceedingly small radio sources with angular sizes $\leq 10''$, so that the ratio of separation to size is $r \geq 200$. No optical identifications have been made for these sources, but their curved radio spectra strongly suggest that they are quasi-stellar objects. Moffet has estimated that there is a probability of about 10^{-6} that the objects are not physically connected. If they are at cosmological distances their separation in space would be so large that physical association would be quite unreasonable. If they are physically connected, one might argue that the objects have a much smaller separation (at a distance of 10 Mpc this would be ~90 Kpc) and that both sources might have been ejected from a local QSO, or might be a pair of identical QSO's that have been ejected from a galaxy. We should also mention the pair of radio sources forming 3C 33 (Moffet, 1964). Here a similar situation prevails. The two sources are small and very similar, and the ratio of separation to size is ~16. A galaxy has been optically identified as the object giving rise to the pair of radio sources, and if this identification is correct the pair lies at a modest distance from our galaxy.

It is well established that many radio sources are double. In fact Arp's hypothesis is in a sense only an extension of the previously well-known observation that the bulk of the radio sources are double, but Arp has attempted to establish the existence of double sources with much wider angular separations than have been accepted before. However, in Arp's cases some of the objects have previously been identified with QSO's and apparently more distant radio galaxies.

Finally, we should also mention that de Jong (1965, 1966) has given evidence suggesting that satellite radio sources of very low power levels are associated with normal spiral galaxies that are weak radio sources. No optical identifications of these satellite sources are available, but if the result is correct it leads to the natural assumption that such sources have been ejected from the parent spiral galaxies. So far only one QSO, 3C 275.1, is known to lie very close in the plane of the sky to a bright galaxy with some optical peculiarities. This QSO lies very close to NGC 4651, so close that the optical identification was originally thought to be with NGC 4651. There is a high a-priori probability that the QSO has a physical association with the optical galaxy; the galaxy has a faint tail or jet extending approximately in the direction of the QSO.

9

The Nature of the Redshifts

When the redshifts of the first quasi-stellar objects were determined the question of their origin arose immediately. There are two mechanisms known to cause spectral line shifts, the Doppler effect and the presence of strong gravitational fields. It is not clear whether there are any other mechanisms that can give rise to such shifts. The Doppler effect can produce either redshifts or blueshifts, depending only on the orientation of the line of sight with respect to the direction of the velocity vector of the emitting object. In the expanding universe, however, we only see receding objects, and hence redshifts. We discuss first the possibility of explaining the redshifts of the QSO's as gravitational shifts.

GRAVITATIONAL SHIFTS

Arguments setting limits to the classes of object that can give rise to large gravitational redshifts can be based either on the observations or on theory. We discuss the observations first. The following argument, for the first two QSO's for which redshifts were measured, is due to Greenstein and Schmidt (1964).

A body of radius R and mass M will, because of the gravitational field, produce a redshift at the surface of the body that is given by

$$\frac{\Delta\lambda}{\lambda_0} = z = \left(1 - 2\frac{GM}{Rc^2}\right)^{-1/2} - 1, \tag{9.1a}$$

and if

$$\frac{GM}{Rc^2} \ll 1,$$

$$z = \frac{GM}{Rc^2} = 1.47 \times 10^5 \frac{M}{M_\odot} \frac{1}{R}, \tag{9.1b}$$

where G and c are the gravitational constant and the velocity of light, $M_\odot$ is the sun's mass, and R is in cm. Suppose a collapsed massive object is surrounded by a thin spherical shell, of thickness ΔR, in which the redshifted emission lines arise. There will be a gradient in gravitational potential across the thickness of the shell; let us assume that the resulting spread in the wavelength of line radiation leaving the object gives rise to the observed widths w of these lines. Then we have, using the widths of the lines measured in 3C 273,

$$\frac{\Delta R}{R} = \frac{w}{\Delta\lambda} = 0.07. \tag{9.2}$$

We may now envisage two possibilities: (1) the object consists of a collapsed star of about 1 solar mass and lies within our galaxy, and (2) the object is more massive, is extragalactic but lies only a moderate distance from our galaxy. The consequences of these two possibilities are given below.

1. The equation of state for collapsed stars requires a radius of $R \sim 10^6 M/M_\odot$ cm in order to yield a gravitational redshift of $z = 0.158$, as observed in 3C 273. If $M/M_\odot \sim 1$, then $R \sim 10^6$ cm and thus $\Delta R \sim 7 \times 10^4$ cm, so that the volume of the shell emitting the line radiation is determined. The volume emissivity in Hβ is known from hydrogen recombination theory; for $T_e \sim 10^4$ it is $\sim 10^{-25} N_e^2$ erg sec^{-1} cm^{-3}. The flux in Hβ measured at the earth from 3C 273 is 3.4×10^{-12} erg sec^{-1} cm^{-2}. We can thus set up a relation between the volume emissivity in Hβ, the volume of the emitting shell, and the measured Hβ flux in which the distance to the object, d, is the only unknown. We have

$$10^{-25} R^2 \, \Delta R \, N_e^2 = 3.4 \times 10^{-12} \, d^2, \tag{9.3}$$

or, since ΔR and R are fixed,

$$N_e^2 = 5 \times 10^{-4} \, d^2. \tag{9.4}$$

A search for a proper motion in 3C 273 has yielded negative results; consequently it is unlikely to be very close to the sun. Greenstein and Schmidt considered that d must be not less than 100 pc, and this yields

$$N_e \geq 6 \times 10^{18} \text{ cm}^{-3}. \tag{9.5}$$

Such a high density is quite incompatible with the appearance of the forbidden line [O III] $\lambda 5007$, and this is therefore a very powerful argument against this hypothesis.

2. Let us now suppose that 3C 273 is a much more massive object lying outside our galaxy but not at a large distance. We can replace the above condition that the distance d should be < 100 pc by the condition that the mass should not be great enough nor the distance small enough for the object to produce detectable perturbations on the motions of stars in our galaxy. To set a number on this, Greenstein and Schmidt postulated that such perturbations should be less than 10% of the gravitational acceleration due to the whole galaxy, so that

$$\frac{M}{M_\odot} \leq 10^{-35} d^2. \tag{9.6}$$

Again using the measured flux in Hβ and the volume emissivity in Hβ, we find, combining equations (9.1) and (9.2) and the inequality (9.6),

$$d \geq 8 \times 10^6 N_e^{-1/2} \text{ pc}$$

and $\tag{9.7}$

$$\frac{M}{M_\odot} \geq 7 \times 10^{15} N_e^{-1}.$$

As we shall discuss in the following chapter, the emission-line spectrum of 3C 273 requires that $N_e \sim 10^7$ cm^{-3}, so that

$$d \geq 2500 \text{ pc and } \frac{M}{M_\odot} \geq 7 \times 10^8. \tag{9.8}$$

The same calculations for 3C 48 yield

$$d \geq 25{,}000 \text{ pc and } \frac{M}{M_\odot} > 7 \times 10^{10}. \tag{9.9}$$

Thus collapsed massive extragalactic objects on this scale could account for the observed redshifts in these two objects, but the conditions are rather stringent.

Now, however, many objects are known with redshifts much larger than those of 3C 48 and 3C 273, and the order of magnitude of the line widths of these QSO's is no larger than those of the first objects that were studied. The value of $\Delta R/R$ in equation (9.2) then has to be reduced by roughly one order of magnitude, making the condition even more difficult to fulfill.

This discussion is based on the idea that limits are placed on the models by the observed widths of the lines, assuming that those widths are due to gradients in gravitational potential through the regions from which the lines are emitted. In the following chapter, however, we discuss the physical mechanisms that are likely to give the line broadening, and since in any case it is hard to avoid the conclusion that these mechanisms are operating, even in a dense body, the limits placed on the value of $\Delta R/R$ are even more stringent than those we have already discussed. Furthermore, a stratified model is required (Chapter 10), and the line widths can be different for different lines, while the absorption lines that are sometimes seen are usually very much narrower than the emission lines, but in some of the QSO's they do not have enormously different redshifts from those of the emission lines. All of these observational arguments tend against the idea that the redshifts could be gravitational in origin, provided that the emitting gas lies in a thin layer on the surface of a highly condensed object.

From the well-known Schwarzschild interior solution for a perfect fluid sphere it is found that GM/Rc^2 has a maximum value of $4/9$, so that from equation (9.1) we find that $z_{max} = 2$. At first sight it is tempting to suppose that this maximum value is related to the apparent dearth of redshifts greater than about 2, though some do exceed this value. It is well known, however, that this theoretical maximum is unreal, since it corresponds to a situation in which the transmission velocity in the fluid is greater than c. If appropriate conditions on the equation of state and on stability are applied, it has been shown by Bondi (1964) (see also Buchdahl (1959, 1966)) that

$z_{\max} \geq 0.62$. It is not clear at present, however, whether models can be made in which larger values of $z_{\max}$ are feasible.

A model in which it is possible to avoid the difficulties brought out by Greenstein and Schmidt has recently been suggested by Hoyle and Fowler. They suggest a model in which the observed line spectrum arises from gas clouds at the center of a massive object, rather than from its surface. Instead of accepting the idea that the system consists of a single coherent cloud of gas they suppose it to be made up of a large number of comparatively compact bodies with radii very much less than the total dimension, R, so that radiation can easily escape from the center. If these objects are highly collapsed stars then a total mass of $\sim 10^{12}$–10^{13} $M_{\odot}$ and a dimension of $R \sim 10^{18}$–10^{19} cm are reasonable. The line spectrum then arises from a cloud at the bottom of the deep gravitational potential well at the center of this distribution, and the light passes freely through the star distribution. In such a system the gas naturally falls to the center. The strong source of continuum radiation is also generated in the central region, whereas the main mass is responsible for the strong gravitational field. Writing the metric in the form

$$ds^2 = c^2 e^{\nu} \, dt^2 - e^{\lambda} \, dr^2 - r^2 \, d\Omega^2, \tag{9.10}$$

we may take e^{ν} as effectively constant throughout the cloud. The emission lines from the cloud are redshifted by an amount

$$z_c = \exp\left(-\nu_c/2\right) - 1,$$

where the subscript c denotes central values. Another important advantage of this model is that the redshift at the center, z_c, can be much larger than the redshift from the surface, z_s. For example, in the Schwarzschild interior solution

$$\frac{1 + z_c}{1 + z_s} = \frac{2}{2 - z_s}.$$

In the limiting case in which the central pressure tends to ∞; $z_s \longrightarrow 2$, and $z_c \longrightarrow \infty$. For a given mass and for a simple equation of state $p = p(\rho)$, there is an infinity of equilibrium solutions corresponding to different values for R. As R decreases, p_c increases until $p_c \longrightarrow \infty$ for a certain R, and then z_c also $\longrightarrow \infty$. If the mass is made up of a large number of subunits, such as collapsed stars or star clusters, a more complicated equation of state will result, but the same property must hold. In another class of model studied by Tooper (1966) it is found that

$$\frac{1 + z_c}{1 + z_s} = (1 + f\alpha)^{4/f},$$

where $2.5 \leq f \leq 4$, and α is proportional to the central value of the ratio of the pressure to the baryon number density. The limiting case is given when $\alpha \longrightarrow \infty$, in which case $z_c \longrightarrow \infty$.

The forces acting on atoms and ions in the gas clouds are gravity and radiation pressure. In normal stellar atmospheres they both have the same dependence on the radial distance, so that radiation pressure cannot come into adjustment with gravity through a change of the radial coordinate, r. However, in this case the situation is different. For ions outside the central gas cloud radiation pressure decreases with r while gravity increases with r, provided that r is not too large. This is because in the metric (9.10) the radial acceleration $d^2r/ds^2 = -\frac{1}{2}e^{-\lambda} \, d\nu/dr$, which increases in magnitude with r because $d\nu/dr = 0$ at the center. Thus stable equilibrium positions are possible for clouds of ions that surround the central cloud. We may then suppose that the absorption-line spectra arise from such floating clouds. In general, this would require that z for absorption lines be less than z for emission lines, and it also might imply that z would be different for different ions.

The observational data on the absorption-line redshifts have been described in Chapter 3. It was the discovery that the absorption-line redshifts nearly all appear to contain a component with $z_{abs} = 1.95$ (Burbidge, 1967) that led Hoyle and Fowler to put forward the gravitational redshift model described here, though they had discovered the model previously. We have already discussed the reasons why this value of 1.95 may very well indicate a gravitational origin for the redshifts, but there are many points that remain unclear at the time of writing. It is the absorption-line redshift that apparently is of the greatest significance, but as yet we have not been able to understand why the value 1.95 is preferred, or indeed whether a realistic model along the lines discussed above that will give emission line redshifts up to 2.2 can be constructed.

If the QSO's are massive objects with $M \simeq 10^{12}-10^{13}M_{\odot}$ and the redshifts are gravitational in origin, the distances of the QSO's are uncertain. Obviously they cannot be at cosmological distances; neither can they be very close to our galaxy, since their tidal effects would then be very large. There are some arguments for supposing that they lie at distances of $\sim$10–100 Mpc; that is, they are "local," but not as close as has been suggested in some hypotheses based on the idea that the redshifts are due to the QSO's moving at relativistic speeds (see Chapter 16). Some 10^6 objects, each with masses $\leq 10^{13}M_{\odot}$, lying within $\sim$100 Mpc would make a contribution to the total mass density of amount $\leq 10^{-29}$ gm/cm^3. Thus they would account for much of the mass of the universe, and possibly considerably more than the contribution z_c made by the normal galaxies. The Doppler contribution to the redshift at a distance of 100 Mpc is about 0.03 so that, if a standard gravitational redshift is produced in the object, we might expect a small dispersion about it of the order $z_c/(1 + z)$ (see Chapter 15).

DOPPLER SHIFTS

Up to the time of writing it has been generally agreed that the redshifts must be due to the motion of the QSO's relative to the observer, though the possibility that the redshifts are gravitational in origin must be seriously contemplated. Greenstein and Schmidt made the assumption that the redshifts are cosmological in origin and are due to the expansion of the universe, and this was a natural assumption to make in an era in which astronomers have been accustomed to interpreting all extragalactic observations of redshift in this way. Moreover, their arguments against the gravitational redshift hypothesis seemed to be very powerful. If we accept this interpretation, then, as is well known, it is possible, depending on the cosmological model used, to calculate luminosity distances for the QSO's with known redshifts. McVittie (1965) has given expressions from which these luminosity distances, D, can be calculated. Here D is defined by $L = P/4\pi D^2$, where P is the power emitted isotropically as measured at the source, and L is the flux received by the observer. Because the redshifts are so large, the luminosity distances, which depend on the redshift and on the cosmological model used, lie in the range 10^9–10^{10} pc. Thus the fluxes emitted at the objects range from 10^{45} to 10^{47} erg/sec.

However, the cosmological interpretation is not the only one possible. Alternatively it may be supposed that the redshifts are Doppler shifts due either to the translational motion of a local object or to the motion of gas within the object. In this case we find that the magnitude of the velocity, v, is given by

$$\beta = \frac{v}{c} = \frac{(z + 1)^2 - 1}{(z + 1)^2 + 1}. \tag{9.11}$$

For $z = 1$, we have $\beta = 0.6$, and for $z = 2$, we have $\beta = 0.8$. Thus, if the objects are moving locally, they must be moving with relativistic speeds and consequently have very large kinetic energies.

The possibility that redshifts might be produced by the motion of gas within an object—for example, by a ring or shell moving at relativistic speeds—has not been explored. Such a possibility requires study and cannot be rejected out of hand, though the absence of a corresponding blue shift must be explained.

Most astronomers have adhered to the view that the redshifts are of cosmological origin and have interpreted the observed properties on this assumption. Terrell (1964, 1967) rejected the cosmological interpretation and argued instead that the objects were ejected from our galaxy at relativistic speeds. Hoyle and Burbidge (1966a) considered the possibility that the objects have been ejected from comparatively nearby radio galaxies in which violent explosions have occurred. If these ideas are correct we cannot derive distances for the objects from the redshifts, as we can if the objects are at cosmological distances, but must use other means. Hoyle and Burbidge considered that distances of 10^6–10^7 pc were probable. In this local hypothesis the total flux radiated by the objects is reduced below the cosmological values by factors ranging from 10^4 to 10^7, but the objects must have very large kinetic energies. The arguments for and against both the local and the cosmological hypothesis will be discussed in detail in Chapter 15.

No alternative suggestions concerning the nature of the redshifts, other than those discussed here, have been proposed. Arp

(1966a,b) has argued that the redshifts are "non-velocity" shifts, but he has not suggested any previously neglected physical mechanism. In fact we are not aware of any other mechanisms compatible with the known laws of physics that will give rise to these large redshifts.

If one takes the viewpoint that the most probable explanation of these objects is the one requiring the least energy, and also that the shifts are Doppler in origin, then a system in which gas is moving at relativistic speed, but remains contained, is to be preferred. But no satisfactory model of this kind has so far been devised.

10

Models for Region
Producing Line Spectrum

We gave in Chapter 3 an account of the emission and absorption lines observed in the spectra of QSO's, and we shall now examine some models that have been proposed to account for these observed features.

The first point to make is that the QSO's by no means form a homogeneous sample. Although it has not been possible yet to study the whole spectral region of any single QSO, we know enough now from putting together the observations of many QSO's with various redshifts to see clearly that there are differences in the line spectra from one object to another. Even in the first two objects for which spectra were obtained, 3C 48 and 3C 273, differences were seen (Chapter 3, Table 3.3). In 3C 48 lines from several forbidden transitions are seen, whereas most of these are absent from the spectrum of 3C 273. Differences in the intensity ratio between the partially forbidden line C III] λ1909 and the permitted resonance line Mg II λ2798 are sometimes quite dramatic; an interesting example is afforded by a comparison of three QSO's that have similar redshifts, PKS 0957 + 00, 4C 20.33, and 3C 309.1. Lynds obtained spectra of all three objects at Kitt Peak and found that although C III] λ1909 is stronger than Mg II λ2798 in PKS 0957 + 00, it is quite weak in 3C 309.1, in which Mg II λ2798 is very strong (see Plate 1).

A glance through Table 3.2 shows other differences of this sort, as well as the wide range of line widths found. Besides these differences in the emission line spectra, some objects have absorption lines and others do not. The task of constructing a model of the line-producing region can therefore be applied either to one particular QSO or to some generalized "average" QSO, and in the latter case we must always keep in mind that this is only an average, and that individual objects may very well differ from the average.

ELECTRON TEMPERATURES AND DENSITIES FROM EMISSION LINES

Let us first consider the emission lines as indicators of the physical conditions in QSO's. The similarity between the ions that are present and the transitions that are seen in QSO's on the one hand and in planetary nebulae (or gaseous nebulae in general) on the other shows that the physical conditions—temperature and density—in both kinds of objects must be rather similar. The presence of forbidden lines, for example, shows that the electron density in QSO's must be lower than in the atmospheres of emission line stars, such as the P Cygni stars, Wolf-Rayet stars, and the like, in which forbidden lines do not appear. The range that is found in QSO's for the relative intensities between forbidden lines and permitted lines shows that the density must lie in a critical range of values—in general, somewhat higher than the densities in planetary nebulae. It is appropriate now to look into this question and consider the mechanisms by which emission lines are produced in gaseous nebulae and how we may determine electron temperatures and densities from them.

In planetary nebulae hydrogen and helium lines are produced by the recombination of ions following photoionization by the ultraviolet light of wavelengths shorter than the limits of the appropriate spectral series. The ultraviolet radiation comes from a central star of high temperature. The strength of an emission line is given by the number of atoms in the relevant upper energy level, $N_{n\ell}$, and the transition probability for the downward transition.

To determine $N_{n\ell}$ we assume that the population of a given level is independent of time—that is, that there is statistical equilibrium. Then the total number of atoms entering a given state per second, by all possible ways of populating the level, must equal the number of atoms leaving that state per second, by all possible routes. For hydrogen the statistical equilibrium governing captures by a proton of an electron into the ground state and a finite number of excited states, followed by downward cascades from the excited states to the ground state, in a field of dilute radiation from a central star, was formulated and computed by Baker and Menzel (1938). Extension to an infinite number of levels is due to Pengelly (1964). The number of atoms $N_{n\ell}$ can be expressed by the equation

$$N_{n\ell} = N_e N_p (2\ell + 1) \left(\frac{2\pi mkT}{h^2} \right)^{-3/2} \exp \left(I_{n\ell}/kT \right) b_{n\ell}, \qquad (10.1)$$

where N_e, N_p are the numbers of electrons and protons per cubic centimeter, $I_{n\ell}$ is the ionization energy for level $n\ell$, and $b_{n\ell}$ measures the departure of the populations from those that would correspond to thermodynamic equilibrium. Pengelly computed the values of $b_{n\ell}$ by solving the equations of statistical equilibrium.

Ionization of the other elements is also caused by the diluted high-temperature radiation from the central star. Forbidden lines are then produced by the following mechanism. Atoms and ions are excited by electron collision from the ground state to fairly low-lying metastable levels, transitions which are radiatively forbidden and can occur only when the energy is supplied by an external electron. Thus atoms and ions excited in this way remain for a relatively long time in the excited level unless the electron density is high enough to cause collisional de-excitation, and then finally they decay to the ground state with the emission of forbidden lines. Determination of the electron density and temperature, N_e and T_e, from forbidden line intensities is discussed by Seaton (1954) and Seaton and Osterbrock (1957). The energy $I(n,m)$ radiated per cubic centimeter per second in the transition $n \longrightarrow m$ is given by

$$I(n,m) = E_{nm} A_{nm} N_n, \qquad (10.2)$$

where E_{nm} is the energy released per transition, A_{nm} is the transition probability, and N_n is the number of atoms or ions per cm^3 in the upper state. The N_n are governed by statistical equilibrium—that is, by equating the number of populations of a given level per second with the number of depopulations; the cross sections for excitation and de-excitation are expressed in terms of dimensionless parameters $\Omega(m,n)$, $\Omega(n,m)$, which have been computed for cases of interest by several people, particularly Seaton and colleagues in recent years.

The upper states of the [O II] $\lambda\lambda 3726$, 3729 lines, with a long lifetime against radiative de-excitation, are particularly sensitive to collisional de-excitation, and their intensities are therefore a good indicator of electron densities.

This type of analysis was applied by Greenstein and Schmidt (1964) to 3C 273 and 3C 48, and by Shklovsky (1964) and Dibai and Pronik (1964) to a spectroscopic study of 3C 273 made with the telescope in Crimea. When spectroscopic observations became available for other objects, Osterbrock and Parker (1966) used them to derive the physical conditions in an average or composite of nine QSO's.

Greenstein and Schmidt *assumed* that the abundances of the elements in 3C 273 and 3C 48 are the same as the average Population I abundances of gaseous nebulae and young stars in the solar neighborhood in our galaxy, and estimated $T_e = 16,800°K$ as a reasonable value for the electron temperature. They then calculated the relative intensities of the lines that were measured, for various values of the electron density N_e, and found the value that gave the best fit to the observations. Somewhat ambiguous estimates of the electron densities resulted (in that the same calculations applied to planetary nebulae yielded relative intensities that needed correction by arbitrary factors to agree with the observations, and the same "correction factors" were applied to the QSO's). The results are as follows:

$$N_e - 3 \times 10^4 \text{ cm}^{-3} \qquad \text{for 3C 48,}$$
$$N_e = 3 \times 10^6 \text{ cm}^{-3} \qquad \text{for 3C 273,}$$

with uncertainty factors of about one order of magnitude either way.

Dibai and Pronik derived a higher value for the electron density in 3C 273 (i.e., $N_e \approx 10^7 \text{ cm}^{-3}$) with a temperature $T_e \approx 10,000° - 15,000°$. Shklovsky pointed out that the smallness of the Balmer discontinuity in the continuous spectrum of 3C 273 (see Chapter 4) suggests that T_e is at least as high as $20,000°$, while the strength of the Hβ emission line relative to the continuum shows that $T_e < 60,000°$. Thus Shklovsky's value of $T_e \approx 30,000°$ seems a good choice. The absence of [O II] 3727 and [Ne V] lines in 3C 273 shows that N_e must be higher in 3C 273 than in 3C 48; later observations have indicated that 3C 48 is more typical of most QSO's than is 3C 273.

Cameron (1965) estimated a still higher value for N_e in 3C 273,

Table 10.1

RELATIVE EMISSION-LINE INTENSITIES FOR MODEL WITH $T_e = 15,000°$,
$N_e = 3 \times 10^6 \, cm^{-3}$, NORMAL ABUNDANCE RATIOS (H TO Mg)
Ionization $x(II) = 0.05$, $x(III) = x(IV) = x(V) = x(VI) = 0.20$,
$x(VII) = 0.15$; for He, $x(II) = x(III) = 0.50$

Ion	Line (Wavelength in Å)	Intensity	Ion	Line (Wavelength in Å)	Intensity
He II	1640	4.2	[O III]	4363	0.4
[O III]	5007	2.6	Hγ	4340	0.4
C IV	1549	2.2	O IV]	1406	0.4
Mg II	2798	2.1	C II]	2326	0.4
[Ne III]	3869	1.7	C III]	977	0.3
[Ne V]	3425	1.6	O III]	1665	0.3
[O III]	4959	0.9	C II	1335	0.2
Hβ	4861	0.8	[Ne IV]	2424	0.2
C III]	1909	0.8	O V]	1216	0.2
[O II]	7325	0.8	O VI	1034	0.2
[Ne III]	3967	0.6	N III]	1749	0.2
He II	4686	0.6	[N II]	6583	0.2
[Ne V]	3345	0.5	N V	1240	0.1

namely $2 \times 10^8 \, cm^{-3}$, but Greenstein and Schmidt thought an upper limit to the acceptable electron density in this object would be $3 \times 10^7 \, cm^{-3}$. This is also the value indicated by Wampler's and Oke's observation of permitted Fe II lines in the spectrum while the corresponding forbidden lines are absent. We accept $N_e = 10^7 \, cm^{-3}$ as probably the best estimate.

Osterbrock and Parker, for their composite average QSO, found a good match with the observations for $T_e = 15,000°$ and $N_e = 3 \times 10^6 \, cm^{-3}$, for an assumed level of ionization. They derived this value of N_e by arguing from the absence of [Ne IV] λ2424 in all QSO's so far observed; the upper level has an unusually long radiative lifetime and must be collisionally de-excited. By setting up the equations of statistical equilibrium, taking account of collisional de-excitations, it is found that for $T \sim 10^4 \, °K$, if $N_e \geq 3 \times 10^5 \, cm^{-3}$ the [Ne IV] line emission coefficient is strongly reduced. Table 10.1

shows the computed line strengths for the model of Osterbrock and Parker (again assuming normal or Population I relative abundances, and considering only the elements up to magnesium in the periodic table of the elements).

Let us now return to the question of the relative abundances of the elements. The fact that the studies just described yield relative intensities that match the measurements reasonably well shows that, with the possible exception of helium, as already discussed, the abundances must be similar to those found in young Population I stars and gaseous nebulae in the solar neighborhood (see Chapter 3 for a discussion of this). If the QSO's are indeed extremely distant objects dating back billions of years in time in an evolving universe, this would be extremely surprising, as we have already remarked.

DIMENSIONS AND MASSES OF GAS GIVING EMISSION LINES IN QSO'S

If the redshifts are of cosmological origin, the luminosity distances of QSO's may be derived from them for any chosen cosmological model. The formulae for different cosmological models may be found in papers by Sandage (1961) and McVittie (1965). For an evolutionary cosmology with the deceleration parameter $q_0 = 1*$, the luminosity-distance is simply $D = cz/H_0$, and fluxes emitted at the source are obtained from the measured fluxes by applying the inverse-square law with this distance. For $q_0 = 0$, $D = cz(1 + \frac{1}{2}z)/H_0$, and the fluxes at the source will be larger by the factor $(1 + \frac{1}{2}z)^2$. Greenstein and Schmidt used $q_0 = 0$ and from the equivalent widths of $H\beta$ in 3C 48 and 3C 273 given in Table 3.3, obtained $H\beta$ luminosities of 6.4×10^{42} erg/sec (3C 48) and 8.8×10^{43} erg/sec (3C 273). Shklovsky, using the measures of Dibai and Pronik, found the $H\beta$ flux in 3C 273 to be 8×10^{43} erg/sec.

The volume emissivity in the line $H\beta$ is given by the hydrogen recombination formula:

$$E(H\beta) = 2.28 \times 10^{-19} N_e^2 T_e^{-3/2} b_4 \exp (0.98 \times 10^4/T_e) \text{ erg cm}^{-3} \text{ sec}^{-1}.$$
$$(10.4)$$

* See Chapter 4 for definitions of q_0 and H_0.

Table 10.2

RADII AND MASSES (IN UNITS OF THE SUN'S MASS) OF THE
HYDROGEN EMISSION REGION IN 3C 48 AND 3C 273

Object	N_e (electrons/cm³)	R pc	$M_H/M_\odot$
3C 48	3×10^4	11	5×10^6
3C 273	3×10^6	1.2	6×10^5
3C 48	"local," at	0.48	410
3C 273	distance of 10 Mpc	0.092	270

We now set $T_e = 10^4$ and b_4 (the factor measuring the departure of the population of the upper level of Hβ from the value for thermal equilibrium) equal to 0.16; these are the values used by Greenstein and Schmidt. With N_e determined as we have described, and with the measured fluxes in Hβ converted to energy $L(H\beta)$ radiated at the object for a cosmological model having $q_0 = 0$, we obtain the values given in Table 10.2 for the radii R of the region emitting the line radiation and the masses M_H of the emitting hydrogen. For other values of the luminosity $L(H\beta)$ and electron density N_e, we have

$$R \propto L(H\beta)^{1/3}N_e^{-2/3} \tag{10.5}$$

and

$$M_H \propto L(H\beta)N_e^{-1}. \tag{10.6}$$

If we convert to a model with $q_0 = 1$ the change in $L(H\beta)$ is small for these objects, since they have small redshifts; the value for 3C 273 should be divided by 1.16 and that for 3C 48 by 1.40. If one wishes to use a different value of T_e, equation (10.4) must be used to obtain a new volume emissivity in Hβ.

If the redshifts are not of cosmological origin, and the QSO's are comparatively nearby, then the Hβ fluxes $L(H\beta)$ will be much smaller, by the inverse-square ratio of the distances and the $(1 + z/2)^2$ factors, and the radii R and hydrogen masses M_H will be correspondingly less according to equations (10.5) and (10.6). For distances of

10 Mpc, the values of R and M_H are given in Table 10.2. The estimates of N_e and T_e come from the line intensities and are of course independent of distance. Is there any other observational limitation to the sizes of the regions in which the spectral lines arise? To answer this we must turn to the question of the variability of QSO's, discussed in Chapter 6.

In general, if radiation of any frequency is emitted symmetrically, and is seen to vary in a time interval τ, then the dimension of the source of the varying radiation should be less than $c\tau$, so that the increased energy coming from the far side of the object may arrive at the observer in phase with that from the near side. Table 10.2 shows that dimensions of 11 pc and 1.2 pc have been calculated for the hydrogen-emission region of 3C 48 and 3C 273, respectively, on the assumption that they are at cosmological distances, and this would set lower limits of 38 years and 3.9 years, respectively, to times for variation of hydrogen line intensities coming from the whole gaseous envelope. No variations at all in these line intensities have been detected in 3C 48 and 3C 273.

The most rapidly varying QSO so far discovered is 3C 446, and we saw in Chapter 6 that its total radiation has fluctuated appreciably in periods of about 1 day. But when the object is bright in the continuum radiation, the spectral lines become relatively weak and hard to see, and Sandage, Westphal, and Strittmatter (1966) showed that the line intensities relative to the continuum changed in a way that was consistent with the supposition that the absolute flux emitted in the lines stayed constant while the continuous radiation fluctuated up and down. Thus there is no contradiction here.

The other QSO that has varied over short periods is 3C 345, and here rapid changes in the structure of the Mg II λ2798 line were found. We shall see in the next two sections that there are good reasons for believing that the Mg II emission comes from a different region from that giving rise to the hydrogen emission, and in fact it may come from small blobs. An ingenious explanation for a rapid variation in the emission of this line alone, coming from regions of small dimensions, has been proposed by Shklovsky, and we shall describe this after discussing empirical models for the region giving the spectral lines.

WIDTHS OF THE EMISSION LINES:
ELECTRON SCATTERING OR MASS MOTIONS?

We saw in Chapter 3 that the emission lines in the spectra of QSO's are usually broad, whereas the absorption lines that have been seen are narrow. Permitted emission lines are in general broader than forbidden lines, and the resonance transitions of Ly-α, C IV $\lambda1549$, and Mg II $\lambda2798$ are the broadest.

The emission line spectrum somewhat resembles the characteristic spectrum of the nuclei of Seyfert galaxies, in which very broad emission lines are seen and the hydrogen lines are the broadest. In the Seyfert nuclei we have good reason to believe that the lines are broadened by the Doppler effect, and are produced in gas undergoing large turbulent or mass motions. An explanation in terms of velocities for the widths of lines in the spectra of novae is also familiar to stellar spectroscopists. If a gravitational origin for the redshifts in QSO's is ruled out, or if the gas cloud lies at the bottom of a deep gravitational potential well, then we do not need to consider a gradient in gravitational potential across the line-emitting region as a possible line-broadening mechanism. Let us first consider mass motions, which were thought by Greenstein and Schmidt to be the most likely explanation.

The line widths in 3C 48 and 3C 273, if due to the Doppler effect, indicate velocities of 2000–3000 km/sec. These greatly exceed the velocities of escape given by the masses of the hydrogen emission region in Table 10.2, which are only ~100 km/sec. If the gas were free to escape, the time scales would be only 10^3–10^4 years. Therefore, the gas should be kept from escaping by the gravitational attraction of a large mass at the center of the gas cloud, and to do this a mass of about $10^9 M_\odot$ is required.

In one of the physical models proposed for QSO's (see Chapter 17), Colgate and Cameron (1963) suggested that supernova explosions might be occurring with great frequency in the centers of dense star clusters. Then the emission lines would come from shells of gas ejected from the supernovae with characteristic speeds of thousands of kilometers per second; these shells would collide with each other and with quiescent gas in the cluster, and emission lines very much broadened by Doppler shifts would be produced.

Mass motions of this sort, however, do not give any obvious explanation for the different line widths seen in one and the same spectrum, and the narrowness of the absorption lines in, for example, 3C 191 is particularly difficult to account for. We will therefore now examine another possible broadening mechanism—electron scattering.

That electron scattering might be very important in QSO's was realized by Shklovsky (1964). In 3C 273, with the dimensions of the hydrogen-emission region determined for a cosmological distance, the optical depth in electron scattering, τ_e, must be about 10. This holds for a thick spherical shell of radius 1.2 pc. But inside this shell there is presumed to be a small central object emitting the continuum radiation, and this continuum radiation varies. Shklovsky realized that an arbitrarily short pulse of radiation produced in the center would take 10–20 years to escape through such an electron-scattering region, because the velocity of diffusion of the quanta would be c/τ_e. To avoid this difficulty, we should have $\tau_e \leq 1$, but for this to hold for the physical parameters deduced for 3C 273, the hydrogen-emission region must be spread out over a much larger dimension. Shklovsky suggested that the hydrogen-emission region might be a comparatively thin closed spherical shell of much larger radius; in which case its total volume could be kept the same but the length of the path traversed by radiation from the central object would be much reduced.

Schmidt (1964) suggested that the hydrogen-emission region might be in the form of filaments with an electron density N_e embedded in a large region of much lower density. Again, the light from the central object would cross only a few such small filaments and the electron scattering could be kept low.

Shklovsky, who had also suggested a nonuniform or lumpy distribution of the line-emitting gas as a way around the difficulty, rejected this possibility for the following reason. He argued that the total hydrogen radiation from 3C 273, calculated for a cosmological distance from the parameters derived in the preceding sections, is of the same order of magnitude as the total radiation outside the limit of the Lyman series, and concluded that the gas around the central object completely absorbs ultraviolet quanta with $\lambda < 912$ Å and transforms them into quanta of the allowed and forbidden transitions of the various elements. A nonuniform, filamentary distribution of gas would not lead to complete absorption of the ultraviolet quanta. For the present we should probably keep in mind both a large thin continuous shell and a filamentary structure as possibilities if the QSO's are at cosmological distances.

Let us turn for the moment from the problem of how to minimize electron scattering so that τ_e is not larger than unity; we will return to this point later. Let us look at the effect on the spectral lines of an electron-scattering region. Münch (1948) considered the effect on a pulse of monochromatic radiation of its passage through an electron-scattering region. The electrons would have a Maxwellian velocity distribution corresponding to their temperature T_e; each encounter between a photon and an electron would change the frequency of the photon through the Compton process. The net result would be to spread out the monochromatic pulse into a widened spectral line. Münch calculated the profiles of such lines for various values of τ_e and T_e. It is clear that for $T_e = 30,000°$, $\tau_e = 1$, very considerable broadening occurs. Burbidge, Burbidge, Hoyle, and Lynds (1966) looked at the problem quantitatively, and we reproduce the argument here.

The widest lines seen are Ly-α, C IV λ1549, and Mg II λ2798. For permitted resonance lines, such as Mg II λ2798, it is not necessary for the optical depth τ_e to be comparable to unity in order for the line to be broadened. For such lines quanta are emitted and reabsorbed in sequence until electron scattering out of the line center takes place. The opacity within about ± 3 Å from the line center is large, and not until electron scattering takes the quanta sufficiently off resonance can they escape from the nebula. If we consider a line to have disappeared into the continuum when its intensity has declined to one-third of what it is not at the center but at 3 Å from the center, then using Münch's computations of electron-scattering profiles, even with small optical depths along a direct linear path through the nebula, we obtain a width of about 20 Å for an electron temperature of 10,000°K, ~30 Å for $T_e \approx$ 30,000°K, and ~50 Å for $T_e \approx$ 100,000°K. For a really strong line this procedure underestimates the width; a decline in intensity to about one-sixth would then be more appropriate, nearly doubling the width. Thus for the long path lengths that quanta in strong permitted lines such as Mg II λ2798 and Ly-α will traverse before finally escaping, it is clear that great widths can be produced by electron scattering at electron temperatures of 10,000°–30,000°K, which are entirely compatible with the line strengths.

For forbidden lines such as [O III] λ5007 the argument is different, since an ion that gives rise to a forbidden line does not supply a high opacity near its resonant frequency. In order for a forbidden line to be broadened appreciably, τ_e must be ~1. Again using the results of Münch, we find for τ_e = 0.8 a width of about 40 Å at $T_e \approx$ 30,000°K, and about 60 Å at T_e = 100,000°K. For the QSO's in which narrow forbidden lines are seen, we conclude that τ_e must be small. The general tendency for the lines from permitted ground-level transitions to be wider than the forbidden lines is a strong argument in favor of the electron-scattering hypothesis. We also recall the observations of PKS 1217 + 02, described in Chapter 3, in which [O III] λλ4959 and 5007 are much narrower than [O III] λ4363; the first two lines arise from an upper level of 2.50 eV excitation, and the third arises from a 5.33 eV upper level. This strongly suggests a broadening agent that is a function of depth in the object, the λ4363 line being produced at a greater depth than the λλ4959, 5007 lines. Electron scattering provides a natural explanation, whereas mass motions do not. The narrow absorption lines can also be explained if electron scattering, rather than mass motions, is the cause of the broadening of the emission lines. We shall see in the next section that we are forced to use a stratified model to account for the spectra of QSO's, and since the absorption lines would naturally arise in the outer layers of such a model, then need undergo very little electron scattering.

Finally, it should be mentioned that Oke (1965) proposed a very high value for the electron temperature, as high as 160,000°K, to explain his measurements of the continuum radiation in 3C 273, which were given in Chapter 4. But at such a high temperature the broadening by electron scattering would be enormous, particularly for the resonance line Mg II λ2798.

A STRATIFIED MODEL TO EXPLAIN THE LINE SPECTRA

We shall now consider an empirical model to explain the line spectra of QSO's. This will not be a physical model, in that we shall not worry about energy sources, production of continuum radiation, or radio flux. The early line identifications, including [O II] and [Ne V] in 3C 48, already showed that a wide range of ionization potential is encompassed in the ions that must be present, and Shklovsky (1964) pointed out that the line-producing region should be stratified—with [O II], for example, coming from a different layer from that giving rise to [Ne V]. According to Osterbrock and Parker, however, a wide range of ionization could result from photoionization caused by thermal radiation from a very hot super massive star or by ultraviolet synchrotron radiation, since both have a great abundance of high-energy photons.

However, the great strength of the Mg II λ2798 emission line and the narrow absorption lines provide more cogent reasons for considering a stratified model, and Burbidge, Burbidge, Hoyle, and Lynds (1966) proposed such a model with three distinct zones. The zones are:

    I   Optically thick to quanta with $h\nu > 13.60$ ev.
    II Optically thick to quanta with $h\nu > 54.40$ ev.
    III Optically thick to quanta with $h\nu > 24.58$ ev.

In Zone I the gas is thin to quanta of energies less than the Lyman limit, and in Zones II and III it is thin to quanta below the ionization potentials of He^+ and He, respectively. These conditions are regarded as being imposed by the hydrogen and helium. Zone I is an H I region. Zone II is an H II, He II region, while Zone III is an H II, He I region. In all zones, lines other than those due to hydrogen and helium are produced by excitation of their upper levels by electron collisions. The hydrogen and helium lines are produced by recombination.

Zone I is necessary to explain the presence of the Mg II emission. The ionization potential of Mg^+ is only 15.03 ev, and this ion can exist in appreciable abundance only in an H I region. It is an attractive possibility that Mg II $\lambda2798$ might be produced by recombination of Mg^{++} in an H II region. The big gap between the ionization potentials of Mg^+ and Mg^{++} (the latter has I.P. = 80.12 ev) would lead to a big buildup of Mg^{++}. However, the recombination coefficient of Mg^{++}, which is not known, would need to be greater than that of H by a large factor to overcome the difference in abundance and give comparable line strengths for Ly-α and Mg II $\lambda2798$. In Zone I the most abundant ionization stages of the common elements are: H, H^+, C^+, N, O, Ne, Mg^+, Si^+, S, and Ar. Lines from these ions that fall within the ultraviolet wavelength range of interest are H I Ly-α, Hα, . . . , C II $\lambda\lambda1335$, 2325, Mg II $\lambda\lambda2796$, 2803, Si II $\lambda\lambda1190$, 1193, 1194, 1197, 1260, 1265, 1304, 1309, 1527, 1534, 1808, 1817, 1818, 2329, 2335, 2345, 2351, S II $\lambda\lambda1227$, 1233, 1234, 1250, 1254, 1259.

The C II and S II lines are seen in absorption in 3C 191, as are the Si II lines on the short-wavelength side of 1500 Å. The lines of C II, S II, Si II are not seen in emission, however, with the exception of C II $\lambda2325$, which is observed weakly in some QSO's. Small cross sections for electron excitation will account for the absence of some of these lines; but in addition, the electron temperature is probably rather low in Zone I. The energy difference between C II $\lambda1335$ and Mg II $\lambda2798$ is ~4.8 ev, so that the number of electrons capable of exciting Mg II $\lambda2798$ exceeds the number capable of exciting C II $\lambda1335$ by exp $(4.8/kT_e)$, where kT_e is measured in ev. For $kT_e \approx 1$ this is a factor of more than 100, which is sufficient to exclude C II $\lambda1335$.

In Zone II the most abundant stages of ionization of the common elements are: H^+, He^+, He^{++}, C^{+3}, N^{+3}, $O^{++} \longrightarrow O^{+3}$, Ne^{++}, Mg^{++}, Si^{+4}, S^{+4}, Ar^{+3}. If we restrict ourselves to ground state transitions and to the excitation of levels requiring only moderate energies, the possible emission lines are: H I Ly-α, Hα, and the Balmer series, He II $\lambda\lambda1640$, 3204, C IV $\lambda\lambda1548$, 1551, O III $\lambda\lambda4363$, 4959, 5007, O IV $\lambda\lambda1402$, 1405, 1406, 1410, 1413, Ne III $\lambda\lambda1794$, 1815, 3344, 3869, 3968, Ar IV $\lambda\lambda2854$, 2869.

All these lines are seen in QSO's, except for the weak lines of Ne III at $\lambda\lambda$1794, 1815, 3344. These are weak because their electronic excitation probabilities are very small. The gaseous material of QSO's is thus very largely in Zone II, and this is the region that contributes mainly to the emission lines.

We have given the ionization state of oxygen as $O^{++} \longrightarrow O^{+3}$. If all the O^{++} were in the ground state, most of the oxygen would be in this particular ionization stage, since the ionization potential of O^{++} is 54.89 ev, slightly above the ionization potential of He^+. However, O^{++} has metastable states several volts above the ground state, so that O^{++} can be excited in two stages, first to a metastable state, then to O^{+3} through the absorption of a quantum with $h\nu$ less than the ionization potential of He^+. Provided the metastable states of O^{++} become sufficiently populated most of the oxygen will be converted to O^{+3}. This, we believe, must be the situation in QSO's, otherwise the lines of O^{++} would be somewhat stronger than C IV $\lambda\lambda$1548, 1551.

The most abundant ionization stages of Zone III are: H^+, He, He^+, $C^+ \longrightarrow C^{++}$, O^+, Ne^+, Mg^{++}, Si^{++}, S^{++}, Ar^+. The corresponding expected emission lines are: H I Ly-α, Hα, . . . , He I $\lambda\lambda$2830, 2946, 3189, 3447, . . . , C II $\lambda\lambda$1335, 2325, C III λ1909, O II λ3727, Si III λ1206, S III $\lambda\lambda$1190, 1194, 1201, 1202. The ionization potential of C^+, 24.38 ev, is very close to that of He, 24.58 ev, and C^+ has a metastable state nearly five volts above ground level. With the latter sufficiently populated, C^+ will be scoured out to C^{++}. The situation here for $C^+ \longrightarrow C^{++}$ is the same as that for $O^{++} \longrightarrow O^{+++}$ in Zone II.

Zones I, II, and III explain the emission lines of QSO's quite satisfactorily. A few cases requiring an optically thin situation beyond $h\nu = 54.40$ ev remain to be explained, particularly emission lines of [Ne V] $\lambda\lambda$2974, 3346, 3426, and a suspected emission line [Mg V] λ2931 in a few objects. Leaving these aside, the next step is to decide on the spatial ordering of Zones I, II, III.

Burbidge, Burbidge, Hoyle, and Lynds (1966) suggested the ordering I, II, III with increasing distance from a central object. At first sight one might expect Zone I to lie on the outside. But this zone cannot cover Zones II and III, otherwise Ly-α could never appear free of strong self-absorption. If Zone I lies on the outside its structure must be broken into discrete blobs. The disadvantage of placing I on the outside is that, if Mg II $\lambda 2798$ arises in it, the great widths shown by that line in some QSO's would then be hard to explain. With Zone I on the inside, light from it must pass through Zones II and III. If either Zone II or Zone III, preferably Zone II, has $\tau_e \approx 1$ and $T_e \geq 30,000°K$, the Mg II doublet will be substantially widened by electron scattering. The strong ultraviolet radiation field necessary to produce Zone II must then arise outside Zone I—for example, by processes that we shall describe in Chapter 11.

A further reason for placing Zone I on the inside is the absence of [O I] $\lambda\lambda 6300$, 6363 in 3C 273. Andrillat and Andrillat (1964) did not see these features on their infrared spectra, yet they are commonly seen in the spectra of the nuclei of Seyfert galaxies. If the H I region is innermost, then the electron density here may be sufficient to cause considerable collisional de-excitation of the upper level of the [O I] lines, and these lines will be suppressed.

Zone III is placed on the outside because the line [O II] 3727 is emitted most effectively at low densities, and the lowest electron densities should be found on the outside of the object. Moreover, Zone III must contain concentrations of C^+, Si^+, S^+, which, while not sufficient to produce an emission line, may be sufficient in some cases to produce absorption, but all the Mg must here be in the form of Mg^{++}, or an absorption component in Mg $\lambda 2798$ would always be produced by Mg^+. In the above discussion we have been concerned with the most abundant ionization stage. A significant number of ions that differ one stage, up or down, from the most abundant ion are always to be expected. In Zone III we expect moderate concentrations of Si^+ and Si^{+3}. Both of these ions are responsible for absorption lines in 3C 191. To give a deep absorption it is therefore important that Zone III should cover the whole source of the continuum, and this it will do best if it lies farthest out from the source of the continuum. If the redshifts are Doppler shifts, then most QSO's with absorption lines must undergo relative motion between Zone III and the rest of the object, since the emission-line and absorption-line redshifts usually differ. In 3C 191 this difference, measured by Burbidge, Lynds, and Burbidge and by Stockton and Lynds, amounts to an outward motion of Zone III by about 600 km/sec.

An interesting question that will be of importance for QSO's with redshifts appreciably larger than 2 is whether higher Lyman lines—Ly-β and Ly-γ—will be visible. The usual analysis of the transfer of ultraviolet radiation in gaseous nebulae postulates that all the higher Lyman lines will be transformed by repeated absorptions and cascade re-emissions into lines of the Balmer, Paschen, etc., series and Ly-α. Bahcall (1966a) showed, however, that this will not be so; there will actually be appreciable emission in Ly-β and Ly-γ due to leakage from the surface layers of the line-producing region.

Finally, let us consider the permitted O III transitions found in spectra of planetary nebulae. Only those members of the multiplet for which the upper level has a particular value of the J quantum number are seen, and this is due to resonance fluorescence. The energy difference between this level and the ground state of O^{++} is almost exactly that given by the He II resonance line at 304 Å. The O III lines seen in planetary nebulae are absent from the spectra of Seyfert nuclei, and Osterbrock and Parker (1965) argued from this that the emitting gas in Seyfert nuclei must consist of an intimate mixture of neutral and ionized gas, so that all He II $\lambda304$ radiation gets absorbed before exciting the relevant upper level of O^{++}. In several QSO's, however, the O III line at $\lambda3133$ has been observed, although not as a strong line. Consequently, the situation is different from that in Seyfert nuclei.

MODEL TO EXPLAIN VARIABILITY OF Mg II $\lambda2798$

Burbidge and Burbidge (1966) and Dibai and Yesipov (1967a) observed variation in the structure and intensity of the line Mg II $\lambda2798$ in 3C 345, and the scanner measurements by Wampler (1967) indicate that (1) the total flux in this line may be variable and (2) the variations in the line profile, while not very large, do appear to be real and affect only the long-wavelength wing of the line. Shklovsky (1966) has proposed an ingenious model to account for variations in this line. He suggests a dimension of $R \sim 10^{16}$ cm for a region in which Mg is mostly in the singly ionized state. Such a region will be optically thick to Mg II $\lambda2798$ radiation. Suppose now that a powerful flux of relativistic particles impinges on such a condensation. The cross section for excitation of the upper level of Mg II λ2798 is $\sim 2 \times 10^{-15}$ cm²—that is, some orders of magnitude greater than the cross section for second ionization. Therefore, a large flux of Mg II λ2798 quanta will be generated inside the condensation. But this flux cannot immediately escape, as long as most of the Mg exists as Mg^+. This situation will be followed by an increasing degree of double ionization; the plasma inside the condensation will be intensely heated in less than 10^5 seconds, and, once the Mg is in the form Mg^{++}, it will become transparent for the resonance quanta of Mg II λ2798. The effect will be like suddenly opening a window—a burst of line radiation could be emitted, followed by fading, the time scale for the consequent variation being $\sim 10^5$ sec.

ESTIMATES OF FLUX EMITTED
FROM A "STANDARD" QSO

The condition that the optical depth for electron scattering $\tau_e \leq 1$, which will in general explain the widths of the lines in the stratified model, makes it possible to compute the total optical emission from a "standard" QSO. Taking $T_e = 30,000°$K in Zone II, the number of electron-proton recombinations is $\sim 2 \times 10^{-13} N_e^2$, and the emissivity in Ly-α, Hα, etc., and in the Balmer continuum is $\sim 4 \times 10^{-24} N_e^2$ erg cm⁻³ sec⁻¹. If the total optical output is about ten times greater than the total hydrogen emission (this is about the upper limit set by the appearance of a Balmer discontinuity in 3C 273), and if the model is taken to be spherical or of thick-shell form, with dimension R, the total output L is

$$L \sim 10^{-22} N_e^2 R^3 \text{ erg sec}^{-1}. \tag{10.7}$$

Now for $\tau_e = 1$ we have $N_e R \sim 10^{24}$ (the Thomson cross section for electron scattering being $\sigma_e = 1.6 \times 10^{-24}$). Substituting this in equation (10.7), we derive

$$L \sim 10^{26} R \text{ erg sec}^{-1}. \tag{10.8}$$

If $N_e \sim 3 \times 10^6$ cm⁻³, then $R \sim 3 \times 10^{17}$ cm. If we put $R \sim 10^{17}$–10^{18} cm in equation (10.8),

$$L \sim 10^{43}\text{–}10^{44} \text{ erg sec}^{-1},$$

and the lower value is close to the luminosities of the nuclei of Seyfert galaxies, and considerably less than the luminosities of QSO's if they are at cosmological distances. To avoid this discrepancy, we have to use a different model, in which the line-emitting region comes from a thin shell of large radius (Shklovsky's model) or a large low-density region partially filled with filaments. To satisfy the numbers given above and achieve a total optical output of 10^{46} erg sec^{-1}, we need a shell of radius 10^{19} cm and thickness 10^{17} cm.

Whether these dimensions are permissible depends on the data available on variations. The most rapidly varying QSO, 3C 446, does not rule out a radius of 10^{19} cm for the line-emitting region, since variations in absolute flux in the emission lines have not been observed. The variations seen in Mg II $\lambda2798$ in 3C 345, however, do seem to suggest a small dimension for the clouds emitting this line. In this case, we have to postulate, as indeed the stratified model does, that the hydrogen emission comes from an entirely different region from that giving rise to Mg II $\lambda2798$.

CONCLUDING REMARKS ON LINE SPECTRA OF QSO'S

There is diversity in the spectra of QSO's, as well as some general similarities, and therefore a model of the line-producing region, to be successful, must allow for differences from one object to another. The range of widths and intensities seen requires a range in N_e, T_e, and τ_e for the objects. A stratified model such as that described here will account quite well for the line fluxes and widths, and takes into account electron scattering. It will account for the appearance in some of absorption components in resonance lines, and in others not; that is, it explains why strong absorption in Ly-α and C IV $\lambda1549$ is not visible in all QSO's, and why these absorptions (when seen) are often sharp and deep. Further, it explains why a strong narrow absorption has seldom been found in Mg II $\lambda2798$ (in only three objects has an absorption component has been seen in this line, and in two of these, it is weak and fuzzy). In 3C 191, the comparative weakness of absorption in Ly-α relative to absorption in C IV $\lambda1549$

can probably also be accounted for by the fact that hydrogen is largely ionized in Zone III. A progression in the difference between absorption-line and emission-line redshifts with ionization potential, which was noticed in 3C 191 by Bahcall (1966b; see also Burbidge and Lynds, 1967), can also be fitted into this model, if there is further stratification in Zone III and a spread in the outward motion of this region. The considerable differences seen in [O II] $\lambda3727$ also have a natural explanation; in QSO's where this line is quite strong and wide, N_e may be lower, and the line may be produced deeper in the object.

Clearly, a range in the physical parameters of the gas producing the spectrum lines must be present in the QSO's. One advantage of such a stratified model is that the arrangement and maintenance of the zones could be quite sensitive to the size and continuum flux of the central source of energy, about which nothing has been said in this chapter. The only problem is that uniform zones will not allow the large energy output required if the objects are at cosmological distances to be reconciled with the allowable electron scattering. One could avoid this difficulty, however, if the QSO's do indeed prove to be at cosmological distances, by having a nonuniform Zone II in which the line emission comes from filaments embedded in a low-density medium; Zone III, however, will still need to be uniform and cover the object in order to produce the very deep absorption lines. For example, Woltjer (1967) has suggested a nonhomogeneous model that is more detailed than Schmidt's. Small dense regions ($N_e \sim 10^8$ cm^{-3}) are embedded in a more tenuous background ($N_e \sim 10^6$ cm^{-3}), and the lines of H and Mg II are supposed to come from the dense filaments and C IV and the forbidden lines from the tenuous region which has higher ionization.

The development of a stratified model for QSO's has been based on the assumption that the redshifts are all Doppler shifts, and if it turns out that they are, instead, gravitational shifts, then a different model will have to be developed. This will be particularly necessary for the region giving rise to the absorption lines. The general idea, however, that different groups of spectral features will be produced in different physical circumstances and in different locations in the QSO, would still seem to be a useful working hypothesis.

11

Models for Regions
Emitting Continuous Flux

A model that will explain the flux emitted by the QSO's must take into account the radio properties, the flux emitted in the millimeter and infrared parts of the spectrum, and the optical continuous flux. Important parameters required in model calculations are the total flux emitted, dimensions of the object, and the physical mechanism giving rise to the emission. The total flux emitted depends on the distances of the objects, and there is a very large uncertainty according to whether the objects are at cosmological distances (10^9–10^{10} pc) or comparatively nearby (10^6–5×10^7 pc). The same uncertainty is involved in estimates of the sizes of the objects if they are made from angular diameter measurements. However, upper limits to the sizes can be derived from the observations of time variations in the flux and, when they can be obtained, they set much more stringent limits on the sizes than do measurements of angular diameters. Several possible physical mechanisms that may give rise to the flux in different parts of the spectrum have been suggested. These mechanisms are thermal emission from a hot gas, coherent plasma oscillations, synchrotron radiation, and the inverse Compton process. We have shown in Chapter 4 that the bulk of the radiation appears to be emitted by a nonthermal process, though it is impossible to exclude the possibility that some part of the optical continuum is thermal bremsstrahlung.

We have already pointed out that the radio properties of the QSO's are very similar to those of the radio galaxies, and it is well established that the bulk of this radiation is due to the synchrotron process. Thus it is natural to suppose that this mechanism is responsible for the radio emission in the QSO's. Many authors have considered that the synchrotron mechanism is responsible for the bulk of the radiation all the way from radio to optical frequencies. Strong evidence that the optical flux is of synchrotron origin is provided by the recent observations of 3C 446 by Kinman et al. (1966), which show that a high degree of linear polarization is present. As will be shown later, difficulties arise for some classes of models if it is supposed that the radio and millimeter flux (in 3C 273) is emitted by the synchrotron process. Ginzburg and Ozernoy (1966) have therefore suggested that coherent plasma oscillations may be responsible for this radiation.

Given a large flux of low-energy photons it is possible that, in inverse Compton collisions, a fraction of these photons can be lifted in energy. Thus it is conceivable that some part of the flux observed was originally emitted at much lower frequencies and has been lifted by this process.

In what follows we shall discuss the models proposed to explain the radio flux in general, and the radio and millimeter radiation from 3C 273. We shall then consider the models required to account for the optical flux, and the infrared and optical flux in 3C 273.

Much of the argument depends on the size limits of the regions, which have been set by the observation of flux variations in the centimeter wavelength range in a number of QSO's, in the millimeter range in 3C 273, and in optical wavelengths in many QSO's. We give first a brief account of the way in which these size limits are set.

LIMITS SET ON SIZE BY FLUX VARIATIONS

The question of size limits set by flux variations has been considered by Terrell (1964, 1966), Williams (1965), and Noerdlinger (1966) for theoretical models in which the emitting surface is moving nonrelativistically. We follow here the discussion by Terrell. We consider a fluctuating source consisting of a spherical surface of radius R oscillating in brightness with a period $\tau_0 = 2\pi/\omega_0$ measured in its own reference frame. It is assumed that all parts are fluctuating in phase, and the surface brightness is given by

$$I = \bar{I} + I_f \sin \omega_0 t \tag{11.1}$$

and

$$\bar{I} \geq I_f \geq 0. \tag{11.2}$$

The total luminosity L is then calculated by an integration over the surface, using for simplicity Lambert's cosine law of surface brightness. It is then found that

$$L = \pi R^2 [\bar{I} + I_f F(\alpha) \sin (\omega_0 t - \theta)], \tag{11.3}$$

where

$$\alpha = \frac{2\pi R}{c\tau_0}, \tag{11.4}$$

$$\tan \theta = \frac{\alpha - \sin \alpha}{1 - \cos \alpha}, \tag{11.5}$$

and

$$F(\alpha) = \frac{2}{\alpha^2} [2 + \alpha^2 - 2 \cos \alpha - 2\alpha \sin \alpha]^{1/2}. \tag{11.6}$$

For large values of α,

$$F(\alpha) \simeq \frac{2}{\alpha} = \frac{c\tau_0}{\pi R}, \tag{11.7}$$

where $F(\alpha)$ is the fraction of the true fluctuation, which is observable at a distance. From (11.2) and (11.4) we see that the fractional change in luminosity ΔL is given by

$$\frac{\Delta L}{L} \leq 2F(\alpha) \tag{11.8}$$

or using (11.7),

$$\frac{\Delta L}{L} \leq \frac{2c\tau_0}{\pi R}, \quad \text{so that} \quad R \leq \frac{2c\tau_0}{\pi} \left(\frac{L}{\Delta L} \right). \tag{11.9}$$

If we wish to consider fluctuations as rates of change of luminosity, then, since $|dL/dt| < \pi \, \Delta\overline{L}/\tau_0$ for sinusoidal fluctuations, we have

$$R \leq 2c\overline{L} \left(\left| \frac{dL}{dt} \right| \right)^{-1}, \tag{11.10}$$

and this expression applies to nonsinusoidal fluctuations. It can also be derived as a limit for fluctuations with arbitrary time dependence. For an observer not in the reference frame of the source the observed period τ will be related to the period in the object τ_0 by the relation

$$\tau = \tau_0(1 + z), \tag{11.11}$$

so that (11.9) and (11.10) become

$$R \leq \frac{2c\tau}{\pi(1 + z)} \left(\frac{\overline{L}}{\Delta L} \right)$$

and

$$R \lesssim \frac{2c\overline{L}}{(1 + z)} \left(\left| \frac{dL}{dt} \right| \right)^{-1}. \tag{11.12}$$

For 3C 273, we have $(1 + z) = 1.158$, and the correction required by (11.11) is negligible. For 3C 446, however, $(1 + z) = 2.403$. For variations in flux to be well established observationally, it is usually the case that $\Delta L \sim \overline{L}$. We see that under these conditions it is appropriate to use the simple condition

$$R \lesssim c\tau \tag{11.13}$$

in order to set an upper limit on the size of the object.

Equations (11.9), (11.10), and (11.12) can also be applied to more general cases in which a combination of sources is considered. For example, if we have n sources, each of diameter R', with random phases, the effective maximum size will be $R'n^{1/2}$, instead of R. If the sources are varying sinusoidally but are uncorrelated, the maximum variation will be proportional to $n^{-1/2}$.

It is of some interest to estimate the value of $c\tau/R$ for variable stars—the only other astronomical objects in which variations in the integrated flux are seen, apart from explosive phenomena. The most rapid variations are seen in flare stars, which exhibit significant brightness variations in periods of $\sim$1 hour. In this case we have that $c_T/R \simeq 10^8$. We do not know the true sizes of the QSO's, and in the subsequent discussion we will use values of R obtained by setting $R = c_T$. It should be borne in mind, however, that R *may be* very much less than c_T.

The problems associated with this limit for R become so acute if the objects are at cosmological distances that it has been proposed (Rees, 1966) that the emitting surface is moving relativistically. In this case the surface will appear to be moving faster than the speed of light, and condition (11.13) can be relaxed to the form

$$R < 2c_T\gamma,$$

where $\gamma = [1 - (V^2/c^2)]^{-1/2}$. Models involving matter moving relativistically will be discussed later in this chapter. It should be stressed that these limits on R are most important in restricting the models if it is assumed that the QSO's lie at cosmological distances. If the objects are local the size limitations do not place such severe restrictions on the models; nevertheless, whether the objects are cosmological or local the mechanism that gives rise to the variations must be explained.

MODELS REQUIRED TO ACCOUNT
FOR THE RADIO FLUX

For the radio galaxies in which the emitting volumes are large, the synchrotron process has been shown to be operating, and it has been shown from the synchrotron theory that the minimum total energy contained in magnetic flux and relativistic particles must often be in excess of 10^{60} ergs. If the QSO's are at cosmological distances, those with radio sources of large diameter (3C 47, MSH 14 − 12*1*, 3C 9, etc.) are intrinsically as powerful as the strongest radio galaxies. Consequently, the energy requirements are similar. Since the minimum energy required to explain a given radio source is obtained when there is approximate equipartition between relativistic particle energy and magnetic energy—and for a given power level this equipartition value is proportional to $R^{9/7}$, where R is the dimension of the system (Burbidge, 1959)—we see that for the simplest kind of model, where the magnetic field is assumed to be uniform, the minimum total energy required to explain the source is considerably reduced if it is very small. The time scale is also reduced by a factor $R^{9/7}$. Thus, if the energetics of a powerful radio galaxy are such that the minimum total energy $E_{min} = E_m + E_p = 10^{61}$ ergs ($E_m \simeq E_p$) and $R = 100$ kpc, a QSO emitting the same flux, but with $R \simeq 100$ pc, will require $E_{min} = 1.5 \times 10^{57}$ ergs. Values appropriate for 3C 273 and 3C 48 have been calculated by Greenstein and Schmidt (1964). However, the structure of the small sources often associated with the QSO's and the frequency dependence of the structures strongly suggests that the models are much more complex than this.

The first indications that there were difficulties with simple homogeneous models came with Dent's discovery of the time variations of 3C 273B at 8000 Mc/s and the interpretation of the data. The frequency ν_m at which synchrotron self-absorption sets in is related to the size of the object, the flux radiated at that frequency, and the magnetic field strength by relation (5.1). For the parameters thought to be appropriate for 3C 273B at that time, it can be shown that the angular size of the source θ (seconds of arc) is given by

$$\theta = 3 \times 10^9 B^{1/4} \nu^{-5/4}. \tag{11.14}$$

If we assume that the objects lie at cosmological distances d, and assume a linear redshift-distance relation, which is appropriate for the small redshift of 3C 273, then

$$d = \frac{cz}{H}, \tag{11.15}$$

where H is the Hubble constant. From the data on the variation at 8000 Mc/s, we have $R \leq c\tau$, so that

$$\theta = \frac{2.06265 \times 10^5 R}{d} \leq \frac{2.06265 \times 10^5 \tau H}{z}. \tag{11.16}$$

If we substitute the numerical values for H and z and set $B \geq 10^{-5}$ gauss and $\nu = 400$ Mc/s, then from (11.16) and (11.14) we find that $\tau \geq 23$ years. In his original calculation of this result Dent made a numerical error, which was corrected by Field (1965). If we suppose that the radio emission at 400 Mc/s, to which the spectrum extends with no cutoff, comes from the same region as that giving the secular variations at 8000 Mc/s, then the value $\tau \geq 23$ years is conceivably just compatible with Dent's result that the flux has increased by 40% in $2\frac{1}{2}$ years. Otherwise it must be concluded that either the synchrotron mechanism is not operating or the object is not at a cosmological distance—the conclusion that Dent reached. If we use just the value 8000 Mc/s for ν in equation (11.14), thus considering this component alone, we find that $\theta \simeq 6 \times 10^{-5}$ seconds of arc = 0.5 l.y. for 3C 273B at a cosmological distance. With reference to 3C 273B, Hoyle and Burbidge (1966a) and Rees and Sciama (1965a) have inquired into the complication involved in devising a model for which it is assumed that the synchrotron process operates and that the objects are at cosmological distances. Rees and Sciama made the obvious assumption that the source contains an exceedingly small component with a dimension of $\sim 10^{-3}$ seconds of arc buried in a much larger source with a dimension of $\sim 0\overset{''}{.}5$. The large halo source gives rise to the flat spectrum of 3C 273B down to about 200 Mc/s. Then for a large enough magnetic field in the central source, $B \geq 1$ gauss, they were able to account for the variable flux at 8000 Mc/s. They attributed the variations with time to variations in the injection of relativistic electrons. They considered some variants of a model of this type and outlined the conditions that would be required if the inverse Compton process acting on the radio photons to give some optical photons was to be important.

Hoyle and Burbidge considered a more general class of models for which it is assumed that the magnetic field in the object is not constant and that the radio spectrum is controlled by variations in the magnetic field. They supposed that a spherical volume in which the relativistic particles are generated has a magnetic field distribution of the form $B = B_0(a/r)^n$, where B_0, a and n are constants; that the electron spectrum is everywhere the same; and that the energy density of the electron distribution has the form $W = W_0(b/r)^m$, where W_0, b and m are constants. The electron distribution is assumed to be optically thin. It then can be shown that the flat form of the electron spectrum observed in 3C 273B can be obtained and that the spectrum continues down to 200 Mc/s without being self-absorbed. This type of model effectively leads to a situation in which different shells are contributing to the radio flux in different energy ranges. Hoyle and Burbidge concluded that such a model for 3C 273B could satisfy the requirement that the process operating be the synchrotron process and that it could be at a cosmological distance. Ginzburg and Ozernoy (1966) have attempted to compare the energy requirements in terms of magnetic flux and relativistic particles for the homogeneous and nonhomogeneous models. They have concluded that under certain conditions, and provided that the equipartition condition $(E_p \approx E_m)$ holds, more energy is required in a nonhomogeneous model to give the observed flux.

For the QSO's in general, however, it appears that the very small source sizes require that if the synchrotron mechanism is operating, the conditions are very far from the equipartition condition. Assuming a homogeneous source and knowing an upper limit to the source size enables us to set an upper limit to the magnetic field, if we suppose that a maximum in the flux spectrum is due to the onset of synchrotron self-absorption.

On the assumption that the objects lie at cosmological distances Williams (1966) has made calculations for QSO's for which θ and ν_m (the frequency at which the flux density is a maximum) are known. For 3C 48, 119, 138, 208, 286 and 287 he found that $B \leq 10^{-4}$–10^{-5} gauss, whereas the equipartition values are in general $\geq 10^{-3}$–10^{-4} gauss. This has the result of increasing the total energy in relativistic particles by factors of 10–100 over the equipartition values, and for many QSO's, including 3C 273B, the total energy must be 10^{60}–10^{61} ergs. The structure of the source as a function of frequency may complicate this picture, since by analogy with 3C 273B we might suppose that a compact component showing strong self-absorption even at high frequencies might be associated with an extended source with a normal spectrum. In such a case the angular diameter observed at high frequencies where the compact source is operating might erroneously be associated with the source giving rise to the low-frequency component.

It does appear reasonable from these results to suppose either that the objects are not at cosmological distances or that the synchrotron mechanism is not operating in such small sources.

In 3C 273B the radiation above 3000 Mc/s is polarized (Dent and Haddock, 1966), suggesting that the synchrotron mechanism is operating. We shall neglect this point for the moment, however, and consider the possibility that the synchrotron mechanism is not operating. As an alternative we may suppose that the radiation near 10^9 c/s is emitted through coherent plasma oscillation, or as Cerenkov radiation. These mechanisms have been proposed by Ginzburg and Ozernoy (1966). Plasmas will radiate near the plasma frequency (Langmuir frequency)

$$\omega_L = 2\pi\nu_L = 5.64 \times 10^4 n_e^{1/2} \text{ c/s.} \tag{11.17}$$

The Cerenkov mechanism will give rise to radiation in the frequency range ν_L to $(\nu_L^2 + \nu_g^2)^{1/2}$, where ν_g is the electron gyrofrequency

$$\nu_g = 2.8 \times 10^6 B \text{ c/s.} \tag{11.18}$$

Thus, for radiation at a frequency near 10^9 c/s, with $n_e \approx 10^{10}$ cm^{-3}, Ginzburg and Ozernoy have considered these processes in the context of a cosmological model in which it is supposed that the radiation is emitted from the atmosphere or magnetosphere of a massive object ($M \sim 10^8 M_\odot$) that would have a scale height of $h \sim 10^{12}$ cm (Chapter 17). The problem, then, is to ask whether the radiation could escape from the object. It is therefore necessary to calculate the optical depths for electron scattering, τ_e, and for absorption, τ_a, in such a plasma. They found that $\tau_e \sim 10^{-2}$ for $\nu_L \approx 10^9$ c/s and $L \sim 10^{12}$ cm, but $\tau_a \sim 10^6$, which makes it hard to see how radiation emitted near the plasma frequency could escape. As an alternative it was proposed that n_e is small ($\sim 10^6$ cm^{-3}) and that the radiation is emitted at the electron gyrofrequency ν_g. From (11.18) it can be seen that to obtain radiation near $\nu = 10^9$ c/s, then $B \sim 10^3$ gauss. Thus we see that if we are prepared to suppose that the magnetic field is very strong, a mechanism of this type may be effective and the difficulties encountered—if we suppose that the objects are at cosmological distances—can be relieved. Since the emitting volume is very small, the radiation density will be exceedingly high.

We can summarize this discussion of the radio models as follows. If the objects are comparatively close by there are no difficulties encountered whether we suppose that the objects emit by the synchrotron mechanism or by coherent plasma mechanisms. If they lie at cosmological distances, however, the size limitations set by angular diameter measurements show that if the synchrotron mechanism is operating, then $E_p \gg E_m$ and $E_p \sim 10^{61}$ ergs. For QSO's in which the size of the region is set by the variations, as in 3C 273B and in other objects discussed in Chapter 6, structure in the source must be assumed in the sense that the high-frequency varying components must come from much smaller regions than the lower frequency radiation. Coherent plasma mechanisms may be invoked but very strong magnetic fields must then be assumed to be present.

MODELS REQUIRED TO EXPLAIN THE MILLIMETER RADIATION FROM 3C 273B

As has been described in Chapter 4, radiation in the millimeter region ($\nu \approx 10^{11}$ c/s) has been measured in 3C 273 and 3C 279. In 3C 273 this flux is known to have varied in intensity by a factor of 2 in less than a month. Thus from the condition $R \lesssim c\tau$ we find that $R \lesssim 10^{17}$ cm. The models that can possibly explain the millimeter radiation have been investigated by Stein (1966). He has considered plasma oscillations and Cerenkov radiation, thermal bremsstrahlung and the synchrotron process. If we invoke plasma oscillations or Cerenkov radiation the arguments are very similar to those just discussed, except that radiation of much higher frequency is involved. Thus to obtain coherent plasma radiation, values of $n_e \sim 10^{15}$ cm^{-3} are required. With this much higher electron density the optical depth for scattering or absorption is very much larger than it was even for radiation with $\nu \sim 10^9$ c/s, and it is therefore obvious that this mechanism must be rejected. It is thus necessary to turn to the idea that the radiation is emitted near the electron gyrofrequency, in which case magnetic fields near 10^5 gauss must be invoked. This, then, is a possible explanation for this limited part of the spectrum if very strong magnetic fields are allowed. But to suppose that immensely strong fields are present raises many problems.

Thus we turn to other possible mechanisms. Thermal bremsstrahlung has been mentioned, but the shape of the spectrum over the whole range up to optical frequencies (Chapter 4) is quite different from that expected if this mechanism is operating, and thus it must be ruled out. This leaves us with the synchrotron process, which appears to be most plausible. Stein has pointed out that if this mechanism is operating, then we must explain the sharp drop in the millimeter spectrum between 10^{11} and 3×10^{11} c/s (Fig. 4.2) as due to an absorption process, since the synchrotron flux cannot fall off more steeply than $\nu^{1/3}$. Stein, then, has investigated the two possible absorption mechanisms—synchrotron self-absorption and absorption by a hot plasma. If synchrotron self-absorption is invoked, then we can use the argument given earlier in this chapter to set an upper limit to the magnetic field. This is determined as a function of the angular size of the source, R/d, in which case the condition $R \lesssim c\tau$ gives $R \lesssim 10^{17}$ cm. If 3C 273 is assumed to be at a cosmological distance ($d = 470$ Mpc) we find that the upper limit is $B \leq 10^{-3}$ gauss. But we must also fulfill the condition that the synchrotron process dominates over the inverse Compton process (this will be discussed in detail in the following section), and this means that $B \geq 60$ gauss. Thus there is a contradiction, which Stein concludes can only be resolved either by supposing that the QSO's are local or by supposing that the absorption is not due to the synchrotron process.

We can now analyze the thermal absorption mechanism and set limits on the models allowed in this case. The absorption might take place either in the gaseous envelope that gives rise to the line spectrum or in the source that gives rise to the millimeter radiation. If we consider the first alternative, then, since the temperature of the gas is determined, the luminosity in the hydrogen recombination spectrum is measured, and the limitation set by electron scattering places an upper limit on $n_e R_1$, where R_1 is now the dimension of this region (Chapter 10), and we find that $(d/R_1) \sim 7 \times 10^7$. If $d = 470$ Mpc, then $R_1 \simeq 7$ pc. This shows that if 3C 273 is at a cosmological distance, the region giving rise to the line spectrum will be $\sim 10^{19}$ cm, a possible situation if variations due to this region are not seen over short time intervals. But if $R \sim R_1$ there is a contradiction, which can only be resolved by supposing that the object is local.

Thus a model that can be used to explain the millimeter flux from 3C 273B must, if the object lies at a cosmological distance, include a very strong magnetic field of $\sim 10^5$ gauss. Alternatively, if the synchrotron process is responsible for the emission and also for the absorption, the object must be local. Otherwise the synchrotron process could be responsible for the emission, provided that $B \geq 60$ gauss in a region $R \leq 10^{17}$ cm, and the absorption must be due to the hot gas surrounding the source, which then must have $R_1 \sim 10^{19}$ cm.

MODELS REQUIRED TO EXPLAIN
THE OPTICAL AND INFRARED FLUX

Most observations have been made only in the optical frequency range 3×10^{14}–3×10^{15} c/s (here we have taken account of the redshift factor), but measurements of flux out to 10μ (3×10^{13} c/s) have been made for 3C 273, and here the bulk of the energy is emitted between 10^{11} and 10^{13} c/s. The distribution of energy with frequency indicates that only a small fraction of this radiation can be of thermal origin. Moreover, it is improbable that thermal emission could give rise to rapid variations because the heating and cooling times are likely to be too long. The only possible nonthermal processes are the synchrotron process and the inverse Compton process. The observation of polarization in the variable optical flux in 3C 446 is strong evidence that the synchrotron process is operating. We shall consider this process first. We suppose that a volume with dimension R set by (11.13) is filled with magnetic flux, relativistic electrons, and optical and infrared photons emitted in the synchrotron process. It is then possible for some of the photons to make Compton collisions with the high-energy electrons before they escape. Since it is necessary that the synchrotron source be maintained, we require that the synchrotron losses dominate over the inverse Compton losses. A detailed comparison of these processes is given by Felten and Morrison (1966). It is easily shown (Hoyle, Burbidge, and Sargent, 1966) that for an isotropic radiation field this condition will be maintained, provided that

$$\frac{8\pi U_{\text{rad}}}{B^2} < 1, \tag{11.19}$$

where U_{rad} is the energy density of photons in the object,

$$U_{\text{rad}} = \frac{L}{\pi R^2 c}, \tag{11.20}$$

and L is the luminosity of the source. Thus we require that

$$B^2 > \frac{8L}{R^2 c}. \tag{11.21}$$

Let us now consider some appropriate numerical values for L and R. If the objects are at cosmological distances, then integration of the flux emitted by 3C 273B gives a value of $\sim 10^{47}$ erg/sec, the bulk of the energy being emitted between 10^{11} and 10^{13} c/s, whereas the optical flux emitted by 3C 273B, and by QSO's in general in the range 10^{14}–10^{15} c/s, is about 10^{46} erg/sec. At the same time we find from Chapter 6, expression (11.13), and the variations in such QSO's as 3C 345 and 3C 446, that R must be less than values in the range 10^{15}–10^{17} cm.

Thus, to give two examples, if $L = 10^{47}$ erg/sec and $R \leq 10^{17}$ cm, we find from equations (11.20) and (11.21) that $U_{rad} \geq 100$ erg/cm^3, and $B \geq 15$ gauss (values appropriate for 3C 273B) and if $L = 10^{46}$ erg/sec and $R \leq 10^{15}$ cm, $U_{rad} \geq 10^5$ erg/cm^3 and $B \geq 400$ gauss (values appropriate for 3C 446). If the objects are not at cosmological distances, so that $L \leq 10^{43}$ or 10^{42} erg/sec, then in the two examples considered, for $R \leq 10^{17}$ cm and $R \leq 10^{15}$ cm, we find that $U_{rad} \simeq 10^{-2}$ erg/cm^3, $B \sim 10^{-1}$ gauss, and $U_{rad} \geq 10$ erg/cm^3, $B \geq 4$ gauss.

If the objects are at cosmological distances the energy density of radiation is immense; the photon densities are $\geq 10^{16}$ cm^{-3}, and are comparable with or greater than energy densities in lasers. The lifetime t_e of an electron emitting synchrotron radiation is given by

$$t_e = 10^{12} \nu^{-1/2} B^{-3/2} \text{ sec}, \tag{11.22}$$

and thus the distance that a relativistic electron can travel while radiating photons in the appropriate frequency range is

$$r = \tau_e c = 3 \times 10^{22} \nu^{-1/2} B^{-3/2} \text{ cm}.$$

Using the values of the magnetic field arrived at above, and assuming that the objects are at cosmological distances, we find for $\nu = 10^{13}$ c/s (for 3C 273) and $B \geq 15$ gauss, that $r \leq 1.5 \times 10^{14}$ cm, and for $\nu = 10^{14}$ c/s (for 3C 446) and $B \geq 400$ gauss, that $r \leq 3.5 \times 10^{11}$ cm. But if the objects are local, then $r \leq 3 \times 10^{17}$ cm for 3C 273 and $r \leq 3.5 \times 10^{14}$ cm for 3C 446. Thus $r \ll R$ if the objects are at cosmological distances, whereas $r \simeq R$ if they are local. This means that if the objects are local, injection of electrons from a single central object with energies of order 10^9 ev (which will give flux in the observed range) will be adequate to explain the observations.

If, however, the objects are at cosmological distances a much more complex situation arises. It is clear that much lower energy electrons are required, since to radiate near a given frequency the electron energy E must be proportional to $B^{-1/2}$. Thus the minimum values of magnetic field in the examples given above show that electron energies $\leq 10^8$ ev are required. Since $r \ll R$ if the objects are at cosmological distances, it is impossible to suppose that the particles are all injected into the region of radius R from a single central object of very small radius.

If this were so the radiation would all be emitted from a volume with a dimension of light hours or less, and in this region the radiation density would be higher according to (11.20), so that the inverse Compton process would appear to dominate, thus leading to a further contradiction. If the magnetic fields are to be as strong as this we must conclude either that the electrons are generated continuously at a large number of injection points separated by dimensions measured in light minutes at most or that they are continuously accelerated over these small dimensions. It also is a requirement that the radiation from each of this very large number of subregions be cophased. A very large number (n) of coherent subregions must be invoked, and all of these must be fitted into an overall dimension less than or equal to R (where R is 10^{17}–10^{15} cm). It is easily shown that $n \geq 10^6$ for $R \approx 10^{17}$ cm.

Thus we conclude that if the QSO's are assumed to be at cosmological distances, then their magnetic fields must be very large; the relativistic particles must be generated or accelerated *in situ;* and the very large number of subregions, each with its own injection or acceleration point, must be phased together.

It is important to realize that these difficulties cannot be avoided if we suppose that the flux observed is generated largely by the inverse Compton process rather than by the synchrotron process. Let us consider this situation briefly. We require that an immense flux of low-frequency radiation be generated by some unspecified device at the center of the object, or perhaps throughout the volume of size R. Unless a much more powerful coherent plasma mechanism than that required to give the radio flux can be invoked here, no one has the slightest idea what could be responsible. Neglecting this problem for the moment, however, we see that the energy density of radiation in the object is clearly so high that inverse Compton collisions will degrade the electrons in exactly the same time as is given by (11.22), though in this instance the magnetic field is negligible. Consequently, we still find that r, which is now the distance traveled by the electrons in losing their energies through inverse Compton collisions, is very small compared with R, so that we still require that the electrons are generated or accelerated *in situ* in millions of separate injection points that must be cophased to give the observed flux variations.

It may well be asked whether there is any mechanism known by which relativistic particles might be generated *in situ*. One possibility is that quarks are involved. This possibility will be discussed in Chapter 17. Another possibility is that they are generated from oscillations in the magnetic field. In order to explain the optical fluctuation data, we must assume that such oscillations propagate with essentially the speed of light—the oscillations would need to be electromagnetic, not hydromagnetic.

A mechanism for generating electromagnetic waves has been discussed by Hoyle, Narlikar, and Wheeler (1964). They regarded the waves as being emitted in the dynamical oscillations of a highly collapsed star, the wavelength being a few kilometers. Such waves do not propagate unless the electron density is very low. Hence in a model based on this mechanism there would have to be an inner region of dimension $\sim 10^{17}$ cm, largely devoid of matter, surrounding a collapsed object. To keep the waves from radiating freely into space it would also be necessary to trap the waves within the inner region by surrounding it with a gas cloud of comparatively high density. It may be added that the distinction between synchrotron emission and the Compton process is now lost; the two processes are the same in a purely electromagnetic field.

In all of the discussion so far, we have supposed that the radiation field is isotropic, in which case the relative importance of the inverse Compton process as compared with the synchrotron process is determined by the energy densities of radiation and magnetic flux. In an attempt to avoid the difficulties and the peculiarities of the model discussed here, Woltjer (1966b) has considered the effect if the radiation field is nonisotropic. The simplified expression (11.19) corresponding to an isotropic radiation field is derived by supposing that there is a random distribution of pitch angles ψ for electrons moving in the magnetic field. The Compton process becomes less important for small values of ψ corresponding to close alignment of the light beam with the magnetic field. For an assumed value of sin $\psi = 0.1$, Woltjer (using $R \leq 10^{17}$ cm, and $L < 10^{47}$ erg/sec based on a cosmological distance for 3C 273) has shown that the synchrotron process will dominate over the inverse Compton effect for values of the magnetic field about one order of magnitude smaller than those given in the example discussed earlier. Of course this result is derived by making the special assumption that the magnetic field is essentially radial and that the electrons have very small pitch angles, so that the radiation is emitted nearly parallel to the magnetic field. The particle energies for such fields are correspondingly somewhat higher than the values we gave earlier, and it must be supposed that they are generated *in situ* in the central object and stream straight out, drawing out the magnetic lines of force with them.

We shall briefly discuss another kind of model—one for which it is supposed that the flux is emitted from coherent blobs of matter moving at relativistic speed (Hoyle and Burbidge, 1966c).

We have already mentioned that Rees (1966) pointed out that a relativistically expanding cloud can increase its apparent angular size at about γ_V times the rate given by the usual nonrelativistic formula, where $\gamma_V = [1 - (V^2/c^2)]^{-1/2}$ and V is the expansion velocity. By combining this kinematic result with synchrotron self-absorption Rees showed that a large increase in radio emission could occur in a time (*our* time) substantially less than R/c. The issue is less clear for the optical radiation, but a model could probably be constructed involving the acceleration of emitting material that gave a similar result. The fluctuation data, however, involve *decreases* of light as well as increases, and the situation for a decrease in brightness is not so clear in a simple radially expanding model. Rees was attempting to account for the increase in radio emission from 3C 273B, and for this object there was no rapid decrease in emission to be explained.

A situation similar to that discussed by Rees occurs if we consider radiation emitted by a discrete blob of radius R_1 moving at relativistic speed V. To a stationary observer radiation from the blob appears largely concentrated in a forward cone of angle $\sim \gamma_V^{-1}$. Deflection of the direction of motion causes the axis of the cone to move, the axis being always in the direction of motion. The minimum time required for the axis to turn through angle γ_V^{-1} is $\gamma_V^{-1} R_1 / c$. The effect of the cone turning across the line of sight would be to give both an increase and a decrease in the observed light. In this way the fluctuation time is again reduced below R_1/c.

To follow this idea further we note that inside the forward cone the radiation intensity is very much higher than it is outside, essentially by γ_V^4. Fluctuations of this large amount ($\sim 10^4$ for γ_V as low as 10) are not observed, but the radiation intensity typically varies by a factor of about 2. This forces us to use many such blobs—indeed so many (about γ_V^2 blobs) that the cones overlap. But there must not be too much overlapping, otherwise the effect of the turning of a single cone would be too small. To explain the fluctuation data it would be necessary for the cones to just about fill the whole solid angle, 4π, neither too much nor too little.

The limitation on size in such a model is for a single blob. The whole distribution of blobs could be much larger than $c\tau\gamma_V$, where τ is the observed fluctuation time. In principle this overcomes the inverse Compton problem. Other difficulties have to be faced, however, since the emitted radiant energy is largely derived from the internal energy of the blobs. It is found that the internal energies are rapidly damped (in our time) unless the synchrotron efficiency within the blobs is very small—that is, unless the magnetic field is weak. This means that it is hard to see why the distribution does not simply fly radially apart, without substantial deflections in the directions of motion of the individual parts. It is also necessary that the relativistic blobs do not have the effect of dissipating or transferring too much energy to the surrounding gaseous shell in which the line spectrum is produced. This probably means that the blobs must be small as compared with the size of the region giving rise to the lines, so that the effective interaction cross section for each blob is small.

A further difficulty concerns the internal energies of the blobs. It is hard to see how the internal energies, necessary for radiant emission, can be derived directly from a central object of small dimension, because internal energies disappear in expansion—the usual adiabatic effect. If we require internal energies to be generated in collisions between blobs, more care is needed in discussing fluctuation times; it is not clear that these can be appreciably reduced below R_1/c.

CONCLUSIONS ABOUT THE MODELS PROPOSED TO EXPLAIN THE CONTINUOUS FLUX

In summary, the models that have been proposed to explain the continuous energy distribution depend largely on the distances assumed for the quasi-stellar objects. If the objects are close by then the synchrotron mechanism can account for all of the radiation emitted without posing any obvious problems. However, the possibility is not precluded that some part of the flux in the frequency range 10^9–10^{11} c/s could arise through coherent plasma processes.

If the objects lie at cosmological distances then the very high densities of photons that must be involved mean that the inverse Compton process is of extreme importance. We are again left with the possibility that some part of the radiation may arise through coherent plasma oscillations or the Cerenkov process, but it appears that for the radiation to escape it must be generated near the electron gyrofrequency, which means that very strong magnetic fields of 10^3–10^5 gauss are required. The bulk of the radiation almost certainly is synchrotron radiation, and for this process to work it is required that very strong magnetic fields ≥ 100 gauss be present and that electrons be generated *in situ* throughout the object or be accelerated in exceedingly small regions. Alternatively, the radiation is emitted by relativistically moving blobs. It is not certain whether some of these conditions are mutually exclusive. For example, if some part of the radiation is emitted by coherent processes in exceedingly strong magnetic fields, it is clear that no relativistic electrons can pass through this strong field without losing their energy. Thus any synchrotron source that lies outside such a region must generate electrons by some process that does not involve injection from a central object.

The suggestion that relativistic blobs and directed beams of radiation may be required imposes the further condition that the sources must be very short-lived and much more frequent than has previously been assumed. We note the rather ironic point that a system of relativistic blobs flying apart corresponds very much to the kind of process that one must invoke for the origin of the QSO's in the local hypothesis if they have been ejected from our galaxy at relativistic speeds.

Woltjer (1966) has suggested that the existence of at least one galaxy (NGC 1275) that shows variations in high-frequency radio flux similar to those seen in a number of QSO's can be used as supporting evidence for the view that the QSO's are at cosmological distances. But, as we have just shown, the difficulties encountered with the cosmological models of the QSO's stem from the very high densities of radiation that arise because of the very great distances of the objects. No difficulties are encountered if the objects are nearby, and none are encountered with NGC 1275, simply because it lies at a distance of only about 50 Mpc. Thus we may as well argue that the similarities between the QSO's and NGC 1275 indicate that the QSO's are not at cosmological distances.

We shall discuss in Chapter 17 the various mechanisms proposed for generating energy in the QSO's, and it will become clear there that we do not really understand how the energy is pumped in. From our analysis here it will be seen that if the objects are local their energetic characteristics are rather similar to the nuclei of Seyfert galaxies, and the synchrotron process can be used to explain the phenomenon without requiring very extreme models. If the objects are at cosmological distances, much more stringent conditions are required, involving very strong magnetic fields and a "machine" that must be able to feed energy in directly as relativistically moving matter. Even these models are based on the idea that the actual size of the object is very close to the upper limits required by the variation data. If variations of even shorter period are seen then the conditions required will be correspondingly more extreme.

Since we do not know the true nature of the energy-producing source, it is at present a matter of taste whether one decides that the class of model required for cosmological objects is reasonable or not. If one believes that very strong magnetic fields cannot be maintained in such an object, or that the generation of relativistic blobs is an unreasonable requirement, then one is forced to the conclusion that the QSO's are local. We tend to believe that these arguments do point in this direction. Other investigators, however, have taken a different approach. They have been working on the assumption that the objects must be cosmological and thus feel that the conditions needed for such models to work must be fulfilled. We shall return to a review of the evidence for the local and the cosmological hypotheses in Chapter 15.

12

Absorption and Scattering
of Flux from Quasi-Stellar Objects

The detection of interstellar absorption lines in the spectra of stars is one of the best-known methods of investigating the properties of the interstellar gas, whereas in the radio frequency range 21-cm absorption techniques have provided a useful tool for galactic investigation. Thus when quasi-stellar objects were found, and it seemed reasonable to suppose that they were at very great distances from us, it appeared possible to use them as probes to investigate the properties of the intergalactic medium. This medium may absorb or scatter photons emitted by the QSO. The specific processes that may be important are:

1. The scattering of photons emitted by the QSO at wavelengths shorter than Ly-α by neutral hydrogen atoms, which see these photons at the Ly-α wavelength in their frame of reference.

2. The scattering of photons as in (1) for any resonance transition involving other atomic species.

3. The absorption of photons emitted by the QSO at wavelengths shorter than 21 cm by neutral hydrogen atoms, which see these photons at a wavelength of 21 cm in their frame of reference.

4. The absorption of photons that are emitted by the QSO at wavelengths shorter than the Lyman band in H_2 (the edge of which is at 1108 Å) and are then absorbed by H_2 along the light path.

5. Absorption due to dust in the intergalactic medium.

6. Thomson scattering by free electrons in the intergalactic medium.

For each absorption or scattering involving a discrete line, such as Ly-α or the 21-cm line, we should see a discrete absorption feature in the spectrum of the QSO on the blue side of the position of the redshifted line in the QSO, provided that the absorbing or scattering material is concentrated in a cloud with a discrete redshift relative to the observer. If the absorbing or scattering material is distributed uniformly throughout the path length, all of the radiation lying between the position of the redshifted line in the QSO and the wavelength of the line in the laboratory will interact with the material in the medium. An absorption trough will be produced that extends from the redshifted wavelength in the object down to the rest wavelength. We consider the specific processes individually.

1. Prior to the discovery that some QSO's have redshifts large enough so that Ly-α is shifted into the normally observed photographic spectrum, E. M. Burbidge (1965) realized that it might be possible to detect absorption of quanta due to this transition by intergalactic hydrogen atoms if one could obtain ultraviolet spectra of nearby galaxies, and discussed the problems associated with this approach. Immediately following the discovery that the Ly-α line is shifted to a wavelength of λ3666 Å in 3C 9, Scheuer (1965), who had not seen the spectrum of 3C 9, pointed out that if the spectrum showed a continuum below 3660 Å, either the mean density of neutral atomic hydrogen is exceedingly low or the ionization is nearly complete. He also did not exclude a third possibility—that the object is comparatively nearby, in which case no appreciable absorption is to be expected. A more extensive investigation, in which Schmidt's first observational material on 3C 9 was used, was made by Gunn and Peterson (1965). They showed that if the intergalactic medium is distributed uniformly with density n in the scattering region, then the optical depth p is given approximately by

$$p = \frac{n}{(1 + z)(1 + 2q_0 z)^{1/2}} \left(\frac{\pi e^2 f}{m \nu_\alpha H_0} \right)$$

$$= \frac{n}{(1 + z)(1 + 2q_0 z)^{1/2}} \times 5 \times 10^{10}.$$

Here H_0 is the Hubble constant set equal to 10^{-10} year^{-1}, and q_0 is the deceleration parameter. Gunn and Peterson concluded that immediately on the blue side of Ly-α the continuum was depressed by an amount that they estimated to be 40%. Thus they estimated $p \simeq \frac{1}{2}$, giving a value for $n = 6 \times 10^{-11}$ cm^{-3}, or a density $\rho = 1 \times 10^{-34}$ gm/cm^3. They assumed $q_0 = \frac{1}{2}$. Since the first spectra of 3C 9 were obtained, however, a considerable number of QSO's with Ly-α in the photographic region have been observed (Chapter 3) and more accurate scanner observations of 3C 9 have been made by Oke and Wampler. The observers now agree that the interpretation of Schmidt's observations originally made by Gunn and Peterson is not correct and that there is no evidence for any significant depression on the blue side of Ly-α. Since the position of the continuum is uncertain to an accuracy of about 5%, this means that the only conclusion that can be drawn is that $\exp(-p) \geq 0.95$, or that $p \leq 0.05$. Thus if we assume that the objects are cosmological, $n \leq 6 \times 10^{-12}$ cm^3 or $\rho \leq 10^{-35}$ g/cm^3.

2. Shklovsky (1964) pointed out that a similar argument could be applied to set a limit to the intergalactic density of Mg$^+$, since absorption due to the resonance doublet of Mg II at $\lambda 2798$ would be expected on the blue side of the position of this emission line in QSO's. Since no absorption is detectable, he concluded that the density of Mg$^+ < 8 \times 10^{-13}$ cm^{-3}. Since the ionization potential of Mg$^+$ is very close to that of hydrogen, then provided that the temperature of the intergalactic medium is not very high or low, the abundance ratio H/Mg = H$^+$/Mg$^+$, and if this is taken to be the same as that in our galaxy we find that an upper limit $n = 2 \times 10^{-7}$ cm^{-3} is set on the intergalactic hydrogen density. If the temperature were high or low enough so that the bulk of the Mg would be multiply ionized or neutral, the limit set on the intergalactic abundance would be governed by the temperature assumed.

Bahcall and Salpeter (1965, 1966) have considered more generally the possibility that resonance lines due to ions such as Li, C, C$^+$, O, Mg, Mg$^+$, Al$^+$, Al^{++}, Fe, and Fe$^+$ might be used to investigate the intergalactic medium by the absorption method. Rees and Sciama (1966) also considered absorption by some ions other than hydrogen. It was considered possible that the intergalactic gas is condensed into clusters of galaxies, so that instead of giving rise to an absorption trough with a frequency width of $\nu z/(1 + z)$, which will be the case if the material is uniformly distributed, a number of discrete absorption features will be seen, each with a width corresponding to the local velocity dispersion.

The major observational problem, then, is to detect and identify absorption features in the spectra of QSO's; we have described the observations in Chapter 3. The first QSO in which an absorption feature was identified was BSO 1 (Sandage, 1965), and the feature was C IV $\lambda1549$—a sharp self-absorption near the center of the broad emission line, which obviously has nothing to do with the external medium. With the discovery of 3C 191 (Burbidge, Lynds, and Burbidge, 1966) the situation changed, since in this object a considerable number of absorption features are seen, and it might be thought at first sight that these are due to absorption in an intergalactic cloud. Most of these lines can be identified with resonance transitions in common ions, and the mean redshift z obtained from the absorption features is 1.947, whereas that from the broad emission features is 1.953. The difference is so small that there is no question but that the absorption and emission features both arise in the QSO.

When Bahcall, Peterson, and Schmidt (1966) found an absorption component in PKS 1116 + 12 at a wavelength about 200 Å less than that of the Ly-α emission, they thought this might well be due to absorption in an intergalactic cloud. If the absorption were produced in a shell of gas expanding outward from the QSO, the difference in wavelength would give a very large expansion velocity, about 17,000 km/sec, whereas that in 3C 191 would be only about 600 km/sec. That large velocity gradients can indeed be present, however, is suggested by the remarkable spectrum of PHL 5200 (Plate 12), in which Lynds (1967a) found very broad absorption bands on the short-wavelength side of the broad emission lines. Moreover, in PKS 0119 − 04, Kinman and Burbidge (1967) found the absorption line of C IV $\lambda1549$ on the *long*-wavelength side of the center of the emission line, by an amount that would correspond to a shell of gas falling inward into the QSO at about 2000 km/sec. Here the absorption obviously could not be intergalactic. Indeed, the accumulation of QSO's with absorption-line redshifts near $z = 1.95$, which was described in Chapter 3, suggests that perhaps it is the absorption-line redshift that is to be taken as the standard, and then the differences between absorption-line and emission-line redshifts, when they occur, could be due either to relative motion of the two regions or to differences in gravitational potential.

Bahcall and Salpeter (1966) pointed out that intergalactic gas should produce absorptions only from the zero-volt atomic levels of the relevant ions, because the fine-structure levels with energies slightly above the zero level will have a negligibly small population. Of the absorptions that arise from ground states with fine structure, all those so far observed in the spectra of QSO's give evidence for a normal population of the fine-structure levels. This shows that the gas cannot lie in a region of very low density and very dilute radiation; it must therefore be associated with the QSO's.

Sciama and Rees (1966b) have attempted to interpret some features in the spectral region of 3C 9 below 3300 Å as being due to Ly-α absorption and an absorption line of N V with a redshift of $z = 1.62$. This, they argue, is due to a hot intergalactic cloud. They made these identifications, however, from a reproduction of the spectral intensity in this region published in the Astrophysical Journal (Field, Solomon, and Wampler, 1966) without taking into account all of the uncertainties involved in making identifications without investigating the raw observational material in detail. Nor have they considered alternative interpretations of apparent absorption (or emission) features—for example, that the features, if real, may be due to the material of the QSO. We conclude that little weight can be placed on this result.

3. Besides Ly-α and the resonance lines of the common ions we can consider the possibility of attempting to detect 21-cm absorption due to the intergalactic medium. Koehler and Robinson (1966) have reported the detection of 21-cm absorption in the spectrum of 3C 273 at a wavelength corresponding to absorption by gas with a redshift of $z = 0.0037$. This is almost exactly the mean redshift of the galaxies in the Virgo cluster, and thus they have concluded that this absorption is caused by a neutral hydrogen cloud associated with the Virgo cluster. Now 3C 273 lies in a direction about 6° from

the center of the Virgo cluster, which itself lies about 10 Mpc from our galaxy. Thus this observation suggests that 3C 273 lies behind a neutral hydrogen cloud, which lies a few Mpc away from us. It certainly does not establish that 3C 273 lies at a cosmological distance (470 Mpc is the distance derived from the redshift), as has been stated by Rees and Sciama (1965a). Koehler and Robinson's observation must be treated with great caution, however, as it is marginal, and so far it has not been confirmed by other radio astronomy groups.

4. There is another measurement that can be made to attempt to set a limit on the amount of H_2 in the intergalactic medium. As was pointed out by Bahcall and Salpeter (1965), limits may be set on the abundance of intergalactic molecular hydrogen by considering the absorption that it will produce in the Lyman band on the short-wavelength side of 1108 Å. Again, objects with $z \geq 2$ are required. Field, Solomon, and Wampler (1966) have attempted this test with 3C 9. They have not been able to detect any absorption, and have therefore taken $\tau_{H_2} < 1$, a very conservative approach. This has led them to the result that the intergalactic density of H_2 is less than about 10^{-32} gm/cm³.

5. Kardashev (1966) has attempted to argue that intergalactic absorption by dust can account for some part of the shapes of the continua in QSO's. As was discussed in Chapters 4 and 11 this is an unlikely possibility, since the forms of the spectra are explicable as due to a nonthermal continuum with superposed line radiation.

6. It is of some interest to consider the effect of Thomson scattering on the radiation emitted by distant sources. This question has been discussed by Bahcall and Salpeter (1965). They have shown that the optical depth τ against electron scattering is given by

$$\tau = 6.5 \times 10^3 n_e \ln (1 + z) \text{ [steady state]}, \quad \text{or}$$

$$\tau = 6.5 \times 10^3 n_e (6q_0^2)^{-1}[1 + 2q_0 z)^{3/2} + (6q_0 - 3)(1 + 2q_0 z)^{1/2} + (2 - 6q_0)].$$

Here n_e is the local intergalactic electron density. For $z \simeq 2$ and values of q_0 near unity this effect is not yet important. Only if the QSO's have values of z very much greater than this can it be expected that Thomson scattering will be of significance. Bahcall and Salpeter have also discussed the possibility that if the intergalactic material shows density fluctuations, multiple small-angle scattering of radio quanta may be of importance.

The observations made so far show no evidence for any absorption or scattering due to a uniform distribution of intergalactic gas or dust. Most investigators have therefore used this result to set very low limits on the density of neutral gas, and have then concluded that the bulk of the mass energy in the universe (which most people assume is near 10^{-29} g cm^{-3}) is present in the form of ionized gas, mainly hydrogen. There are, of course, two major flaws in this argument. First, the absence of any effect can equally well be interpreted as being due to the fact that the radiation has only traversed a very small path in the intergalactic medium—that is, that the QSO's are local rather than cosmological. Second, even if the objects are cosmological, one cannot logically jump to the conclusion that the bulk of the mass is in the form of ionized gas. This is only one of several possibilities. Others are that the matter is in the form of stars, uniformly distributed, or condensed into small star clusters or in low-luminosity galaxies, or in the form of solid matter, or even in the form of neutrinos. The only advantage associated with the ionized-gas hypothesis appears to be that further investigations concerning the state of this gas are possible, and the reader who pursues this subject must be continuously aware that the investigations are often designed to fit in with one or another cosmological prejudice or hypothesis.

We have so far been concerned with ways in which propagation through a low-density intergalactic medium might redistribute the radiation emitted from the QSO's. Wagoner (1967b) has looked into the possibility that the path of the radiation from a QSO might intersect a foreground galaxy. For redshifts $z > 1$, the probability of intersection of the light path with a galaxy becomes significant for a number of cosmological models. Provided that the galaxy contains a considerable amount of uncondensed matter the effects that have just been described will occur and in some cases they may be detectable. A detectable amount of Faraday rotation may also be found in some cases.

The radio and optical absorption lines are again likely to be the best indicators of the nature of the intervening matter and also of where it is. It is possible that one might be able to see the nucleus of an absorbing galaxy that appears to lie very close to the QSO. Wagoner has considered the case of 3C 287. This object has colors and a Faraday rotation measure that are not in disagreement with the idea that the electromagnetic radiation has passed through a galaxy on the way to us. He has also noticed that there is a very faint "star" with $m_v \simeq 21$ separated by $3''$ from the optical image of 3C 287. If identifiable absorption lines were found in the spectrum of 3C 287 at a much lower redshift than that of the emission lines, this would give some weight to the possibility that we are observing the QSO through a foreground galaxy. Even this discovery, however, would not settle the question unless the redshifts in the QSO's had been conclusively established to be Doppler shifts. As has been mentioned earlier, if the redshifts are gravitational in origin then it may be expected that in some cases we may find a QSO (with a large gravitational redshift) physically associated with a galaxy (with a small redshift).

13

Correlations Between Redshifts and Optical and Radio Magnitudes

We have described in earlier chapters the optical and radio properties of the QSO's. In this chapter we shall briefly consider whether correlations exist between these observed quantities. The properties that can be used are the redshifts, colors, optical luminosities, radio luminosities, and radio spectra.

It has already been shown in Chapter 4 that correlations do exist between the redshifts and the colors of the QSO's, and it seems probable that these correlations are due to the presence of the emission lines. This correlation arises from the intrinsic properties of the QSO's; we shall not discuss it further.

CORRELATION BETWEEN REDSHIFTS AND APPARENT OPTICAL MAGNITUDES

The correlation between the redshifts and the optical luminosities is of considerable interest. If the quasi-stellar objects are at cosmological distances then this relation may be used to investigate cosmological models. For fairly small redshifts the plot of log z against magnitude should give a straight line, as in Hubble's original diagram for galaxies, whereas for large redshifts various cosmologies predict departures from the straight-line relation by different amounts. Sandage (1965) made a plot of the relation between apparent magnitude and redshift for the ten QSO's whose redshifts were known at that time, alongside a similar plot for the radio galaxies. The latter, after correction for the K-effect (see Chapter 4 for the definition of this) showed a good, tight, straight-line relation, but the ten QSO's already showed considerable scatter. No correction for K-effect was applied to the magnitudes of the QSO's; as discussed in Chapter 4, this correction is very small for QSO's unless their continua have slopes differing considerably from the slope given by $F(\nu) \propto \nu^{-1}$ (Sandage, 1966a).

An alternative way of correlating optical luminosity with redshift is that adopted by Schmidt (1965). For a chosen cosmological model (evolutionary, with $q_0 = +1$) he calculated the monochromatic flux from nine QSO's at an emitted frequency of 10^{15} c/s (i.e., at a rest wavelength of 3000 Å) and then saw whether these fluxes were approximately the same for all the objects. The problem with this approach is that to employ it properly, over the whole range of observed redshifts, one needs spectral scans of QSO's ranging all the way from near the ultraviolet atmospheric cutoff for objects with small z to the infrared at $\lambda > 9000$ Å for objects with large z; as we saw in Chapter 4, the time-consuming work of producing such spectral scans has been performed for relatively few objects. Schmidt made use of the U,B,V photometry, and computed flux densities at the wavelengths $3000(1 + z)$ Å by means of the relations derived by Matthews and Sandage (1963) (see Chapter 4). In the circumstances, it is probably preferable to use the U,B,V measurements as they stand, in the way Sandage has done, because quantities derived from these are that much further from the observed quantities and carry the additional uncertainty in the steps used to make the derivations. As far as it goes, however, Schmidt's calculation shows that the fluxes of the nine objects are consistent with an evolutionary cosmology with $q_0 = +1$, with a scatter whose extreme range is a factor 20.

As new redshifts have become available, the scatter in the apparent magnitude-redshift relation has become larger instead of smaller (Hoyle and Burbidge, 1966b). Figure 13.1 shows the plot with all the redshifts in Table 3.1; what little correlation there is shows a scatter of a similar order of magnitude to that of the total span of the relation. Indeed, with the luminosity variations shown by *individual* QSO's (more than 3 magnitudes, or a factor of nearly 20 for 3C 446), such scatter is not surprising. The plot represents,

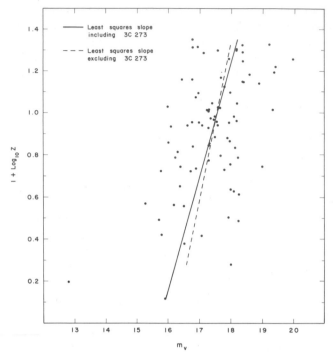

FIG. 13.1 *Plot of Redshift against apparent visual magnitude for all QSO's with z known in February 1967. Full line has a slope of about 0.2 as for cluster galaxies and radio galaxies.*

in fact, the quality of the intrinsic luminosity function of the QSO's, rather than a meaningful distance-redshift relation.

CORRELATION BETWEEN REDSHIFTS AND RADIO FLUX

Hoyle and Burbidge (1966b) made a plot of the logarithm of the radio flux (or radio apparent magnitude) at 178 Mc/s against $(1 + \log z)$ for the QSO's in the 3C R catalogue, and this showed even more scatter than the similar plot of redshifts against optical apparent magnitudes. The diagram is shown in Figure 14.2, in connection with the discussion in Chapter 14 of the radio source counts.

In fact, there is in this plot no sign of any correlation, and this implies that the range in apparent radio fluxes is not determined by a range in distances but entirely by the intrinsic spread in the radio properties of the QSO's. The implications of this in interpreting the counts of radio sources down to given flux limits are discussed in Chapter 14.

Bolton (1966) suggested that a plot such as that shown in Figure 14.2, made with radio measurements at the comparatively low frequency of 178 Mc/s, contains objects with a variety of radio spectra, and he made a plot of $(1 + \log z)$ against radio magnitude at a higher frequency, 1410 Mc/s, for QSO's in the Parkes catalogue. Although such a plot shows an equally large overall scatter, one can make a distinct separation into two groups if one considers objects with flat or relatively flat radio spectra as one group and objects with steep radio spectra as another group. The objects with steep radio spectra show a slight negative correlation, with the strongest emitters having the largest redshifts, and Bolton suggests that this is simply a reflection of a very large dispersion in the relevant intrinsic radio luminosities. The QSO's with flat radio spectra may all undergo synchrotron self-absorption (Chapters 5 and 11), and the radio emission may be emanating from a very small volume; Bolton suggests that such objects might have less intrinsic spread in their high-frequency radio emission, and, while there is no very distinct relationship, the scatter for the flat-spectrum sources is considerably lower than in either of Figures 13.1 or 14.2. If this suggestion is correct, one may perhaps find that the so-called radio-quiet QSO's are actually radio emitters at very high frequencies, and that they include objects with the largest values of z.

14

Counts of Quasi-Stellar Objects and the Log N–Log S Curve

We consider a uniform distribution of sources of radiation throughout the whole of Euclidean space at rest with respect to their local reference frame and suppose that they have an intrinsic brightness P. The apparent brightness is $S = P/r^2$, or $r = (P/S)^{1/2}$. Thus the number of sources whose apparent brightness exceeds S, inside a sphere of radius r, is $(4/3)\pi\rho(P/S)^{3/2}$ where ρ is the density of sources. Thus the number N per unit solid angle is $(1/3)\rho(P/S)^{3/2}$. If there is a spread in intrinsic brightness

$$N = \tfrac{1}{3} \sum (\rho P^{3/2}) S^{-3/2}, \tag{14.1}$$

where the sum is over the various brightness classes, and thus the plot of log N versus log S should have a slope of $-\tfrac{3}{2}$ for any luminosity distribution of sources. There are a number of effects associated with the redshift that become of increasing importance as S get smaller. These are the effect of the so-called K term, which we discussed in Chapter 4. We showed there that for spectra of the form $P(\nu) \propto \nu^{-\alpha}$, which applies for the radio sources, the correction is of the form $2.5(1 - \alpha) \log (1 + z)$, and since $\alpha \approx 0.7$ this correction is small. There is also a correction due to the number effect; that is, the redshift reduces the brightness over and above the inverse square law so that the r corresponding to a given S is reduced. This reduces N. The third effect will depend on the cosmological model used to interpret the data. If we live in an evolutionary universe then ρ was much greater in the past than it is now, and for increasing redshift we are looking further and further back into the past, which means that ρ should get bigger and bigger. Thus ρ will increase with increasing redshift, so that N should be increased.

In the steady-state universe this last effect is not present, but in the evolutionary models the second effect overwhelms the third. Thus the prediction is that the cosmological effects will tend to reduce the slope of the log N–log S curve.

It is well known that over the last decade strenuous efforts have been made to investigate cosmological models by making counts of all radio sources. This was done despite the fact that few optical identifications were available so that the nature of the objects was not known.

In the early work on the source counts of all radio sources by Ryle and Scheuer (1955) the slope of the log N–log S curve was about -3, much steeper than any predicted values. Next a survey by Mills, Slee, and Hill (1958) gave a slope that they estimated to be about -1.8, and a comparison of the Ryle-Scheuer survey and this survey suggested that the slope was considerably less than -3. The next survey (Edge et al., 1959) gave a slope of about -2. A further survey was then carried out with greatly increased precision by the Cambridge group (Scott and Ryle, 1961) and this gave a slope of -1.8, which was in good agreement with the results of the survey of Mills et al. More recently a survey has been carried out by Bolton, Gardner, and Mackey (1964) that gives a slope of -1.85. The other sections of the Parkes catalogue (see Chapter 1 for references) give slopes that do not differ significantly from this. Thus there is now good evidence from several independent groups that the slope of the log N–log S curve for all sources is near -1.8.

Since the cosmological effects all tend to flatten the curve to values below -1.5, it is obvious that other effects must be present to explain the observed slope. Either an excess of faint sources or a deficit of bright sources is required. If an excess of faint sources is assumed to be present, then it is reasonable to argue that this is due to the fact that the intrinsic brightness of a source is a function of its time of formation in an evolving universe; were this shown to be correct, the steady-state theory would have been shown to be incorrect. If, however, the slope were due to a deficit of bright sources, this could be explained by the presence of a local irregularity in distribution; Hoyle and Narlikar produced a modified version of the steady-state theory that might do this, though there are now known to be difficulties in such a model.

As we stated earlier all of these investigations were carried out at a time when the majority of the radio sources remained unidentified, though they were largely thought to be associated with galaxies. As was described in Chapter 2 extensive identifications have been made of the objects in the revised 3C catalogue. Of the 328 sources in this catalogue 32 are probably or certainly galactic, and of the remaining 296 Véron (1966) has concluded that 42 lie in fields that show galactic absorption and cannot be easily identified, 144 are galaxies, 60 are QSO's, 36 have no optical object with $m_v < 21$, and 14 remain unidentified.

By plotting the log N–log S curve separately for radio galaxies and QSO's, Véron has found that for the radio galaxies the slope is -1.5, whereas for QSO's it is about -2.2. The slope for all 296 sources in the revised 3C taken together was made earlier by Ryle and Neville (1963), and gives a slope of -1.85. The value of -1.5 obtained for the galaxies is due simply to the fact that the size of the region over which the 3C survey sources have been found is small enough so that the Euclidean space approximation holds. The greatest redshift known so far for a radio galaxy is that for 3C 295, $z = 0.46$, and the majority of the radio galaxies so far studied spectroscopically have $z \leq 0.2$. Thus in this survey at least the departure from the $-\frac{3}{2}$ law arises from the QSO's. There are two possible explanations for this. If the QSO's are cosmological, then we must attribute this steeper slope to evolutionary effects in an evolving universe, as has been attempted by Longair (1966). Alternatively, if they are local, this slope might be attributed to the local conditions under which these objects were ejected from galaxies.

Since the slope of -1.85 for all radio sources persists in the counts to much lower flux levels than those of the revised 3C catalogue, the explanations can fall into two categories. If the QSO's are cosmological then the contributions to the slope given by them may arise from evolutionary effects at intrinsically lower power levels, whereas the galaxies will independently depart significantly from the -1.5 slope as we go fainter. The galaxy contribution may modify either positively or negatively the slope for the QSO's. If the QSO's are local and if, for example, we argue that in the 3C catalogue we are sampling in them a wide range of luminosities of objects ejected from local galaxies, and if we have reached some of the faintest ones, then as we go to counts of much fainter sources the following effect will be expected. We shall be detecting sources coming out of more distant galaxies, but under such conditions the objects will not be optically detectable. But they will follow exactly the relation for galaxies, since the sources associated with galaxies and those ejected from galaxies will be indistinguishable. Thus the slope should return to a value of -1.5 corresponding to objects where the Euclidean space approximation holds. The steepening of the slope to -1.85 must be due to evolutionary effects of the now indistinguishable galaxies and intrinsically fainter QSO's.

It should be added that another type of argument to explain the observations and also to save the steady-state theory was proposed (Sciama, 1963, 1965; Sciama and Saslaw, 1966). This involves the idea that there is present another class of intrinsically very faint objects—QSO's with zero redshift, lying at characteristic distances of $\sim$100 pc. There is no direct evidence for the existence of these objects, and since we are concentrating here on possible interpretations of the observed QSO's this type of theory will not be discussed further.

The assumption underlying the studies of the log N–log S relation for cosmological purposes is, as we have shown, that the slope is to be accounted for by a distance-volume effect. With the rapid accumulation of redshift data it is possible to test this generally accepted assumption by considering the log N–log S relation for QSO's in which redshifts have been measured. Hoyle and Burbidge (1966b) did this for a sample of about 30 QSO's from the 3C catalogue. A plot of log N versus log S for these objects is shown in Figure 14.1, and it can be seen that the slope is close to -1.5, not quite as steep as the value of -1.8 obtained from the count of all radio sources and not as steep as the value of about -2.2 obtained by Véron for all QSO's in the 3C catalogue. However, the slope of the curve in this figure is influenced by the two lower points, which are subject to large statistical scatter. Thus no undue significance

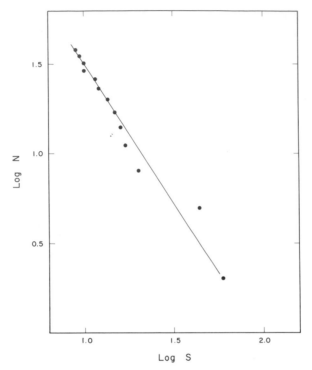

FIG. 14.1   *Plot of log N against log S for 38 QSO's in the 3C catalogue with known redshifts (N = number of sources whose apparent radio flux exceeds S flux units). Straight line, fitted to the points by eye, gives slope −1.5.*

should be attached to the value of the slope that these points happen to give. What does appear to be significant, however, is that even this small sample of QSO's gives a log N–log S slope near −1.5. The distance-volume interpretation requires that the objects with smaller S be at greater distances, and if redshifts are cosmological in origin small S must be correlated with large z. In Figure 14.2 we show a plot of the relation between redshift and apparent radio magnitude for these objects, and from this plot it is obvious that no such correlation exists. Thus *if* it is assumed that the distance-volume interpretation of the log N–log S relation holds, it must be concluded that the redshifts have nothing to do with distances.

RED SHIFT VERSUS RADIO MAGNITUDE

(S = 10   EQUALS m_R = 0.00)

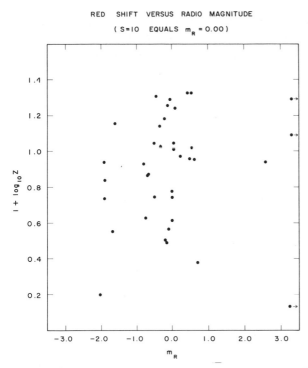

FIG. 14.2   *Plot of redshift against apparent radio magnitude for QSO's in the 3C catalogue.* [*After Hoyle and Burbidge (1966b).*]

Following this investigation several authors (Longair, 1966; Sciama and Rees, 1966a; Roeder and Mitchell, 1966) misquoted Hoyle and Burbidge and implied that they had concluded unconditionally that redshift had nothing to do with distance. The conclusion accurately stated above can, however, be inverted to the following form: If the redshifts are related to distance in the usual cosmological sense, then the distance-volume interpretation of $NS^{3/2} \approx$ constant must be abandoned for the sources in this particular sample. Consider the sources in a shell between distances r and $r + dr$. Provided these sources have an intrinsic scatter in their radio emission they will exhibit a log *N*–log *S* relation. If all such shells have the same log *N*–log *S* curve then summation of all shells will give a curve related to intrinsic scatter, not to distance. This is the point made by Bolton (1966). It must be noticed, however, that in order that all shells give the same log N–log S curve it is necessary for the average emission to vary in a special way from one shell to another. This indeed is what has been suggested by Longair and by Roeder and Mitchell. It requires that the average emission be a function of r, and hence of the epoch. Such an interpretation is evidently in disagreement with the strict steady-state theory (Sciama and Rees, 1966a).*

While one can certainly express a personal preference for this latter form of argument, it is overstating the case to claim support from it for one cosmology or another as has been done by these critics. All their discussions are predicated on the cosmological interpretation of the redshifts of the quasi-stellar objects, in the sense that this interpretation is taken as axiomatic. Conclusions following from it are accepted, essentially whatever they may be, because a noncosmological interpretation is taken to be out of the question. In view of the uncertainties about the nature of the QSO's, this approach is not wise. The result might equally well be interpreted as indirect evidence that the QSO's are local objects.

---

* In passing it may be noted that Kafka (1967) has concluded that the whole of this argument is premature, since he believes that not enough objects with redshifts are available for analysis of the log N–log S curve to give significant results.

15

Quasi-Stellar Objects as Local Phenomena

We have already introduced the idea that the quasi-stellar objects may lie comparatively close by. This concept was introduced in order to avoid the apparent difficulties associated with their small sizes and energetic properties if they lie at cosmological distances. No observations have yet been made that would enable us either to establish that the objects are local or to show that they lie at cosmological distances.

If they are indeed cosmological objects then some of the boundary conditions for possible models have already been described in Chapter 11, and no problem is encountered in explaining the redshifts, since they are due to the expansion of the universe. If the objects are comparatively nearby, however, their intrinsic radiation properties are easily accounted for, but to explain their redshifts we must suppose that they are moving locally at relativistic speeds or that the redshifts are gravitational in origin. If the objects are moving locally at relativistic speeds, then there are two points that must be discussed. The first is the question of the luminosities and spectral shifts to be expected if objects are moving at relativistic speeds, and the second is concerned with the energy that is required to generate large numbers of relativistically moving objects. We shall consider these in turn and then briefly discuss the situation if it is supposed that the redshifts are gravitational in origin.

LUMINOSITIES AND SPECTRAL SHIFTS FOR LOCAL OBJECTS MOVING AT HIGH SPEED

We follow here the analysis by Strittmatter (1966) of a number of possible cases. We first consider briefly the effects of redshift that are independent of the distance to the source. The redshift z is defined as usual by

$$1 + z = \frac{\lambda}{\lambda'} = \frac{\nu'}{\nu},$$ (15.1)

where λ, ν refer to the wavelength and frequency of a particular spectral feature. The prime denotes a value in the rest frame of the emitter, and unprimed quantities refer to the corresponding values in the frame of the observer; this notation will be used throughout. First we consider the effects of redshift on the continuous energy distribution.

Suppose that $N_{\nu'}$ photons of frequency between ν' and $\nu' + d\nu'$ are emitted in time dt' in a solid angle that subtends unit area at the observer. This area will be shown later to be Lorentz invariant. Thus in the emitter's frame the flux per sec per c/s, $F'_\nu(\nu')$, is given by

$$\cdot F'_\nu(\nu') = N_{\nu'} \frac{h\nu'}{dt'},$$ (15.2)

where h is Planck's constant. In the observer's frame, the $N_{\nu'}$ photons will be counted in a time dt and at frequencies between ν and $\nu + d\nu$, where

$$\frac{d\nu'}{d\nu} = \frac{\nu'}{\nu} = \frac{dt}{dt'} = (1 + z).$$ (15.3)

Thus

$$F_\nu(\nu) = \frac{F'_\nu(\nu')}{(1 + z)} = \frac{F'_\nu((1 + z)\nu)}{(1 + z)},$$ (15.4)

from which it clearly follows that

$$F_\lambda(\lambda) = \frac{F'_\lambda(\lambda')}{(1 + z)^3}$$ (15.5)

in an obvious notation. Also the total flux of energy F per second is given by

$$F = \frac{F'}{(1 + z)^2},$$ (15.6)

where

$$F' = \int_0^\infty F'_\nu \, d\nu.$$

The way in which these quantities are related to the total luminosity of the emitter depends, of course, on the intrinsic directional distribution of radiation from the source, and on the effective distance to the observer.

We now turn to the class of problems involving the relationship between redshift and distance. In a cosmological context, redshifts are attributed to the expansion of the universe and are directly related to metric distance in a way that depends on the model adopted. It is therefore possible to "test" the various models by determining observationally the redshift-magnitude dependence for particular classes of objects, the magnitude being a distance indicator. However, apart from the corrections due to time dilations mentioned in the previous sections, the observed luminosity will also be affected by the relativistic change in the angular distribution of energy, which results in a preferential flux in the direction of motion in the observer's frame. This is conventionally accounted for by introducing the concept of a luminosity distance, D_ℓ, which in fact is the metric distance traveled by the photons between the emitter and the observer in the frame of the former. Owing to symmetry properties between observers at different points in the model universe, the luminosity distance is given simply by

$$D_\ell = ra(t_0),$$ (15.7)

where r is the co-moving radial coordinate, t_0 the current time and a the expansion factor for the universe. It is equal to the *current* distance from observer to emitter and can be determined directly from the assumed model. Thus the observed flux, F, at the observer is given by

$$F = \frac{L_{int}}{4\pi r^2 a^2(t_0)(1 + z)^2} = \frac{L_{int}}{4\pi D_\ell^2(1 + z)^2},$$ (15.8)

where L_{int} is the intrinsic luminosity of the source.

However, in the case in which the redshifts are due to high

velocities in a local frame, the redshift-distance relation is more complicated, since a given value of z may correspond to a range of velocities V depending on the angle θ between the direction of motion and the line of sight. In fact the redshift is given by

$$1 + z = \frac{1 + \dfrac{V}{c} \cos \theta}{\left(1 - \dfrac{V^2}{c^2}\right)^{1/2}}. \tag{15.9}$$

However, the luminosity distance of a source at metric distance D from the observer will also depend on V and θ. We now derive the relation between D and D_ℓ.

Let O–$XYZt$, O'–$X'Y'Z't'$ be rectangular four-dimensional co-ordinates in the rest frames of spatial origins at the observer and the emitter, respectively. In the observer's frame the Z axis is along the direction of motion, the plane OXZ contains the emitter, and the time origin is set at the moment of emission; similar definitions apply in the emitter's frame. The positions of observer and emitter in each frame at the moments of emission and reception are given below (Y coordinates are all zero and are omitted).

	Frame of Observer		Frame of Emitter	
	Position of		Position of	
	Observer	Emitter	Observer	Emitter
at emission	(0,0,0)	$(X_e, Z_e, 0)$	$(-X_0', -Z_0', 0)$	(0,0,0)
at reception	$(0,0,t_r)$	(X_e, Z_e, t_r)	$(-X_0, -[Z_0 + Vt_r'], t_r')$	$(0,0,t_r')$

$$\tag{15.10}$$

Thus the Lorentz transformation between the two frames, which is completely specified by our choice of initial conditions, is given by

$$X' = X - X_e$$

$$Z' = \frac{(Z - Z_e) - Vt}{\left(1 - \dfrac{V^2}{c^2}\right)^{1/2}} \tag{15.11}$$

$$ct' = \frac{ct - \dfrac{V}{c}(Z - Z_e)}{\left(1 - \dfrac{V^2}{c^2}\right)^{1/2}}.$$

Hence, from the position of the observer at the moment of reception, we obtain, after writing $D = (X_e^2 + Z_e^2)^{1/2}$ and $\cos \theta = Z_e/D$,

$$D = \frac{D'\left(1 + \dfrac{V}{c}\cos\theta\right)}{\left(1 - \dfrac{V^2}{c^2}\right)^{1/2}} = D'(1 + z) = D_\ell, \tag{15.12}$$

where D_ℓ is the luminosity distance. For a source of intrinsic luminosity L_{int} the flux of energy per second at the observer, F', is given by

$$F' = \frac{L_{int}}{4\pi D'^2} \tag{15.13}$$

assuming that the source radiates isotropically. Thus, using (15.8) and (15.11), we find that in the observer's frame

$$F = \frac{L_{int}}{4\pi D^2(1 + z)^4}. \tag{15.14}$$

Equations (15.10) and (15.11) also enable us to obtain a relation between the angles θ and θ':

$$\cos \theta' = \frac{\dfrac{V}{c} + \cos\theta}{\left(1 + \dfrac{V}{c}\cos\theta\right)}. \tag{15.15}$$

Thus, if we define Ω as the solid angle subtended by angle θ about the Z axis, it can readily be shown that

$$D^2\, d\Omega = D'^2\, d\Omega'. \tag{15.16}$$

This verifies that unit area normal to the photon path is invariant under Lorentz transformations, an assumption implicit in this discussion of apparent luminosity changes.

Perhaps we should comment here on the apparent dissimilarity between equations (15.8) and (15.14) for the observed luminosity in the cosmological and special relativistic cases, respectively. In the cosmological context it is more convenient to work in terms of $D_\ell = a(t_0)r$, since for all sources $a(t_0)$ is the same (i.e., it denotes the present epoch) and since one can solve directly for r in terms of z. The equivalent to D in equation (15.14), the metric distance from the source to the observer in the latter's frame at the time t_1 of emission, is given by $D \approx ra(t_1)$. But since $a(t_0)/a(t_1) = (1 + z)$ it is clear that equations (15.8) and (15.14) are identical except in the specification of D.

The so-called cosmological tests owe their simplicity to the existence of a definite relation between redshift and distance. In the local case, the general situation is more complex and, without some simplifying assumptions, would defy further study. We shall discuss a number of specific models that may be of relevance if the QSO's are not at cosmological distances.

Observer at Seat of Explosion. This model, first proposed by Terrell (1964) and developed in a different context by Hoyle and Burbidge (1966a), would be relevant if QSO's had been ejected from our own galaxy, or a nearby galaxy, and had reached distances large compared with the distance of the observer from the explosion center. If in the observer's frame the ejection took place at time $t = 0$, then for objects seen at time $t = T$ we have

$$T = t_e + Vt_e/c, \tag{15.17}$$

where t_e is the time at which the photons were emitted and V is the velocity. Thus the metric distance to the source at the time of emission is given by

$$D = Vt_e = VT \Big/ \left(1 + \frac{V}{c}\right) \tag{15.18}$$

and the redshift by

$$1 + z = \left(\frac{1 + \dfrac{V}{c}}{1 - \dfrac{V}{c}}\right)^{1/2}. \tag{15.19}$$

Thus the observed luminosity of a source is

$$F = \frac{L_{\text{int}}}{4\pi D^2(1 + z)^4} = \frac{L_{\text{int}}}{4\pi T^2} \frac{1}{z^2(1 + z/2)^2}. \tag{15.20}$$

This, of course, has the same z dependence as cosmological models in which the deceleration parameter, q, is zero—the "empty" universe. The equivalent of the log N–log S relation (N the number of objects observed to be brighter than S) depends entirely on the distribution of velocities imparted in the original explosion. Suppose $n(V)$ objects have velocities between V and $V + dV$ and that all have the same intrinsic luminosity, then

$$N(S) = \int_{V_\ell}^{V_u} n(V)\, dV, \tag{15.21}$$

where V_ℓ is the lowest velocity of ejection and

$$V_u = c \left[1 + \left(\frac{4\pi S}{L_{\text{int}}} \right)^{1/2} cT \right]^{-1}.$$

Thus if $n(V) \propto V^\beta$, for example, we have

$$N(S) \propto \left[1 + \left(\frac{4\pi S}{L_{\text{int}}} \right)^{1/2} cT \right]^{-(\beta+1)}, \tag{15.22}$$

which for uniform space density of objects ($\beta = 2$) and

$$cT > \left(\frac{L_{\text{int}}}{4\pi S} \right)^{1/2} \frac{1}{c}$$

(i.e., light travel time greater than that required in rest frame to reach position of flux density S from source) reduces to

$$N(S) \propto S^{-3/2}, \tag{15.23}$$

the familiar result in a uniform Euclidean space, which was discussed in Chapter 14. Since observations are, in practice, made in a fixed wave band rather than over the whole spectrum, we should consider in this context the appropriate K-corrections. We have already pointed out, however, that the QSO's have radio spectral energy distributions that approximate to the form $F_\nu \propto \nu^{-1}$, so that the K-correction will be small. Thus, if we wished to explain the log N–log S slope for the QSO's obtained by Véron (Chapter 14), a value of $\beta \simeq 3$ would be required, implying that the distribution is nonuniform.

Uniform Distribution of Randomly Moving Objects. This model may be applicable to the QSO's if we are looking at a sample that has been ejected from a variety of galaxies lying within distances of ~ 100 Mpc. It has been treated by Faulkner, Gunn, and Peterson (1966), Noerdlinger, Jokipii, and Woltjer (1966), Zapolsky (1966), and Strittmatter (1966). We follow Strittmatter's treatment here. We first consider the case in which all objects have the same velocity, are ejected in random directions from isotropically distributed centers at rest with respect to the observer, and have lifetimes short compared to the light travel time from the point of ejection to the observer. We assume an intrinsic continuous energy spectrum of the form $F_\nu \propto \nu^{-\alpha}$.

Consider all sources in an element of volume at distance D from the observer; suppose they are n in number. Then from (15.9) the number with redshifts between z and $z + dz$ is given by

$$N(z)\, dz = \frac{nc}{2V}\left(1 - \frac{V^2}{c^2}\right)^{1/2} dz. \tag{15.24}$$

If all such sources can be seen, then the ratio of those with blue shifts to those with redshifts is

$$\frac{N^-}{N^+} = \frac{1}{(1 + z_m)}, \tag{15.25}$$

where

$$(1 + z_m) = \left(1 + \frac{V}{c}\right)^{1/2} \Big/ \left(1 - \frac{V}{c}\right)^{1/2}.$$

But if the finite lifetime is also taken into account, the *observed* life of an object is proportional to $(1 + z)$, and hence the above ratio becomes

$$\frac{N^-}{N^+} = (1 + z_m)^{-2}. \tag{15.26}$$

In practice, however, observations are made down to a limiting luminosity S_e in some particular band pass. For objects at a distance D, the observed luminosity S is given by (15.14) and the distance to which objects of given z can be observed is therefore given by

$$D(z) = \left\{\frac{F_\nu[\nu(1 + z)]}{4\pi S_e(1 + z)^3}\right\}^{1/2}, \tag{15.27}$$

where ν is the effective frequency of the band pass. Thus the number of such sources is

$$N(z) = \frac{nc}{2V}\left(1 - \frac{V^2}{c^2}\right)^{1/2} \left\{\frac{F'_\nu[\nu(1 + z)]}{4\pi S_e(1 + z)^3}\right\}^{3/2}(1 + z) \tag{15.28}$$

if the finite lifetime is taken into account. If we take $F'_\nu(\nu') \propto (\nu')^{-\alpha}$ we then obtain a ratio of blue-shifted to redshifted objects of

$$\frac{N^-}{N^+} = (1 + z_n)^{(2.5+1.5\alpha)}.$$

For $\alpha = 1$, which approximates fairly well to the observed optical distribution in the QSO's and is the value for which the K-correction vanishes (Chapter 4), we find that $N^-/N^+ = (1 + z_m)^4$, which is ≈ 81, taking z_m to be of the order of the maximum redshift (≈ 2) observed so far.

We have shown earlier that so far only redshifted QSO's have been found, so that observationally $N^+/N^- \geq 70$. This result can be interpreted in several ways.

1. It can be supposed that there are very strong selection effects at work that discriminate against the detection of QSO's with blue shifts.

2. It can be concluded that the QSO's are all moving away from us and have therefore been ejected from a nearby source.

3. It can be argued that this absence of blue shifts is evidence in favor of the cosmological nature of the QSO's.

4. It can be supposed that the objects do not radiate isotropically in their own rest frames.

5. It can be supposed that the redshifts are not Doppler in origin.

We discuss these possibilities in turn. As regards the first, selection effects of various kinds may be present. For example, it appears that in many cases synchrotron self-absorption in the QSO's gives rise to a maximum in the radio spectra, and below a certain frequency the flux falls off rapidly. Depending on the frequency at which this maximum occurs, the effect of a blue shift may be to shift the spectrum to high enough frequencies such that the flux at the frequencies of the surveys may be too small to be detected. In this way QSO's searched for first as radio sources may be missed. It appears that only a fraction of objects—those with large blueshifts—would be likely to be excluded in this way.

What about selection effects that may arise if we attempt to detect blue-shifted QSO's through their optical properties alone? To investigate this we need to know the form of the continuous spectrum out into the infrared, and we must consider which infrared lines are likely to be present. This has been done by Burbidge, Strittmatter, and Sargent (1966). Only for 3C 273 have infrared flux measurements been made (see Chapter 4), and the flux there is rising steeply in the infrared region. If all quasi-stellar objects have continuous spectra of this form it is clear that this flux, blue-shifted into the measuring bands, will give rise to some comparatively bright objects, since the apparent luminosities will be greatly increased for large blue shifts. There are, however, very few emission lines in the infrared that can be expected to have great intrinsic strengths. The strongest lines are likely to be Pα, Pβ, He I λ10830, and Hα. It seems probable that, if 3C 273 can be taken as a prototype as far as its infrared continuous flux is concerned, then for a considerable range of blue shifts, either the lines will appear too weak to be detectable against the steeply increasing continuum, or else only one line is likely to be seen in the usual wavelength region observed. For this we tentatively conclude that it may not be possible to measure shifts in objects that have blue shifts of $z > 0.5$. But we should be able to detect objects with such small blue shifts that Hα, Hβ, and [O III] λ5007 still remain within the normal wavelength range observed by the spectroscopists. None have been found, however, and though the fraction of objects with small redshifts corresponding to the same velocity range is small, this fact argues against the existence of blue shifted QSO's.

Although it may not be possible to identify the spectra of QSO's with comparatively large blue shifts, what should these objects look like? They should show continuous spectra with only one line, or perhaps none at all. A few of them will appear bright, and depending on the form of their intrinsic energy distribution in the infrared, they may or may not have colors that fall into the part of the $(U - B)$, $(B - V)$ diagram occupied by the redshifted QSO's (Chapter 4). If they do, then many must have already been discovered. In this case they may be some of the objects that have been identified as QSO's but for which the spectroscopic observers have not been able to identify lines. A number of objects of this type are known, including, for example, 3C 93. Otherwise they might be objects that have previously been thought to be white dwarfs with continuous spectra, or that exist in the catalogues of Luyten and Haro and are only known as blue stellar objects. It is clear that they do not appear frequently, if at all, as optical objects identified with radio sources. A preliminary investigation of a number of blue stellar objects detected by using the color method alone (Chapter 2) was carried out by Lynds (1965), and he noted that a very large proportion of the objects he studied showed only continuous spectra. If the majority of blue-shifted objects show only continuous spectra, how can they be distinguished from highly evolved stars? The only method that we have been able to think of is to observe them over a wider wavelength band, out into the infrared. If they showed strong evidence for nonthermal flux (i.e., if they emit very strongly in the infrared) then we could at least say that they are not stars.

We now briefly consider case 2. This is one obvious explanation for the total preponderance of redshifts. It remains to be shown, however, that our own galaxy, or a nearby galaxy, is able to give rise to a large cloud of quasi-stellar objects. The energetic problems will be discussed later in this chapter. If this explanation is the correct one, a conflict arises when we consider Arp's hypothesis (Chapter 8). Arp has concluded that quasi-stellar objects and radio sources are ejected from a wide population of galaxies, and not from a single nearby source. If this is correct, and if only velocity shifts occur in the spectra, we would expect to see a large ratio of blue shifts to redshifts.

In case 3 little more can be added to what we have already said. The predominance of redshifts probably is the most powerful general argument in favor of the idea that the objects are at cosmological distances. The pros and cons of all of these arguments will be given in Chapter 18.

We now consider case 4. The ratio (N^-/N^+) has been calculated on the assumption that the radiation is emitted isotropically in the rest frame of the QSO. To overcome the very large value of (N^-/N^+) given above, it could be supposed that there is a strong beaming of the emission in the reverse direction of the motion. This appears very unlikely as far as the optical radiation is concerned, but such an effect might occur for the radio radiation. If a large number of QSO's with continuous spectra are indeed objects with blue shifts, such an effect would explain why they are not radio sources. It is interesting that, in the local hypothesis, some part of the luminosity of a QSO may arise from its interaction with the intergalactic medium. It can be shown, using reasonable parameters for the intergalactic density and for the size of the object, that the rate of dissipation of kinetic energy may be comparable to the energy emitted in the radio frequency range. Since the objects are moving with relativistic speed, the energy is released in nuclear collisions in which electrons and positrons will be generated following meson decay. Local acceleration processes may take place, and the radiation characteristics of the object will be determined by the configuration of the magnetic field. In this case it is not implausible that the bulk of the radio radiation would be emitted in the reverse direction of motion.

In case 5, if the redshifts are gravitational in nature this would provide an obvious explanation for the absence of blue shifts.

ENERGETIC REQUIREMENTS OF LOCAL OBJECTS MOVING AT LARGE VELOCITIES

The total energy of a relativistically moving object with rest mass M moving with velocity V is given by

$$E = \frac{Mc^2}{\left(1 - \frac{V^2}{c^2}\right)^{1/2}}. \tag{15.29}$$

Thus for the largest redshifts known we see from (15.19) that the total energy is about $1.6Mc^2$. For objects with the smallest redshifts (near $z \sim 0.1$) we can use the nonrelativistic approximation, in which case $E_{\mathrm{kin}} \approx 10^{-2}Mc^2$. To make realistic estimates of the magnitude of the energy involved we need to know the number of objects ejected from a given galaxy and their masses.

The only other method of estimating the minimum energy content is to calculate the total energy that has been radiated by the object during its lifetime. We consider this method first. If the objects have been ejected from our own galaxy or a nearby system, and lie at a distance D, then the lifetime is $\sim D/V$. We have suggested earlier that in this type of local hypothesis the intrinsic luminosities may be between 10^{42} and 10^{43} erg/sec, and that the distances D are 1–10 Mpc. If we suppose that the average velocities of the objects are $0.5c$, then if the objects have been ejected from sources lying close to us and now are distant 1–10 Mpc, their lifetimes range from 6×10^6 to 6×10^7 years. Thus the total energy emitted, assuming that the luminosity remains constant, lies in the range 2×10^{56}–2×10^{58} ergs, or 10^2–$10^4 M_\odot c^2$.

If we suppose that the objects have been ejected from a variety of galaxies out to distances of ~ 100 Mpc, as is implied by Arp's hypothesis (Chapter 8), then since he is discussing pairs of objects with separations between $1°$ and $3°$, their projected distances from the parent galaxies are in the range 2–6 Mpc. Thus the lifetimes are similar, and the minimum energies lie in the same range. The energies would be reduced if the objects were truly galactic, as Terrell originally suggested, because their distances would then be less than 1 Mpc. But, as we have already discussed, the proper motion data suggest, for at least some of the objects, minimum distances of ~ 1 Mpc. The minimum masses of the QSO's from this argument range from 10^2 to $10^4 M_\odot$, and we can estimate the true masses only if we understand the mechanism of energy conversion. This is not understood, but it seems probable that it is similar to that functioning in explosive events on the galactic scale (Chapter 17), and indeed it may be a scaled-down version of this; there are a number of indirect arguments for supposing that this mechanism is highly efficient. We may hazard a guess that if the objects are local, then on the basis of this argument an upper limit to their masses may be perhaps $10^6 M_\odot$.

We turn now to the methods of estimating the mass of a QSO based on analysis of its line spectrum. In the stratified model described in Chapter 10, the highly energetic object is the small, dense, central source that gives rise to the nonthermal continuum flux. The region giving rise to the emission lines is probably a much larger low-density shell or filamentary structure. The mass of this shell can be estimated from the analysis given in Chapter 10. From equations (10.4) to (10.6) we see that for 3C 48 and 3C 273 the masses required, if the distances of the objects are 10 Mpc, are $300-400 M_\odot$. For distances of 1 Mpc the masses are reduced to about 3 or $4 M_\odot$. Thus only a small fraction of the total mass is required to explain the line emission.

Setti and Woltjer (1966) attempted to estimate the total masses by supposing that the line widths were due to large random motions of gas in the shell and that the central mass must be large enough to stabilize the object gravitationally. From this argument they obtained masses in the range $10^7-10^8 M_\odot$ for 3C 273 and 3C 48 on the local hypothesis. Their argument is entirely vitiated, however, if the line-broadening is not due to mass motions, and we have shown in Chapter 10 that electron-scattering is probably the dominant broadening mechanism in most QSO's.

Another method of estimating the mass of a local QSO is to suppose that it does not conserve its mass and that gas is continuously escaping from it. Bahcall, Peterson, and Schmidt (1966) suggested that the QSO PKS 1116 + 12 might be undergoing a continuous outflow of gas from the surface. We described their observations—and also those by Lynds and Stockton (1966) on this object—in Chapter 3. The clearly seen absorption component 200 Å on the short-wavelength side of the Ly-α emission line, and the less clearly seen absorption component on the short-wavelength side of C IV $\lambda 1549$, would, if produced by such an outflow of gas, correspond to an outward velocity of 17,000 km/sec.

We have seen that there is an accumulation of absorption-line redshifts near $z = 1.95$, and this suggests that it is the absorption lines that somehow give the standard redshift. The gas producing the emission lines would then need to be falling in toward a central region, relative to a stationary absorbing layer farther out, or be located in a region of higher gravitational potential. We shall ignore these considerations for the moment, however, and follow the discussion by Bahcall, Peterson, and Schmidt.

The absorption features that they believed they had identified were Ly-α and C IV $\lambda 1550$. The strength of the lines made it possible to estimate the product of the thickness of the absorbing shell, R, times the number density, n, of the atoms (from the absorption coefficient in, for example, the C IV line). They then argued that since absorption lines are present in about 10% of the QSO's so far studied—and the lifetimes of local objects are $\sim 10^8$ years—then the absorption-line phase lasts $\sim 10^7$ years. From this an estimate of R can be made by supposing that expansion at 17,000 km/sec has taken place for this period. From these two arguments the total mass of gas that has escaped is found to be $\sim 10^9 M_\odot$. We have earlier concluded that the lifetimes of the QSO's, if they are local objects ejected from external galaxies, lie in the range 6×10^6–6×10^7 years, and if they are of galactic origin the lifetimes can be shorter than this. Thus, following the argument of Bahcall et al., we conclude that the values of the ejected masses are less than those they obtained, and lie in the range 10^7–$10^8 M_\odot$.

Of course, the mass actually required to give rise to the observed absorption features is exceedingly small, and the very large masses are obtained simply by supposing that continuous outflow is taking place. The discovery that some QSO's have absorption lines lying on the long-wavelength side of the emission lines—for example, PKS 0119 − 04 (Kinman and Burbidge, 1967)—as well as the clustering of the absorption-line redshifts around $z = 1.95$, clearly indicates that the true nature of the phenomenon is more complicated than is suggested by the simple hypothesis that shells of gas flow continuously outward from QSO's.

We conclude that the masses of local QSO's cannot be determined with precision. Both Setti and Woltjer, and Bahcall et al., having obtained large masses, have argued that the energies required for local rapidly moving objects are very high, and thus they have felt that these are powerful arguments against this type of local hypothesis. It appears to us that the result of Setti and Woltjer is not valid for the reasons given earlier, and that any mass obtained by the method of Bahcall et al. is open to many uncertainties.

In any case, we do not consider that these results can be used as an argument against the local hypothesis in which the redshifts are assumed to be Doppler shifts produced by explosive ejection from a galaxy. As will be discussed in Chapter 17 we do not properly understand the nature of the energy sources that give rise to radio galaxies or QSO's, whether the latter are local or cosmological objects. Thus to conclude at this stage that the energy required in a given case is too large is a purely subjective decision.

LOCAL OBJECTS WITH GRAVITATIONAL REDSHIFTS

We have already discussed in Chapter 9 the possibility that the redshifts of the QSO's are gravitational in origin. This explanation has recently been revived following the discovery of what appears to be a "standard" redshift of 1.95 in the absorption spectra of a considerable number of QSO's. If the redshifts are gravitational then we have no direct means of determining their distances, unless they can be found in association with galaxies whose distances are known (see Chapter 8). But if the objects are very massive (10^{12}–$10^{13} M_\odot$), as Hoyle and Fowler (1967) and Burbidge (1967) have proposed, they cannot be galactic objects but must be at minimum distances of megaparsecs. Otherwise they would give rise to large tidal distortions of our galaxy. At the same time they cannot be at distances so great that the component of redshift due to the expansion of the universe becomes very large; otherwise a "standard" redshift would not have been found. If we denote the gravitational redshift as z_g, and the cosmological redshift as z_c, the redshift observed is given by

$$1 + z = (1 + z_g)(1 + z_c)$$

or

$$z_c = \frac{z - z_g}{1 + z_g} \approx \frac{z - z_g}{3}.$$

As can be seen in Table 3.7 the observed absorption-line redshifts range from $z = 1.91$ to perhaps $z = 1.97$, and these are extreme values. Consequently the total range of z_c that appears to be possible is only about 0.02. For a value of the Hubble constant of 100 km/sec (Mpc)$^{-1}$ this corresponds to a maximum distance of 60 Mpc. If the QSO's are all contained in a volume of this size and have average masses of $10^{12} M_\odot$, their mass density is $2 \times 10^{-34} n$ gm/cm^3. If $n \simeq 10^5$ (Chapter 2) this gives a mass density of 2×10^{-29} gm/cm^3. Most of the values, however, are very close to 1.95, and this may mean that z_c is considerably smaller than 0.02 in most cases. If this is so, the objects must be much closer than 60 Mpc unless the Hubble constant is much smaller than the value used above. Then the masses of the objects must be less than $10^{12} M_\odot$ if the mass density due to them is to be not greater than $\sim 10^{-29}$ gm/cm^3. But if the masses are much lower than $10^{12} M_\odot$ it is difficult to see how a model such as that proposed by Hoyle and Fowler can account for the large red-shifts. We conclude that if the redshifts are gravitational in origin, the objects must lie at distances $\lesssim 100$ Mpc and probably in the distance range 10–100 Mpc. In this case the energetic requirements of the QSO's are rather similar to those of radio galaxies. These distance estimates are also compatible with the suggestion by Arp that the QSO's are genetically related to peculiar galaxies, though if the QSO's are very massive it would seem more probable that they have given rise to the peculiar galaxies, rather than the reverse.

If the redshifts are gravitational in origin, could the QSO's be galactic objects? If z_c is shown to be exceedingly small we may be forced back to this model. It would necessarily mean that they must have masses very much less than the mass of a galaxy, and no models of this sort that could give rise to very large redshifts have yet been devised.

16

Quasi-Stellar Objects and Galaxies

The most massive concentrations of matter known to be present in the universe are galaxies. We are able to observe them because they consist largely of stars that are shining by normal thermonuclear processes. What relation do the quasi-stallar objects bear to galaxies? In what ways are they similar to galaxies, and in what ways are they different?

We shall first discuss the similarities and differences as they can be deduced from the observations and then consider the possible relationships from a theoretical standpoint. The quasi-stellar objects and the normal run of galaxies look quite different when observed directly, because, as their name suggests, the QSO's are hardly distinguishable from stars, and normal galaxies are extended sources. As we have already mentioned, if the QSO's are at cosmological distances they are intrinsically very much brighter than the brightest known galaxies. If they are local objects then their luminosities are comparable with, or smaller than, the luminosities of the nuclei of highly concentrated galaxies.

The intrinsic sizes of the main energy-producing regions of QSO's are only $\leq 10^{-5}$ that of normal galaxies; this conclusion is based on study of flux variations and is thus independent of the distances of the QSO's. The spectra of the QSO's and of normal galaxies are quite different. The line spectrum of a QSO is emitted from a hot gas, whereas the continuum is nonthermal in origin. Although some absorption lines are present there is no evidence for the presence of stars. In normal galaxies, however, the spectra are largely due to stars, and many lines of evidence suggest that the stars are responsible for the total luminosity of the system, though only in the nearest galaxies is it possible to resolve the stars.

More similarities in the spectra are found when we compare the quasi-stellar objects with the radio galaxies. The spectra of the radio galaxies frequently show strong emission lines. These emission lines are stronger relative to the continuum than are those of the QSO's. But the temperatures and electron densities required to explain the spectra of objects like Cygnus A are not very different from those required to explain the line spectra of QSO's. These spectra refer only to the nuclear regions of the radio galaxies. In many comparatively nearby radio galaxies the extent of the objects and their similarities with other systems strongly suggest that the bulk of the light comes from stars with an extended distribution. Thus it may be concluded that the gas in the nuclear region that shows a high degree of excitation has been ejected or excited in the events that have given rise to the radio source, which would mean that this is a comparatively short-lived phase in the life of the galaxy. There are some galaxies that are radio sources but show no evidence for the presence of highly excited gas in their nuclei. Presumably the differences are to be interpreted in terms of the different stages of evolution at which radio galaxies are observed.

There are, however, a large number of radio galaxies of which Cygnus A is the prototype in which there is no direct evidence for the presence of stars. Thus one could conclude that in these cases we are only seeing a hot gas cloud, and whether a concentration of stars is buried in this cloud is not clear.

The Seyfert galaxies form a special class. These are nearly all spiral galaxies with star-like nuclei whose spectra are rather similar to those of the QSO's. The luminosities of these nuclei are comparable to those of the QSO's if the QSO's are local objects. At least one Seyfert galaxy, NGC 1068, has been discovered to be radiating strongly in the infrared. Pacholczyk and Wisniewski (1967) observed the nucleus of this galaxy at wavelengths between 0.9 and 3 microns, and showed that it is emitting much more energy in this range than do normal galaxies. In fact, the energy distribution here is very similar to that of 3C 273 (Chapter 4, Fig. 4.2). Thus the sources of nonthermal radiation in QSO's and in Seyfert nuclei may be similar. If the QSO's are at cosmological distances they are much more powerful sources than Seyfert nuclei, but if they are comparatively local, the intrinsic power output of the two classes may be comparable, since, for example, NGC 1068 lies at a distance of about 10 Mpc from our galaxy.

The so-called N-type galaxies are in some respects rather similar to the QSO's. The main differences are that these objects are not starlike but have finite angular sizes of a few seconds of arc, and that their emission lines are rather stronger than in the QSO's. Only a few of these are known at present, and no detailed studies have been published.

We have already remarked that in their radio properties the QSO's and the radio galaxies show many similarities. In the early radio surveys they were indistinguishable. We now know that the QSO's tend to have at least one radio source component that is very small, but there are a number that have sources as large as those found in typical radio galaxies. If the objects are cosmological, then the power levels of QSO's and strong radio galaxies are comparable, but if they are local, the radio fluxes emitted are comparable with those from the weaker radio galaxies. We now know that at very high frequencies the QSO's are often variable in flux. This indicates that the regions responsible for this variable flux are very small. The radio galaxy NGC 1275, which is at a distance of about 50 Mpc, also shows flux variations.

It is of some interest to consider the plot of the intrinsic radio luminosity, L, against surface brightness, B, since this brings out the differences and similarities between the radio properties of QSO's and radio galaxies. Heeschen (1966) has constructed such a diagram, and we show this in Figure 16.1. The material that has been used is given in Table 16.1, which is adapted from the table by Heeschen. Because there is insufficient material available on the way the structure of the radio sources varies with frequency, L and B are computed at one frequency, 1400 Mc/s, since a large amount of homogeneous material is available at this frequency. The distances of the QSO's and radio galaxies are computed on the assumption that the QSO's are at cosmological distances and that the Hubble constant $H = 100$

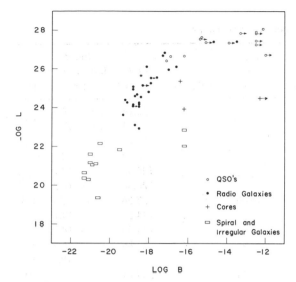

FIG. 16.1   *The absolute radio luminosity L and surface brightness B at 1400 Mc/s for quasi-stellar objects, radio galaxies, and spiral and irregular galaxies.* [*After Heeschen (1966).*]

km/sec (Mpc)$^{-1}$. The strong radio galaxies are denoted by *RG*, and one by *N* (the single *N*-type galaxy that is included), whereas the weak radio galaxies, which are all spiral or irregular systems, are denoted by *Sp* or *I*. The radio luminosities and brightnesses are derived from the relations $L = 4\pi R^2 S$ and $B = 4S/\pi\theta^2$. For an optically thin, spherically symmetric source of radius r and average volume emissivity ϵ, the absolute luminosity $L \propto \epsilon r^3$, and the surface brightness $B \propto \epsilon r$.

The smooth form of the relation that is plotted in Figure 16.1 suggests at first sight that an evolutionary sequence may be present and in such a scheme lends support to the idea that the quasi-stellar objects are at cosmological distances. The sense of the evolution would be that the small intense radio source in a QSO would evolve to the large radio source in a radio galaxy, which would expand and gradually grow weaker. The points that depart most markedly from the smooth distribution shown in Figure 16.1 are those for NGC 1068

Table 16.1

LUMINOSITY–SURFACE-BRIGHTNESS TABLE

Source	R (Mpc)	S_{1400} (flux units)	$\log \theta$ (radians)	$\log L$ $W(c/s)^{-1}$	$\log B$ $Wm^{-2}(c/s)^{-1}$ $ster^{-1}$	Type
3C 33	180	12.84	< -4.0	$\begin{cases} 25.16 \\ 25.55 \end{cases}$	$\begin{cases} > -18.3 \\ > -17.9 \end{cases}$	RG
3C 40	53	5.20	-3.2	$\begin{cases} 23.64 \\ 24.12 \end{cases}$	$\begin{cases} -19.3 \\ -18.8 \end{cases}$	RG
3C 47	1280	3.75	-4.3	$\begin{cases} 26.42 \\ 26.68 \end{cases}$	$\begin{cases} -17.1 \\ -16.9 \end{cases}$	QSO
3C 48	1100	15.60	< -5.4	27.36	> -13.9	QSO
3C 66	64	9.68	-3.2	$\begin{cases} 24.29 \\ 24.60 \end{cases}$	$\begin{cases} -19.1 \\ -18.7 \end{cases}$	RG
3C 71	11	4.97	-4.5	22.86	-16.2	Sp
3C 75	65	6.34	-3.5	24.21	-18.5	RG
3C 78	87	7.14	-3.5	24.81	-18.0	RG
3C 84	54	13.49	$\begin{cases} < -6.3 \\ < -3.2 \end{cases}$	$\begin{cases} 24.50 \\ 24.14 \end{cases}$	$\begin{cases} > -12.3 \\ > -18.8 \end{cases}$	RG
3C 88	91	4.95	-3.3	24.69	-18.6	RG
3C 147	1640	22.49	< -5.3	27.86	> -13.3	QSO
3C 218	160	43.40	$\begin{cases} -4.3 \\ -3.7 \end{cases}$	$\begin{cases} 25.39 \\ 25.98 \end{cases}$	$\begin{cases} -16.4 \\ -17.0 \end{cases}$	RG
3C 219	520	7.95	-3.6	26.11	-18.1	RG
3C 231	3.2	8.67	-4.4	22.03	-16.2	I
3C 245	3084	3.16	< -5	27.56	> -15.4	QSO
3C 254	1635	3.08	-4.8	26.69	-16.2	QSO
3C 270	11	17.85	-3.1	23.11	-18.7	RG
3C 273	470	39.6	< -6.3	26.72	> -12.0	QSO
3C 274	11	200	$\begin{cases} -4.0 \\ -2.8 \end{cases}$	$\begin{cases} 23.94 \\ 24.07 \end{cases}$	$\begin{cases} -16.2 \\ -18.5 \end{cases}$	RG
3C 278	43	7.90	-3.2	24.24	-18.5	RG
3C 279	1620	8.67	< -6.3	27.28	> -12.5	QSO
3C 286	2547	15.20	-6.3	28.07	-12.1	QSO
3C 287	3165	6.99	-6.3	27.92	-12.5	QSO
3C 295	1380	23.07	-5.3	27.42	-13.5	RG
3C 310	160	7.82	-3.2	25.08	-18.8	RG
3C 315	320	3.91	-3.5	25.68	-18.4	RG
3C 338	90	3.58	-3.5	24.54	-18.4	RG

Table 16.1, concluded

LUMINOSITY–SURFACE-BRIGHTNESS TABLE

Source	R (Mpc)	S_{1400} (flux units)	$\log \theta$ (radians)	$\log L$ $W(c/s)^{-1}$	$\log B$ $Wm^{-2}(c/s)^{-1}$ $ster^{-1}$	Type
3C 345	1785	6.43	< -5.0	27.39	> -15.1	QSO
3C 348	470	45.32	-3.7	26.70 / 26.84	-17.3 / -17.2	RG
3C 353	91	57.34	-3.4	25.28 / 25.58	-17.9 / -17.6	RG
3C 380	2079	14.39	< -6.3 / < -4.8	27.48 / 27.65	> -12.5 / -15.3	QSO
3C 386	10	6.96	-3.3	22.92	-18.5	RG
3C 405	170	1490	-3.7	27.41	-14.7	RG
3C 433	300	11.91	-4.1	26.11	-16.6	RG
3C 442	79	3.36	-3.1	24.40	-19.2	RG
3C 445	170	5.33	-3.4	24.97	-18.8	N
CTA 102	3100	6.6	< -6.3	27.88	> -12.5	QSO
NGC 253	3.2	5.6	-2.9	21.84	-19.5	Sp
IC 342	1.8	3.3	-2.4	21.11	-20.7	Sp
NGC 598	0.72	3.1	-2.2	20.29	-21.1	Sp
NGC 2903	6.9	0.70	-2.5	21.60	-21.0	Sp
NGC 3031	3.2	1.2	-2.4	21.17	-21.0	Sp
NGC 5457	3.5	0.82	-2.5	21.08	-20.9	Sp
NGC 5907	4.0	0.24	-2.6	20.66	-21.3	Sp
NGC 7331	14.4	0.58	-2.8	22.16	-20.5	Sp
LMC*	0.055	620	-0.9	20.35	-21.3	I
SMC†	0.055	67	-1.8	19.38	-20.6	I

* Large Magellanic Cloud.
† Small Magellanic Cloud.

and M82, both of which are comparatively nearby weak radio galaxies containing radio sources of very small angular diameter, and the core components of the radio galaxies 3C 84 (NGC 1275), 3C 218, and 3C 274 (M87). If the QSO's are not at cosmological distances but are much closer, their luminosities will be lower but their surface brightness will remain constant. Thus they will all move down in Figure 16.1 to form a cluster of points at much lower values of $\log L$

in a region at the same levels but to the right of NGC 1068 and the other four core objects.

The diagram is physically meaningful only if the surface brightness calculated in the way described is the true surface brightness of a coherent source. If a large radio source is really made up of a number of small sources of high surface brightness, then the value of B plotted here comes from an average involving the number of subunits and the (much higher) surface brightness of each. Wade (1966) has recently shown that Cygnus A and some other sources do contain such structures, so the physical significance of this diagram, even for radio galaxies, is not clear at present.

These observational similarities and differences can be looked at in different ways. In all cases we must suppose that the events that give rise to the QSO and radio galaxy phenomena lead to the release of energy, which produces a hot cloud of gas and a large flux of relativistic matter. In addition, there is generated a tremendous flux of nonthermal radiation. If the QSO's are cosmological the nonthermal flux is very much greater than the total flux generated in the radio galaxies, but the radio fluxes are comparable. If the objects are local then both the nonthermal optical and infrared fluxes and the radio flux are smaller than the total fluxes generated in radio galaxies. These questions will be considered in more detail in Chapter 17.

Of course the bulk of the faint radio sources remain unidentified with optical objects. They could be much more distant or intrinsically fainter radio galaxies, as has been suggested by Bolton (1966), or they might be intrinsically fainter or more distant quasi-stellar objects, either local or cosmological. This question can only be settled by taking photographs centered on the radio source positions and reaching to much fainter limiting apparent magnitudes than has yet been done, and then by obtaining spectra of any objects found at the positions. The very preliminary results indicate that, if anything, fuzzy and nonstarlike images are present, thus suggesting that the unidentified radio sources may be associated with galaxies.

We have shown in the previous chapters that the masses of the QSO's cannot be obtained with any precision from observations. If the objects are cosmological these masses are $\geq 10^8 M_\odot$, probably, but if they are local, smaller masses may be invoked. Whether they are local or cosmological there is no *direct* evidence that the masses present are comparable with those of the bright galaxies, which lie in the range 10^{10}–$10^{12} M_\odot$.

We shall discuss in the next chapter the various proposals made to account for the energy released in the quasi-stellar objects. In some theories it is assumed that the QSO is an evolutionary phase in the life of a galaxy, so that the presence of stars is invoked. In other theories it is argued that the QSO is a galaxy in the process of formation. It is important to emphasize that these are theoretical assumptions, and that there is no direct observational evidence to support them. What evidence we have suggests that if the QSO's are cosmological objects they are not associated with galaxies in clusters (Chapter 8). If they are local they must be associated with galaxies, and if they are moving rapidly they cannot have galactic masses, and they must have dynamical properties quite different from those of normal galaxies.

Thus we see that there are some similarities and many differences between QSO's and galaxies. Many of these comparisons may be superficial, and no real understanding of the relationship can be expected until we have a reasonably good theoretical understanding of the mechanism that gives rise to the QSO's. We turn to this problem in the next chapter.

17

Theories to Account for the Energy Requirements of Quasi-Stellar Objects

We have described in earlier chapters the schematic models required to explain the observed radio and optical properties of QSO's. Here we shall attempt to give a critical review of the proposals made to account for the remarkable energetic characteristics of these objects.

In Chapter 16 the properties of QSO's and radio galaxies were compared and contrasted, and we saw that in their radio properties great similarities exist between the two classes of objects. From the radio spectra of QSO's there is every reason to believe that the synchrotron mechanism is responsible for the emission, as is certainly the case for the radio galaxies. If the QSO's are at cosmological distances then the *minimum* total energies required to give rise to the radio sources are of the same order of magnitude as those for the radio galaxies and are $\sim 10^{61}$ ergs (see Burbidge and Burbidge, 1966). Since many arguments suggest that the total energy released is far above this minimum value it may be necessary to account for an energy release in the range 10^{62}–10^{63} ergs, largely in the form of relativistic matter. For the very small radio components of QSO's, the minimum total energy required can be much smaller, since for a given synchrotron flux this total energy is proportional to $R^{-6/7}$, where R is the dimension of the system, so that it might be as low as 10^{58} ergs. As was discussed in Chapter 11, however, there are other arguments in this case to suggest that this minimum total energy condition cannot be fulfilled, and that the total energy, largely in the form of particles, must be in the range 10^{60}–10^{61} ergs and confined in a dimension of a few parsecs or less. All of these arguments are based on the assumption that the magnetic field is fairly homogeneous. If one considers a nonhomogeneous model (Hoyle and Burbidge, 1966) somewhat lower total energies may be feasible.

If the QSO's are moving at high speeds and are comparatively nearby then the minimum total energy in the relativistic particles and magnetic fields in a given object is much reduced—to perhaps 10^{55}–10^{56} ergs in an individual source. But a very large amount of kinetic energy must be contained in a relativistically moving QSO. For a mass of $\sim 10^4 M_\odot$ and $V/c = 0.6$, for example, the total energy is $\approx 10^{58}$ ergs, and we must suppose that a number of QSO's are ejected in a galactic explosion. Thus in any case very large releases of energy are required.

Let us now turn to the magnitude of the energies required to explain the bulk of the radiation emitted *outside* the radio frequency range. Consider first the QSO's. If these lie at cosmological distances then their luminosities in optical frequencies range from 10^{45} to 10^{46} ergs/sec, whereas in 3C 273 the total flux emitted is $\sim 2 \times 10^{47}$ ergs/sec, most of it being radiated in the form of photons with frequencies in the range 10^{11}–10^{13} c/s. We have described earlier the arguments suggesting that this flux is generated by a nonthermal process. If the QSO's are local a flux less by a factor of 10^4–10^6 is needed. For the radio galaxies it is commonly believed that most of the optical luminosity is thermal radiation coming from stars, but it is possible that a considerable component may be due to radiation from a hot gas (Burbidge, 1967).

If the QSO's are emitting optical, infrared, and millimeter radiation by the synchrotron process, then in the most extreme situation, in which the magnetic fields are as large as 100 gauss (Shklovsky, 1965), the total energy present in the electrons must be about 2×10^{52} ergs, and this must be renewed every 10^5 seconds. Thus, if the objects last for about 10^6 years, the total energy release is about 10^{61} ergs. If the inverse Compton process is operating (and it is not clear whether such a model can be devised), two components are required: an intense source of low-frequency photons and a supply of high-energy electrons. Since in such a model the photons must be raised many octaves in frequency, the bulk of the energy must probably reside in the electrons. If, for example, a "machine" generating photons with frequencies as low as 10^4 c/s were operating, it would require electrons with energies of 10 Gev to lift the photons by the inverse Compton process to $\nu \sim 10^{12}$ c/s. It is really not possible to estimate how the energy is divided, but the total energy release must at least $\sim 10^{47} t$, where t, the lifetime of the source, may be about 10^6 years, which means that the total will be about 10^{61} ergs.

The various theories proposed to account for the energy emitted in the radio sources have been summarized earlier by Burbidge, Burbidge, and Sandage (1963) and by Burbidge and Burbidge (1965). Since the time that these reviews were completed a number of suggestions have been put forward in later investigations. We shall therefore revise the earlier discussions in what follows. The majority of the theories attempt to account for the QSO's as objects at cosmological distances, but some are compatible with the idea that they are objects thrown out of galaxies. Some attempt is made to explain the properties of the radio galaxies as well. In very few, if any, of the theories is there a satisfactory explanation of the physical mechanism that leads to the release of energy largely in the form of relativistic matter. If the QSO's are coherent objects ejected from radio galaxies, or indeed objects ejected in galactic explosions in general, the underlying mechanism is as obscure as the mechanism of the release of individual high-energy particles in many theories.

A fundamental assumption made in nearly all of the hypotheses so far put forward is that matter is present in a highly condensed form. We consider first the theories based on the idea that dense galactic nuclei are present.

SUPERNOVA THEORIES

An idea of this sort was first proposed by Shklovsky (1961), who argued (without supporting theory) that in a radio galaxy the rate of supernovae in the nucleus must be very high, and by Burbidge (1961), who suggested that the star densities in galactic nuclei could be so high that a supernova evolving in the normal way could trigger explosions in nearby stars, thus giving rise to a chain reaction of explosions. Following this, Cameron (1962) argued that rapid star formation must occur, and for fairly massive stars the rate of evolution would be rapid enough so that supernovae would continuously be erupting. But like Shklovsky, Cameron had not derived a satisfactory mechanism for star formation in such a region. In all of these theories it was supposed that the energy released per supernova was of the same order as that observed to have been released in individual supernovae. We have evidence from the light curves of supernovae in external galaxies and from the remnants of old supernovae in our own galaxy that this energy is of the order 10^{50} erg/$M_{\odot}$. The only observational evidence concerning the magnitude of the energy contained in the flux of relativistic particles released in a supernova outburst comes from the study of radio emission from supernova remnants in our own galaxy, and the energies are $\leq 10^{49}$ ergs per supernova. Furthermore, at the time that these ideas were put forward it was generally believed, following Burbidge, Burbidge, Fowler, and Hoyle (1957), that the energy of a supernova explosion was largely of thermonuclear origin, so that the absolute upper limit of energy released was of the order 10^{52} ergs/$M_{\odot}$, and that this upper limit could never be reached because the initial reaction in the p-p chain cannot take place rapidly. (A realistic upper limit of $\sim 10^{51}$ ergs/$M_{\odot}$ is indicated.) Consequently, it appeared that in order to release energies of the order 10^{61} ergs and higher—to account for the strong radio sources—supernova explosions involving 10^{10}–10^{12} or more stars were required. It was this result that suggested (Burbidge, 1962) that another more powerful source of energy—gravitational energy—be explored, and thus Hoyle and Fowler (1963a, 1963b) were led to the mechanism of gravitational collapse of a large super-star. Before turning to this theory, however, we shall continue the discussion of the supernova hypotheses.

For several years the group at Livermore, under the direction of Stirling Colgate, has been considering the hydrodynamics of the final stages of evolution of a supernova, using as their starting point the final stages of nuclear evolution discussed by Burbidge et al. (1957) and by Fowler and Hoyle (1965). They start with a hot evolved star with a mass of $10M_{\odot}$, which is dense enough to be unstable against gravitational collapse, and follow it as it falls inward (Colgate and White, 1966). A shock is formed, heating results, and nuclear reactions take place. The core begins to fall in very rapidly, and the outer part falls in more slowly. The energy released in the collapse is emitted largely in the form of neutrinos. These will escape if, and until, the outer parts of the star have collapsed to a high enough density so that a significant opacity to the neutrino flux is produced. At this point the neutrinos will exert sufficient force to halt the collapse of the outer parts of the star, and these will be ejected. At the same time the inner parts of the star will continue to collapse and will be able to form a stable neutron configuration, if the division of mass between the infalling part and the ejected part is such that most of the mass is ejected, leaving a mass less than the critical mass for a neutron star. This critical question, and the question of whether the energy released in an explosion can be as great as 10^{-3} of the rest mass energy of the star, can only be answered by treating the problem relativistically. It also depends on the stiffness of the equation of state of matter at nuclear densities. So far it has not been possible to solve the problem using relativistic hydrodynamics and a realistic equation of state. With the approximations chosen, and using Newtonian gravitational theory, Colgate and White concluded that about 10^{-3} of the total mass energy could be ejected; that is, they found that the energy released from a $10 M_\odot$ star, largely in the form of kinetic energy of gas, was about 10^{52} ergs, whereas about 2×10^{51} ergs was ejected in the form of relativistic particles. This is more than 100 times the energy for which we have direct evidence of release in a supernova, and it is not likely that we can find a method of directly observing it. If we accept this argument, however, then we see that this much larger release of energy makes the supernova hypothesis for strong radio sources and QSO's more attractive again. It should be remembered, of course, that the energy is gravitational in origin.

Colgate and Cameron (1963) (see also Cameron (1965)) first applied the argument to attempt to account for the light variations in QSO's. They suggested that the very large luminosities were produced by the heating of the surrounding interstellar gas by the ejected gas. A more ambitious attempt to explain the flux radiated by a cosmologically distant QSO (3C 273 is taken as the prototype) has recently been made by Colgate (1966). He began by assuming that some 4×10^7 stars of solar mass are contained in a volume of radius 0.17 pc (5×10^{17} cm); that is, he assumed a star density of

$\sim 10^{10}/\text{pc}^3$. Given this star density, Colgate argues that stars of greater mass, $\sim 50 M_\odot$, will be formed by inelastic collisions between the original stars. It is then argued that these stars will evolve to the supernova stage in times of $\sim 10^6$ years and that supernova explosions will occur at a rate of ~ 3 per year. The kinetic energy ejected from the supernovae then heats the gas remaining from previous explosions, and it is this excited gas that gives rise to the high luminosity with a variable component. The radio emission is assumed to arise from the material at very high kinetic energy ($0.1 \ c^2/\text{gm}$). This will pass through the bulk of the gas cloud with little loss of energy, but when it passes through the boundary region of the dense cloud it is argued that a counter-streaming plasma oscillation instability will occur in which ions and electrons share kinetic energy. The radio emission is then assumed to arise from electrostatic bremsstrahlung, and this is scattered from coherent plasma oscillations, giving the spectral characteristics of 3C 273B. It is claimed that this model avoids the difficulties associated with synchrotron emission models (see Chapter 11). A component of still higher energy gas ejected from supernovae at relativistic speeds is then invoked to give rise to the radio source 3C 273A, and such components will also be required for any QSO's that have extended radio sources. Unfortunately, many of the details of this model are not easily understood, but the whole concept is highly ingenious. The underlying model, involving many supernovae, may also be considered for the strong radio galaxies.

Aizu, Fujimoto, Hasegawa, Kawabata, and Taketani (1964) have considered a possible mechanism of explosion in a galactic nucleus that contains a high density of stars together with gas. They suppose that the gas may have the effect of speeding up the evolution of the stars, also of inducing collective explosions of stars. They call this a "pile theory," but have not worked out the consequences of their ideas in detail.

STELLAR COLLISIONS

Given a very high star density in a galactic center, the sequence of events runs as follows. The stars interact more and more rapidly, through inelastic collisions; it is at this stage that Colgate believes stars of greater mass will be formed and will be able to evolve before further interactions occur. As the velocity dispersion of the stars gets larger as the cluster shrinks, the violence of the star collisions increases, and at high enough energy the stars will completely disrupt. During this process some stars will be ejected from the cluster at higher and higher velocities. These stages have recently been considered in some detail by Spitzer and Saslaw (1966), and the approach to them has been explored by Ulam and Walden (1964). Some authors (Gold, Axford, and Ray, 1965; Woltjer, 1964) have suggested that the energy for the strong radio sources and QSO's is derived from the star collisions themselves, though they have not discussed in any detail the mechanisms that convert this kinetic energy of collision into the energy modes in which it is seen. Very high star densities of $\sim 10^{11}$ stars/pc^3 (Woltjer, 1964) may be required in such a model. If the collision velocities are $\sim 10^4$ km/sec, the kinetic energy available is some 10^{51} ergs/$M_\odot$. This class of model, however, suggests that the violent phase in which most of the energy is released will be exceedingly short, since most of the star collisions will occur in a period that is a few times the size of cluster divided by the velocity dispersion—that is, in 10^9–10^{10} seconds. Thus the QSO phase is very short-lived.

In such violent star collisions the major part of the kinetic energy will be dissipated by radiation processes, and some mass will be ejected from the cluster. Most of the matter will fall back together, however, and the agglomeration process will eventually give rise to a massive cloud, with a small net angular momentum. This is perhaps not the only way in which a very condensed object can be produced. Nevertheless, it is the final evolutionary phase of a dense galactic nucleus of stars. How long it takes to evolve to this state depends on the initial density assumed. If this is low, comparable to the densities seen in nearby galaxies, the total time involved may be much longer than the Hubble time.

Given such a large dense mass, which is unstable against gravitational collapse, the question arises whether its very large store of gravitational energy can be released.

MASSIVE SUPER-STARS

The foregoing discussion leads us naturally to the investigations of Hoyle and Fowler (1963a,b) (see also Hoyle, Fowler, Burbidge, and Burbidge, 1964), who first considered the problem of the release of gravitational energy in the collapse of a super-star. They specifically excluded any discussion of the possible modes of formation of such a massive object, but it is clear that if we restrict ourselves to conventional mechanisms, such an object can only be formed (1) by the evolution of a galactic nucleus through the processes previously described or (2) by condensation out of a low density intergalactic medium. The second process, which in itself will release a large amount of energy, has been discussed by Field (1964) and in a different context by Sturrock (1966). We shall describe their hypotheses later.

The basic idea of Hoyle and Fowler is well known and we shall only discuss it briefly here. It is that in the gravitational collapse of a massive object it may be possible to release an amount of energy that is a small but significant fraction of the rest mass energy. The well known difficulty associated with the idea is that in order to release energy by this mechanism it is necessary to consider collapse to a radius nearly the size of the Schwarzschild radius. At this stage general relativity shows that it is very difficult for energy to be emitted and an object in this predicament gets closer and closer to the situation in which quanta cannot escape, with the result that the object cuts itself off from the remainder of the universe. No escape from this situation is known if we are dealing with spherically symmetrical collapse, unless it is supposed that the theory of general relativity is modified in this extreme condition. The role of rotation in the relativistic regime is unclear, though there has been some suggestion (Wagoner, 1965) that expulsion of matter can occur in extreme configurations.

Modification of the theory of relativity has been attempted by Hoyle and Narlikar (1964) who introduced a C-field (a field of negative energy) that they had considered in their cosmological investigations. This has the effect of halting gravitational collapse, and it was then proposed that the object would carry out radial oscillations, which would take it for some part of the time outside the Schwarz-schild radius, and in this phase energy could be emitted.

In the models in which energy is released in gravitational collapse of a massive object it is not clear in what form the energy will be emitted. The most efficient process as far as the strong radio sources in galaxies and QSO's are concerned is the ejection of energy already in the form of high-energy particles, since there are many arguments which suggest that the further process of conversion of energy from any other form to high-energy particles will be rather inefficient.

If the QSO's are local objects ejected from galaxies, then it must be argued that the energy is emitted in coherent lumps with cores of very high density. These are most likely to be produced in a process of fragmentation, perhaps due to rotation in the final collapse phases. Obviously a proper theoretical treatment of such ideas will be required if this hypothesis for QSO's is to be pursued.

Although the idea that gravitational collapse is responsible for the generation of the large energy of radio sources remains a popular one, despite the difficulties discussed earlier, Fowler (1964, 1965, 1966) has also attempted to account for the optical properties of the QSO's by considering the early collapse phases of a massive object.

He first showed that in the early collapse phases, normal hydrogen burning through the CNO bi-cycle will give a luminosity $L \approx 2 \times 10^{38} (M/M_\odot)$ ergs/sec, so that for $M \sim 10^8 M_\odot$ the luminosity $L \approx 2 \times 10^{46}$ ergs/sec will be comparable with the optical flux emitted by a cosmological QSO. The hydrogen-burning would take place at a temperature near 8×10^7 degrees, and the surface temperature would be near 70,000 degrees, so that a large flux in the ultraviolet would be emitted. Since this model was first proposed, it has become apparent that at least for 3C 273 the bulk of the energy is radiated in the infrared and millimeter regions, only $\leq 10\%$ arising in the optical region, and also that the radiant energy is largely due to a nonthermal process (see Chapter 4). These results argue against the massive star model for the observed flux. There has been some suggestion, however, that 3C 273 shows cyclic variations with a period of order 10 years (Chapter 6), and this, if confirmed, would certainly be an argument in favor of the idea that a single, massive, pulsating star is involved. The random variations in flux in both optical, radio, and millimeter ranges could equally well be explained by flares in a single massive object, by individual supernova outbursts, or by variations in the magnetic field or in the ejection of high-energy particles in other types of models.

Setting aside these observational difficulties, there first appeared to be severe difficulties associated with the concept of a single massive object, as follows. Fowler estimated that the total thermonuclear energy available in a massive star would enable it to radiate for $\sim 10^6$ years. But it also became clear that the general relativistic instability of a nonrotating star means that it cannot be stable for a time anywhere near as long as 10^6 years, but must undergo essentially free-fall collapse (Fowler, 1966; Chandrasekhar, 1964a, 1964b, 1965). However, it has now been shown (Fowler, 1966; Roxburgh, 1965) that a small amount of rotation can stabilize the massive star against gravitational collapse for a limited period. It has also been shown that turbulent or magnetic forces will also be able to stabilize the star as long as it contains nuclear energy sources. It therefore appears that a massive star may be able to exist for a period of $\sim 10^6$ years in its thermonuclear burning phase, provided that its mass does not exceed 10^8–$10^9 M_\odot$.

Fowler (1965) has shown that relaxation oscillations of such massive stars might then be able to account for any periodic flux variations that are seen. In order to explain the nonthermal components of the flux and their variations, it is then necessary to suppose that high-energy particles are ejected from the object and that variations in flux are produced by variations in the magnetic field or by fluctuations in the rate of injection of particles. This part of the problem has not been studied in detail within the framework of this model, and still remains a severe difficulty.

Although the massive star model might still appear attractive as far as the flux radiated in a very small volume is concerned, it should be remembered that for any QSO's in which very extended radio sources are seen, at least two massive objects are required. One must have formed, evolved to the gravitational collapse stage, and emitted enough high-energy particles to give rise to the extended source, while a second must currently be passing through its thermonuclear phase to produce the quasi-stellar component. To explain the strong radio galaxies by this mechanism we must assume that the massive object evolved and collapsed to give rise to the extended radio source.

THE ROLE OF MAGNETIC FIELDS
IN MASSIVE OBJECTS

The ideas described so far—of the release of energy in supernovae, in stellar encounters, and in gravitational collapse of massive objects—were all conceived to account for the vast amounts of energy required to explain the radio galaxies and QSO's. Little attention has been paid until recently to the problem of the magnetic fields that are an integral part of the phenomenon to be explained. Of course one of the major difficulties is that we really do not know what the strengths of the magnetic fields are, either in the extended radio sources or in the very small QSO's. For the extended sources most theoreticians have been content to take the minimum total energy conditions required to explain the observed synchrotron emission. These normally require the existence of homogeneous uniform magnetic fields with strengths of 10^{-4}–10^{-5} gauss. However, as has been discussed—for example, by Woltjer (1966a)—it is very difficult to see how the magnetic fields can be as strong as this, whether they have been ejected in the relativistic plasma cloud in the central explosion or have been amplified from a much weaker intergalactic field by the explosion. If, for example, the fields have strengths of $\sim 10^{-6}$ gauss then it necessarily follows that the total energy requirement of the source is much increased above the minimum total energy, and that a very large part of the energy resides in the relativistic particles; energetically, the magnetic field is negligible.

There are strong arguments for believing that a nonhomogeneous magnetic field is present in the highly condensed QSO's, also there is no reason to believe that the equipartition condition is fulfilled (Chapter 11). In order to avoid many difficulties, particularly if the QSO's are at cosmological distances, it may be necessary to invoke very strong magnetic fields ≥ 100 gauss in some regions. But here again no unambiguous estimate of the magnetic field strength can be made.

It is natural to suppose, however, that if the relativistic particles gain energy by a conventional acceleration mechanism—for example, the Fermi process or the betatron mechanism—then the magnetic field plays an important role in energy transfer, and of course its configuration is one of the main factors determining the synchrotron radiating properties of the source. If when the particles are injected from the condensed object they already have energies at which they can radiate in the observed range, then the first point made above is irrelevant. However, we shall confine ourselves here first of all to conventional acceleration mechanisms, in which case an obvious possibility is that gravitational energy released in the condensation and collapse of a massive object is converted to magnetic energy and through it to the relativistic particles. Thus a number of authors (Ginzburg and Ozernoy, 1964; Ginzburg, 1964; Ozernoy, 1966a,b; Kardeshev, 1964; Piddington, 1964, 1966; Sturrock, 1965, 1966) have explored some possibilities using this approach.

Both Piddington and Sturrock attempt to discuss in a qualitative fashion the condensation of a mass of galactic size out of the intergalactic medium. Piddington (1964) started with the natural hypothesis that galaxies condense from gas clouds with frozen-in magnetic fields and argues that the form of the galaxy will depend on the orientation of the rotational vector ω with respect to the magnetic field vector $\mathbf{B}$. He believes that when they are parallel, spiral systems will be formed, and when they are orthogonal, radio galaxies will result. In the latter case it is argued that stars form while the uncondensed gas continues to shrink, giving rise to a condensed mass, whereas if star formation is inhibited by some process the whole galactic mass will shrink to "nuclear" dimensions and a QSO will result. Of course there is a serious question how such an evolution can take place—a question that is bypassed by Piddington. For example, in the case of the radio galaxies the bulk of the stars are thought to be old ($\sim 10^{10}$ years), but it is unreasonable to suppose that the central plasma cloud, which is supposed to give rise to the radio source, has remained in a state of activity for the life of the galaxy, since the energetic requirements of the source go up enormously in this case. If the gas cloud is to collapse completely to the dimension of a QSO ($\sim 10^{18}$ cm or less), a condition inherent in the theories of both Sturrock and Piddington, and if the gravitational energy given up in this process is only to be released by the types of plasma instability suggested by these authors, then it still remains to be shown that all of the other possible mechanisms, including fragmentation and re-expansion—which have bedeviled earlier attempts to understand the formation of protogalaxies—will not be important.

Sturrock's argument is based on a model of the solar flaring mechanism proposed earlier by him that must be scaled up by an enormous factor, a point that may or may not be one of the attractions of the hypothesis. It is argued that a galaxoid, defined by Sturrock as a protogalaxy, a compact elliptical galaxy, a galactic nucleus, or a QSO, is condensed from the intergalactic gas in such a way that it maintains a connection with the intergalactic magnetic field. It is not clear how this object is originally formed, since Sturrock does not discuss the problem of gravitational instability, or thermal instabilities in the original diffuse gas; he considers a situation in which, given a primary condensation, material can be accreted by it. It is supposed that the intergalactic material is at least partially ionized, that the magnetic field has an hourglass configuration through the object, and that accreted matter will be "funneled" into the condensed object. The angular momentum problem is briefly mentioned, and it is argued that provided the velocity of the gas being accreted is less than the Alfvén velocity, the magnetic field has the effect of removing angular momentum from the forming object. The well-known difficulties associated with condensation in an ionized medium containing a magnetic field, and the question of stability with the condition that the gravitational and magnetic forces remain comparable throughout the shrinking process, are not discussed.

The situation is reached in which the galaxoid or QSO is highly condensed and contains magnetic energy that supports it against gravitational collapse. Sturrock then finds that this condition implies that $\Phi \approx 10^{-3}M$, where Φ is the flux in gauss cm^2 and M is the mass in grams of the condensed object. He then concludes that the masses of the central objects must be of the order of 10^{10}–$10^{12}M_\odot$, and these are much greater than the masses required to explain the energy input in terms of gravitational collapse. For the extended radio sources he uses the values of Φ computed by Maltby, Matthews, and Moffet (1963). These have been obtained by *assuming* the equipartition condition $E_p \approx E_m$ to give the minimum total energy in particles plus magnetic field, and as we have stressed earlier there is no physical basis for this result. In fact the recent observation by Wade (1966) that in Cygnus A there are a number of small sources with high surface brightnesses, which contribute much of the observed flux, shows directly that the source must be very far from equipartition between magnetic and particle energies in the source taken as a whole.

Sturrock then argues that energy release from the QSO will be the tearing mode instability in the region of the sheet pinch, which in his assumed magnetic field configuration is perpendicular to the axis of the hourglass. It is then argued that this instability will give rise to ejection of a pocket of magnetic field and high-energy particles which comprise the jets seen in QSO's and radio galaxies; such a jet will eventually divide into two clouds, which will be the double radio source. The main interest in this model lies in the plasma instability mechanism. Given the condensed object together with the magnetic field configuration required, the model has some attractions. However, it is not clear to us from Sturrock's discussion how this situation can be reached in nature.

Piddington has paid more attention to the problems of rotation in a contracting cloud. He has argued that when ω and **B** are orthogonal the field will be wound in a spiral of ever-increasing strength until electromagnetic forces control the size and shape of the system. It is then supposed that the rotational energy is converted to magnetic energy so that further collapse can occur. This process continues without sudden collapse. The ω dimension is at first much smaller than the radius of the disk, but the object eventually reaches a spherical state followed by explosions along the $\pm\omega$ axis. The particles are accelerated in a neutral sheet at the expense of magnetic energy in a process bearing some resemblance to that postulated by Sturrock. Piddington has argued that the hourglass-magnetic-field model is one that gives rise to a normal spiral galaxy (ω parallel to $\mathbf{B}$) and thus he reaches quite a different conclusion from Sturrock in this respect. The difference lies in Sturrock's comparative neglect of the effect of rotation in his model while using the condition that the magnetic flux and gravitational energy are in equilibrium according to the virial throughout the contraction.

We must conclude that although the flare models of this type have some attractions, they require initial conditions that we certainly cannot deduce from observation nor unambiguously derive by theoretical argument.

Ginzburg and Ozernoy started with the idea that QSO's and strong radio galaxies get their energy from the gravitational collapse of a massive super-star. They begin by supposing that a very large spherically symmetric mass has condensed into a small volume, and then consider the effect of further collapse on the magnetic dipole moment trapped within the object. The magnetic energy is assumed to be small compared with the gravitational energy of the initial star. As the star collapses, the magnetic field grows, reaching enormous values in the star's interior. It is argued, however, that in the lower-density atmosphere surrounding the star, conditions may develop such that a current-carrying shell may become detached. Thus the collapsing magnetic star may develop very powerful "radiation belts" within a magnetosphere, and it is argued that it is these regions that give rise to the flux of optical and radio emission that we see in quasi-stellar objects. Ozernoy (1966a,b) has developed a model of what is called a magnetoid—a quasi-stationary configuration in stable rotation along the lines of force of a toroidal magnetic field. It is argued that such a model can explain some of the variable features of QSO's, particularly if they are quasi-periodic. Although Ginzburg and Ozernoy stress that the development and structure of this type of model involve many complex and unsolved problems, the model does have some attractive features. It may be able to account in a natural way for the very strong magnetic fields required to avoid some of the difficulties discussed in Chapter 11. It is not clear, however, how the bulk of the gravitational energy is to be transformed to the high-energy particles that radiate in this field.

Layzer (1965), however, has argued that any gas cloud, provided that it is sufficiently massive, will, before it becomes unstable, generate a magnetoturbulent field whose energy is comparable to its own rest energy. It must then be presumed that a considerable part of this energy is converted with a very high efficiency to relativistic particles, which then radiate in local strong magnetic fields.

From discussion of the first three kinds of theories—supernova theories, stellar collisions, and massive super-stars—we see that, given a nucleus of very high density, there are a number of processes, all involving release of gravitational energy, that may be able to explain some of the observed properties of the QSO's and the radio sources. The two mechanisms that have so far been considered to account for such high-density nuclei are (1) the normal evolutionary processes of energy loss and shrinkage of a galactic nucleus of stars and (2) the formation of a dense gas cloud by condensation in the intergalactic medium. The first of these is more firmly based on observation, since we know that at least some of the strong radio galaxies contain large concentrations of stars. Even in galaxies, however, the maximum star densities that can be deduced directly from observation are only $\sim 10^3$ stars/pc^3. This does not mean that much higher densities may not exist, but merely means that much higher densities extending over a few parsecs at the centers of galaxies could not be detected (Burbidge, 1961). As has been shown by Spitzer and Saslaw, the time for the evolution of a galactic nucleus with a comparatively low star density will be very long, and unless we assume a rather high density to start with, it is not clear that the very large star densities required for the theories surveyed earlier will be reached in periods of less than 10^{10} years. If, however, we *postulate* that higher densities are present from the beginning, then the reason why they exist in the first place is not clear.

The idea that a dense gas cloud can form out of the intergalactic medium and form a QSO also is difficult to understand theoretically. Ginzburg (1961) first proposed that gravitational energy released in the formation of proto-stars might be used to explain the radio galaxies, and Field (1964) proposed that the QSO's were galaxies in the process of formation. His was a very idealized model and clearly could only account for the high-luminosity phase of a QSO at a cosmological distance. It could not explain a radio galaxy that contains old stars, nor the extended radio sources associated with some QSO's. As has previously been discussed, the flare theories do not give a convincing picture of the way in which the condensed object is formed from the diffuse medium.

From all of this discussion we must conclude that the formation of a dense object is not well understood. Bearing this in mind we turn to a class of theory in which no attempt is made to understand the formation of a dense object from the gas or galaxies as we see them in the universe today. In fact McCrea (1964) has suggested that the problem of the formation of condensations may be man-made and that there is no evidence that nature poses such problems. It is then either argued that the dense phase is a remnant of the very early evolution of the universe, in which all of the mass energy was contained in a very small volume, or else it is supposed that matter is continuously created in conditions of high density. These ideas relate the QSO's and the radio galaxies directly to cosmological models. We turn to these models next.

THEORIES USING THE CONCEPT THAT MASSIVE OBJECTS HAVE A COSMOLOGICAL ORIGIN

Proposals along this line have been made by McCrea (1964), Hoyle and Narlikar (1966), Stothers (1966), Novikov (1965), and Ne'eman (1965).

McCrea has considered a modification of the steady-state theory in which it is supposed that matter is only created in the presence of already existing matter. Thus it is argued that all matter is contained in galaxies, and that continuous creation simply has the effect of increasing the galactic mass. He supposes that occasionally a galaxy may eject a fragment, which is then the embryo from which a new galaxy is grown. Such embryos of galaxies are then very closely related to the quasi-stellar objects, and the phenomena of outburst and ejection from galaxies to produce radio sources are to be associated with the creation and ejection process. Such a model would easily explain the QSO's if they have a local origin.

A rather similar proposal has been made by Hoyle and Narlikar, who have discussed it within the framework of their C-field cos-

A problem not covered in these theories is associated with the apparently normal composition of the gas cloud giving the line radiation in the spectra of QSO's. Since it is not reasonable to suppose that matter is created or expands from a superdense state with a composition similar to that of normal stars and gas in our galaxy, it must be supposed either that extensive nucleosynthesis has gone on in the evolution of these objects leading to normal composition— a highly unlikely situation—or that the object has managed to accrete material with normal composition.

QUARKS AS ENERGY SOURCES IN MASSIVE OBJECTS WITH A COSMOLOGICAL ORIGIN

Since it was first proposed that a classification of the elementary particles is obtained in a natural way from the assumption that all the particles are composed of three types of truly fundamental particles, which Gell-Mann named quarks, many attempts have been made to detect them, with no success so far. The limit placed on the masses is that they are ≥ 5 Gev/c^2; this limit is placed by attempts to produce them in accelerators. If such particles exist, then one can suppose that bare quarks form the major constituent of the universe in a stage in which matter has not evolved. Thus if the universe was once in a highly condensed state it may have been one in which bare quarks predominated, whereas if the universe has a steady-state character, so that matter is continuously created, then this matter might be created in the form of quarks. The situation in an evolving universe has already been discussed by Zeldovich, Okun, and Pikelner (1965) and by Saslaw (1966). Zeldovich et al. have discussed the situation in which it is supposed that the quarks burned out in the first few microseconds of the expansion, and Saslaw has considered that we may be able to obtain cosmological information by considering the role of the quarks in this very short epoch.

If we accept the view that quarks are of importance in these cosmologically dense configurations and suppose that such massive objects containing bare quarks are left behind in the initial expansion, or are present in newly created material, then it is easy to see that as the objects evolve they can give rise to the major constituents of mology. They are able to calculate the rate of the creation of matte using this theory and have shown that the growth in "pockets" o creation is likely to be an unstable process, since the growth of a mass to infinity takes only twice the time for the mass to double itself— a time that they adjust to the order of the Hubble time. They suggest that such a runaway process will be prevented by a fragmentation of the growing mass, and that each fragment will act as an individual pocket of creation—the embryo in McCrea's formulation.

Stothers takes a rather different view concerning the places in which matter is created. He argued that this occurs where matter is lacking (between clusters of galaxies) just because it *is* lacking, and that the QSO's (which may not occur in clusters) are the manifestation of this creation. He also considers other phenomena that may be explained through such a hypothesis. For a variety of reasons, however, the McCrea-Hoyle-Narlikar hypothesis is more attractive.

If one adheres to the view that we live in an evolving universe, then it is possible to argue that the superdense objects are inhomogeneities remaining in the general expansion of the universe, and once again the problem of forming condensations out of a diffuse intergalactic background is bypassed. Ne'eman has proposed that the QSO's, which he supposes are cosmological objects, are in an expanding state, having lain near the singular state for some 10^{10} years. Thus in its own coordinate system a QSO behaves as a miniature expanding universe. It is argued that extremely large energies must have accumulated from strong interactions in the superdense state with no outlet for the decay of various mesons. But having attained a lower density in the slow expansion these mesons and hence high-energy particles may be released.

The argument of Novikov is rather similar to this, though he considers that energy is released when shells of matter moving outward in the expansion collide with shells ejected earlier, or with matter falling onto the object from outside (Ambartsumian, 1966).

In this whole class of theory conventional acceleration mechanisms for high-energy particles are not invoked, but it is supposed that the high-energy particles are directly injected. The ideas contained in these theories are foreshadowed in the early papers of Ambartsumian (1961, and earlier references given there).

the radio sources and QSO's. The only previous mention of this possibility has been made by Pacini (1966).

In such evolution we suppose that the quarks go through what we may now call the primary process of nucleosynthesis, the formation of baryons and mesons and hence, after decay, of stable nucleons together with electrons, positrons, γ-rays, and neutrinos, through the processes in which three quarks combine to form a baryon and mesons form from quark-antiquark pairs. The great attraction of such a hypothesis lies in the fact that because the quarks are so massive, the packing fraction of the nucleons and mesons is very large, so that in this primary process of nucleosynthesis, very large amounts of energy, some ten times the rest mass of the baryons or greater, will be released and will reside finally, after the baryons and mesons decay, in the form of high-energy protons, electrons and positrons, γ-rays and neutrinos. This proposal has been foreshadowed by a remark made by J. R. Oppenheimer at the Galileo Quadricentennial Symposium in Padova, September, 1964 (Oppenheimer, 1966). Moreover, the energies of the electrons and positrons that give rise to the synchrotron emission are already in the Gev range. It will not be possible to calculate the energy spectrum of the resulting particles until the masses of the quarks are determined. However, from the lower limits set at present it is already clear that the energies are likely to be high enough so that, for radio emission at least, the magnetic fields calculated from the synchrotron theory may be less than the equipartition values. This in turn means that the bulk of the energy required to explain the observations will be contained in the particles.

It is not clear what the role of the high-energy γ-rays and neutrinos will be in such a model. It cannot be supposed that the γ radiation is heavily degraded by the redshift effect in its escape, in which case it might account for some part of the optical flux, because if such a condition prevailed the particles would also be degraded.

We have found here a mechanism for releasing energy directly in the form of relativistic particles, thus producing such particles with very high efficiency, which as we discussed earlier is one of the major requirements to be satisfied by any theory that attempts to account for the origin of the strong synchrotron sources. If we suppose that the whole of the rest mass of primitive matter is originally in the form of bare quarks, then the rest mass energy is converted at an efficiency of 100 percent into high-energy particles, though the energy in the neutrino component may be lost. If matter is originally in the form of bare quarks, what determines the conditions under which it is transmuted into baryons and mesons? The lower limit to the bare quark mass shows that matter composed of bare quarks must have a density greater than that of nuclear matter and a temperature $\geq 5 \times 10^{13}$ degrees. Under such extreme conditions of density gravitational forces are dominant, as is well known; a mass of galactic size (say $10^{10} M_\odot$) has a Schwarzschild radius of 3×10^{15} cm, whereas the same matter at nuclear densities would be contained within a radius of $\sim 10^{10}$ cm. It is thus not possible to discuss the properties of such dense configurations without relating general relativity to the theory of the elementary particles underlying the quark hypothesis.

It is obvious that given such extreme conditions the period of primary nucleosynthesis will be exceedingly short. However, the estimates that have been made of the characteristic time scales associated with the quasi-stellar objects and strong radio sources suggest that their properties cannot be explained by supposing that there was produced a single burst of particles that expanded with a velocity close to c, but that there has been continuous injection of relativistic particles over periods ranging from 10^3 to 10^6 years. To explain such a phenomenon we must suggest, as did Ne'eman, that the object is in a slowly expanding state and is gradually enlarging until its material lies outside the Schwarzschild radius. The primary nucleogenesis will have already given rise to the large flux of relativistic particles, which are then able to escape over a period determined by the rate of expansion.

We have already discussed in Chapter 10 the conclusion that the regions giving rise to the line spectra of the QSO's have chemical compositions not very different from those of stars in our own galaxy. If these objects arise from a very dense state we must suppose that following the production of baryons by the primary process of nucleosynthesis, extensive nucleosynthesis occurs in the massive super-star. It is entirely possible, however, that the composition of this material made in this way will be quite different from that seen in the QSO's. If this is the case then the material that we are observing directly may be an outer shell of normal material that has been accreted by the object.

Is it possible to obtain evidence that an object composed of bare quarks is the ultimate source for the QSO's and radio galaxies? Although the primary nucleosynthesis may have been complete, so that no quarks remained, it is possible that some quarks survived and are stable. If this is the case we may expect that atoms in which the quarks are the nuclei may be formed, and that line radiation may be emitted from them. If, for example, we take the case in which the quarks are fractionally charged, and consider an atom with a nucleus consisting of a quark with charge $2e/3$ and a single electron (quark hydrogen) the Lyman series wavelengths will be $L\alpha = 2735$ Å, $L\beta = 2307$ Å, $L\gamma = 2188$ Å, assuming that the quark has a mass of $10m_p$. This wavelength region has been extensively studied in QSO's with fairly large redshifts, but there are no features that can be attributed to this series. Little can be deduced from this, however, since as we have previously described, the part of the QSO from which the line spectrum arises is an outer shell which, because of its composition, may have been formed from normal material.

It is obviously not possible at present to make quantitative calculations using the model proposed here, because we do not yet understand how the gravitational field is coupled to the force fields of the strongly interacting particles. However, it is only in violent events in the universe at large that we may be able to study (experimentally) such interactions, though of course the observational evidence will necessarily be indirect.

As an aside, we may consider the relationship of this idea to the general problem of the generation of relativistic particles.

If relativistic particles are produced on the extragalactic scale by a mechanism as fundamental as this, how can such particles be produced in the galaxy? We know directly from the studies of the radio sources in our galaxy that large fluxes of such particles are produced in supernova remnants. Colgate and White (1966) have shown that it may indeed be possible to produce a large flux at the time of the explosion. However, the continued existence of energy sources that give rise to very high-energy electrons long after the explosion is strongly suggested in some cases—for example, in the Crab Nebula, where the optical flux, and probably the x-ray flux, is of synchrotron origin. Moreover, in the Crab Nebula the existence of the rapidly moving wisps indicates that energy sources still remain. Is it possible to suppose that these energies are derived also from the primary nucleosynthesis process? All that we can say is the following: We have every reason to believe that the remnant left after a supernova explosion may often be an object whose mass is greater than the critical mass required for its stabilization by degenerate neutron pressure. Under such conditions gravitational collapse will continue without end according to relativity theory. To get energy out, the following ad hoc proposal, which is related to earlier ideas, can be made. Gravitational energy of collapse is converted to bare quarks, which in turn go through the primary nucleosynthesis process, giving rise to relativistic nucleons, electrons, and positrons, together with γ-rays and neutrinos. All of these processes must take place close to or within the Schwarzschild radius, which classically is never reached, so that we are invoking a coupling between the gravitational and elementary-particle fields of a kind that is not yet understood. On the basis of classical theory it appears that stars may evolve to a state in which the bulk of their mass energy may become inaccessible to the rest of the universe (Hoyle, Fowler, Burbidge, and Burbidge, 1964). If this mechanism is possible then such mass energy might reappear in the form of relativistic particles.

MATTER-ANTIMATTER ANNIHILATION

The idea that matter-antimatter annihilation might be a powerful mechanism for explaining the energy release in radio galaxies was first proposed by Burbidge (1956) and Burbidge and Hoyle (1956). The idea is, at first sight, an attractive one, since the annihilation of matter and antimatter with low kinetic energy will give rise to neutrinos, γ-rays, and electrons and positrons. The electrons and positrons take up about 15 percent of the energy released in the annihilation, and thus mass energy is released at about 15 percent efficiency into one of the components responsible for the synchrotron radiation. Moreover, it is not necessary to suppose that any high-energy nuclear component is present, thus reducing the minimum energy requirement in the synchrotron source by a factor of ~ 10 or more. The difficulties with the hypothesis were thought to be associated with (1) the plausibility of the assumption that antimatter is present in the universe and (2) the problem of understanding how matter and antimatter could be created or evolve and remain separated, and then later be brought into interaction with each other in isolated events.

In recent years Alfvén and Klein (1962) have proposed a model universe in which matter and antimatter enter in a symmetric way. Alfvén (1965) has developed the concept of an "ambiplasma," which contains both kinds of matter, and he has shown that a mechanism of separation involving the magnetic field is possible. If one accepts this type of cosmology then the difficulties mentioned earlier can be removed. But this type of cosmological model, based on the old theoretical model of Charlier, is probably not compatible with present views. Setting aside this objection for the moment we consider the consequences of the annihilation proposal further. Ekspong, Yandagni, and Bonnevier (1966) have used this idea to attempt to account for the radio spectra of some QSO's and radio galaxies. They have calculated the electron-positron spectrum through the decays of the π and μ mesons produced in $p\bar{p}$ annihilation and have then used this spectrum to calculate the resulting synchrotron spectra. These they have compared with observations of the radio spectra of such QSO's as 3C 48, 3C 147, 3C 286, CTA 102, and the radio galaxies Cygnus A and 3C 295. The calculated spectra are curved and show a tendency to get flatter at low frequencies. We have discussed earlier (Chapter 11) the generally accepted reason for this flattening—that it is an approach to the synchrotron self-absorption, which naturally gives a maximum in the spectrum, particularly for the sources containing very small components. In this hypothesis, however, the curvature has an entirely different origin; it is due to the form of the energy spectrum of the electron-positron component produced in the annihilation, which has a peak at about 30 Mev, below which very few electrons are produced. A much more serious difficulty is that very large magnetic fields are required to give radiation in the observed frequency range using electrons with energies in the range 30–100 Mev with a tail extending to several hundred Mev. Ekspong et al. have used field strengths of $\sim 10^{-2}$ gauss. But particularly for the extended sources, which include 3C 147, Cygnus A, and 3C 295, and are among the sources these investigators have used, the minimum total energy condition gives magnetic fields in the range 10^{-4}–10^{-5} gauss. If the magnetic field is much larger than this, as it has to be in this theory because very low-energy electrons are used, then there is a strong departure from the minimum total energy condition. This in itself does not mean that it is not a plausible hypothesis, but it does mean that the total energy residing in particles and in the magnetic field is many orders of magnitude greater than the minimum, and that the bulk of the energy resides *in the magnetic field*. Thus these investigators have proposed a model in which the electron-positron component is produced by annihilation at comparatively high efficiency, but in which nearly all of the energy is present in the magnetic field. If, for example, we take the volume of the radio source 3C 295 as $\sim 10^{70}$ cm^3, its total magnetic energy is $\sim 4 \times 10^{64}$ ergs (assuming $B \sim 10^{-2}$ gauss). Thus they have not solved the energy problem at all, but are left with the difficulty of explaining the origin of a fantastic amount of energy in the magnetic field, which cannot arise from annihilation. On this ground alone it appears that this model must be rejected. To avoid the difficulty it is necessary to argue that the annihilation energy can somehow be put into electrons with much higher average energies, perhaps ~ 1 Gev, with an approximately equal amount of energy present in the magnetic field, so that $\epsilon_p \geq \epsilon_m$.

GRAVITATIONAL FOCUSING

Barnothy (1965, 1966) has suggested that the very high luminosities of the QSO's, which are assumed to be at cosmological distances, are due to amplification by gravitational focusing. He argues that a large concentration of mass (a galaxy or other object) lies very close to the light path between the QSO and the observer. It is well known that the gravitational lens effect is inversely proportional to the transverse distance between the object exerting the strong gravitational field and the light path. The objects must be dark; otherwise their own radiation would swamp the flux that is to be gravitationally focused. Moreover, they must occur quite frequently in space if the chance of this effect occurring is to be non-negligible. Both of these conditions are inherently implausible. Furthermore, it is still necessary to postulate the existence of objects with the spectral properties of the QSO's, since this effect only increases the apparent luminosities. Therefore, Barnothy has argued that the QSO's are the nuclei of very distant Seyfert galaxies. It is known, however, that although the spectra of the nuclei of Seyfert galaxies bear some resemblance to those of the QSO's, the two classes of objects are clearly distinguishable. The main difference lies in the fact that the emission lines in the QSO's are weak relative to the continuum, whereas in the Seyfert nuclei they are very strong. Thus Seyfert nuclei cannot be invoked, and the hypothesis of Barnothy is reduced to the idea that two new components in the universe are present—large numbers of dark massive objects, and objects which emit much less flux than the cosmologically distant QSO's but in all other respects are the same. Thus the proposal should probably be discarded.

18

Conclusion

It is now several years since the first quasi-stellar object was identified, and as more observational facts are gathered, these strange phenomena seem only to become more enigmatic. We have devoted a greater amount of space in the preceding chapters to summarizing the observed properties of the objects, and attempting empirically to link these with the physical conditions in the objects, than we have devoted to trying to account for them theoretically. It is on the observational side that most has been learned; for example, successively larger and larger redshifts have been discovered, light variations have been found involving large changes in shorter and shorter periods of time, and variations have been discovered in the radio flux also. On the theoretical side we have been hard put to produce even qualitative models to explain the properties of the objects.

Let us summarize the salient observational properties. Most of the QSO's so far identified are radio sources, and of these the majority have at least one radio component with a very small dimension. Some of the sources are double—the characteristic found so commonly in radio galaxies. The radio spectra generally have a form consistent with the emission being synchrotron radiation, often with self-absorption, while the continuous radiation in the optical region, with its strong ultraviolet output, is consistent either with an inverse power-law frequency dependence, as is often found for the radio flux, or with a spectrum of exponential form.

The emission lines in the spectra are broad, and the redshifts range from about $z = 0.1$ to values of z slightly greater than 2; the relative strengths of the lines are consistent with their being emitted by gas of "normal," or solar-neighborhood, composition at a slightly higher temperature than that of a typical planetary nebula and with about 100 times the electron density. Absorption lines that are sometimes narrow and deep are being found in an increasing number of QSO's with $z \approx 2$; these absorption spectra suggest that we are often seeing a standard redshifted spectrum in the object.

Luminosity variations as large as three magnitudes are now known (in 3C 446), with changes by a factor of about 2 in times as short as 1 day. Also in 3C 446, linear polarization of the optical radiation is quite strong. It is these variations, together with those observed in the radio and microwave regions of the spectra of other QSO's, that lead to real problems in accepting the large redshifts as distance indicators. Who would have expected to find a galaxy-like object varying in this way? It is true that a galaxy can approximately double its overall radiation in a few days if it is a galaxy of modest luminosity and a bright supernova explodes in it, but no supernova has ever been seen to *decrease* in brightness in the same short period of time.

At first the discovery that the QSO's have large redshifts led nearly all astronomers to the immediate conclusion that the objects must be at very large distances, and thus it was expected that they would be a new and powerful tool for cosmological investigation. At present it is still true that most astronomers would like to accept this interpretation. There are a variety of reasons for this, some of an historical or subjective nature. It has been remarked elsewhere (Burbidge and Hoyle, 1966) that the situation regarding the QSO's at the present time is rather similar to that existing about fifty years ago when the first redshifts of the spiral nebulae had been measured. At that time their extragalactic nature had not been established, and astronomers attempted to interpret the redshifts in terms of galactic objects streaming in preferred directions (similar to the concept of star streaming with which they were familiar). It took more than a decade before their extragalactic nature was firmly established.

The quasi-stellar objects may be:

1. Objects that lie at the cosmological distances indicated by their redshifts.

2. Objects that do not lie at cosmological distances but whose redshifts are Doppler shifts, so that they must either be moving at relativistic speeds or contain matter moving at relativistic speeds.

3. Objects that do not lie at cosmological distances but have redshifts that are gravitational in origin.

4. Objects that do not lie at cosmological distances, whose redshifts are due to some as yet undiscovered mechanism.

We have described the evidence bearing on these different hypotheses.

There are three qualitative arguments in favor of serious consideration of the proposal that the QSO's are not at cosmological distances:

1. This is a completely new class of astronomical object, and one should at least be prepared to find a new explanation for the existence of large redshifts.

2. The objects are highly variable in energy output and are therefore very small, and if they are at very great distances the resultant exceedingly high energy-densities in small volumes lead to model restrictions that may be unacceptable.

3. The recent discovery of a considerable number of objects with absorption-line redshifts close to 1.95 is very difficult to explain if the objects are at cosmological distances.

Two qualitative arguments that carry considerable weight have been used against the second hypothesis:

1. The origin of relativistically moving objects is difficult to understand; moreover, the amount of energy that must be ejected from galaxies in the form of such objects is high (it is hardly reasonable to argue that it is excessively high, as some have done, since no one knows what "excessive" means in this context).

2. All the line shifts are redshifts; no blue shifts have been found.

If the shifts are Doppler shifts, this is probably the strongest observational argument in favor of the objects being at cosmological distances, but it can also be argued that the center of explosion is comparatively nearby, as was originally suggested by Terrell and by Hoyle and Burbidge, in which case the objects must have passed us and must all be receding. It is also possible that observational selection is at work, so that blue-shifted objects are not being detected.

As has been discussed earlier, however, the assumption that many galaxies have ejected local QSO's leads to the conclusion that if the objects are emitting with spherical symmetry, then provided the Doppler effect is invoked for the shifts in spectrum lines, blue-shifted objects should predominate. If we reject the idea that the objects are radiating largely in tails pointing along the velocity vector in the backward direction, in which case the theoretical blue-shift/redshift ratio can be changed, then we are forced to conclude that peculiar or radio galaxies are not contributing generally to the local population of QSO's, so that only a local explosion is involved, or that the objects are cosmological. This brings us completely in conflict with the data of Arp (1966a,b).

The work of Arp has given rise to one of the most baffling aspects of the QSO's and radio galaxies to date. We are inclined to believe that although the statistics of the argument may still not be clear, there are enough good examples to merit considering the effect seriously. If Arp is right then the local nature of the QSO's has been established. We then have to argue that the blue-shift difficulty can be overcome by taking into account the effects mentioned earlier, or that the spectral shifts are not due to the Doppler effect. We are then led directly to the remaining two hypotheses. Arguments for and against the redshifts being gravitational have been given in Chapter 9. With regard to the fourth hypothesis, it is always possible to take the view that the redshifts may be due to some as yet undiscovered mechanism, but unless both Doppler and gravitational shifts can be completely ruled out, one should probably not spend too much time on this approach.

There are some observational results that are inconclusive in the sense that they are compatible with either the local or the cosmological hypothesis. These include:

1. The apparent absence of absorption due to the intergalactic medium in the flux from the QSO's. From this it can be argued either that the objects are comparatively nearby, with the result that absorption at the relevant wavelengths cannot be seen, or that the intergalactic matter is absent or is in such a form that no absorption occurs.

2. The forms of the log N–log S, redshift-apparent magnitude, and redshift-radio flux relations. We have shown that these do not support or rule out either hypothesis. The slope of the log N–log S curve must be determined by a property of the QSO's, either a large-scale evolutionary effect or a local luminosity function effect.

It is generally agreed that there is no theoretical argument that can, as yet, enable us to decide whether the objects are nearby or are at cosmological distances. Apart from Arp's work and the results already available on the absorption lines, there are three observations that may settle which of the hypotheses is correct:

1. The detection of a blue shift.

2. The detection of a QSO in the position of a cluster of galaxies, and spectra showing that the redshift of the cluster is the same as that of the QSO. Alternatively it might be possible to detect absorption features in the spectrum of the QSO that could be shown to have the same redshift as the cluster galaxies. This would show that the QSO was a background object.

3. The obtaining of an ultraviolet spectrum covering the Ly-α region of the nucleus of a comparatively nearby galaxy. One would have to choose an object with a redshift of at least 1000 km/sec, so that Ly-α would fall clear of interstellar absorption in our own galaxy, and the object must have an appreciable ultraviolet flux; from this it might be possible to see whether there is any intergalactic neutral atomic hydrogen to cause intergalactic Ly-α absorption. The nucleus of a Seyfert galaxy might be a suitable object to observe, since these nuclei are

bright and starlike, and they probably emit a considerable ultraviolet flux. This would not, however, be a completely conclusive test.

The situation may be summed up as follows. Many of the observed properties of the QSO's are still consistent with the view that they lie at cosmological distances. Even if this is so, however, they cannot easily be used as cosmological probes. For example, if there were no galaxies in the universe could the expansion of the universe have been detected from the QSO's alone? The answer is emphatically no. Presumably the observers, having found them among the galactic stars, would have explained them as stars being ejected from the galaxy at high speed.

The evidence against the idea that they are cosmological objects consists of the correlations between pairs of radio sources and galaxies discovered by Arp, the apparent anisotropy of redshifts as a function of position, and the discovery of absorption spectra with a unique value near 1.95. In addition, the rapid flux variations are more easily explained if the objects are not at cosmological distances. All this evidence, if taken at its face value leads to the idea that the QSO's lie at distances < 100 Mpc and strongly suggests that the redshifts are not Doppler shifts. But none of the arguments is watertight, and much of the observational evidence is highly incomplete. Consequently no firm conclusions can be drawn at present. And of course no satisfactory theoretical models have yet been constructed for cosmological or local QSO's.

We conclude with a few remarks about the subjective nature of this topic. It is obvious that all of us have been pretty well conditioned to interpret extragalactic redshifts as due to the expansion of the universe. This is simply because of the age in which we live. The local hypothesis has bothered those who may have believed consciously, or subconsciously, that if the quasi-stellar objects are local they are not such great discoveries as if they are cosmological; if they are local they are not available for cosmological investigation (for example, the arguments using them which apparently rule out the simple steady-state theory disappear); if they are local many of the theoretical investigations concerned with energy production are irrelevant (in our opinion this is only partially true, since such models are often appropriate for the radio galaxy problems). But if they are comparatively nearby they are exceedingly interesting in the problems that they pose. In any case the objects are of great cosmogonical significance.

In writing this book we have swayed from side to side in our own beliefs. At the time of writing we can see no conclusive answer, though our own prejudices, which we cannot objectively evaluate, remain.

REFERENCES

Adgie, R. L. 1964, Nature, **204,** 1028.
Adgie, R., Gent, H., Slee, O. B., Frost, A., Palmer, H. P., and Ronson, B. 1965, Nature, **208,** 275.
Aizu, K., Fujimoto, Y., Hasegawa, H., Kawabata, K., and Taketani, M. 1964, Pr. Th. Phys. Supp. No. 31, p. 35.
Alfvén, H. 1965, Rev. Mod. Phys., **37,** 652.
Alfvén, H., and Klein, O. 1962, Arkiv f. Fysik, **23,** 187.
Allen, L. R., Anderson, B., Conway, R., Palmer, H. P., Reddish, V. C., and Ronson, B. 1962, M.N.R.A.S., **124,** 477.
Ambartsumian, V. A. 1961, Astron. J., **66,** 536.
Ambartsumian, V. A. 1966, Structure and Evolution of Galaxies (13th Solvay Congress), New York: Wiley, p. 172; Soviet Astron., **41,** no. 6.
Anderson, B., Donaldson, W., Palmer, H. P., and Ronson, B. 1965, Nature, **205,** 375.
Andrillat, Y., and Andrillat, H. 1964, Compte Rendus, **258,** 3199.
Arp, H. C. 1965, Ap. J., **142,** 402.
――― 1966a, Science, **151,** 1214.
――― 1966b, private communication, Ap. J., **148,** 321 (1967).
――― 1966c, Atlas of Peculiar Galaxies, Ap. J. Suppl., **14,** 1.
Arp, H. C., Bolton, J. G., and Kinman, T. D. 1967, Ap. J., **147,** 840.
Bahcall, J. N. 1966a, Ap. J., **145,** 684.
――― 1966b, Ap. J., **146,** 615.
Bahcall, J. N., Peterson, B. A., and Schmidt, M. 1966, Ap. J., **145,** 369.
Bahcall, J. N., and Salpeter, E. E. 1965, Ap. J., **142,** 1677.
――― 1966, Ap. J., **144,** 847.
Baker, J. G., and Menzel, D. H. 1938, Ap. J., **88,** 52.
Barber, D. R., Donaldson, W., Miley, G. K., and Smith, H. 1966, Nature, **209,** 753.
Barnes, R. C. 1966, Ap. J., **146,** 285.
Barnothy, J. M. 1965, Astron. J., **70,** 666.

—— 1966, Astron. J., **71,** 154.

Barnothy, M. F., and Barnothy, J. M. 1966, Astron. J., **71,** 155.

Bennett, A. S. 1962, Mem. R.A.S., **68,** 163.

Bolton, J. G. 1966, Nature, **211,** 917.

Bolton, J. G., Clarke, M. E., and Ekers, R. D. 1965, Austr. J. Phys., **18,** 627.

Bolton, J. G., Clarke, M. E., Sandage, A. R., and Véron, P. 1965, Ap. J., **142,** 1289.

—— 1966, Ap. J., **144,** 860.

Bolton, J. G., and Ekers, J. 1966a, Austr. J. Phys., **19,** 275.

—— 1966b, Austr. J. Phys., **19,** 471.

—— 1966c, Austr. J. Phys., **19,** 559, 713.

Bolton, J. G., Gardner, F. F., and Mackey, M. B. 1964, Austr. J. Phys., **17,** 340.

Bolton, J. G., and Kinman, T. D. 1966, Ap. J., **145,** 951.

Bolton, J. G., Shimmins, A. J., Ekers, R. D., Kinman, T. D., Lamla, E., and Wirtanen, C. A. 1966, Ap. J., **144,** 1229.

Bondi, H. 1964, Lectures on Relativity (Brandeis Summer Institute in Theoretical Physics), Englewood Cliffs: Prentice-Hall, 456.

Buchdahl, H. A. 1959, Phys. Rev., **116,** 1027.

—— 1966, Ap. J., **146,** 275.

Burbidge, E. M. 1964, Proc. Liège Symposium, Ann. d'Ap., **28,** 164.

—— 1965a, Ap. J., **142,** 1291.

—— 1965b, Ap. J., **142,** 1674.

—— 1966, Ap. J., **142,** 612.

—— 1967, Ap. J., **147,** 845.

Burbidge, E. M., and Burbidge, G. R. 1966, Ap. J., **143,** 271.

Burbidge, E. M., Burbidge, G. R., Fowler, W. A., and Hoyle, F. 1957, Rev. Mod. Phys., **29,** 547.

Burbidge, E. M., and Kinman, T. D. 1966, Ap. J., **145,** 654.

Burbidge, E. M., and Lynds, C. R. 1967, Ap. J., **147,** 388.

Burbidge, E. M., Lynds, C. R., and Burbidge, G. R. 1966, Ap. J., **144,** 447.

Burbidge, E. M., and Rosenberg, F. D. 1965, Ap. J., **142,** 1673.

Burbidge, G. R. 1956, Ap. J., **124,** 416.

—— 1959, Paris Symposium on Radio Astronomy, ed. R. N. Bracewell, Stanford University Press, p. 541.

Burbidge, G. R. 1961, Nature, **190,** 1053.

—— 1962, Ann. Rev. Nuclear Sci., **12,** 507.

—— 1967a, Ap. J., **147,** 851.

—— 1967b, Ap. J., in press.

Burbidge, G. R., and Burbidge, E. M. 1965, The Structure and Evolution of Galaxies (13th Solvay Congress), New York: Wiley, p. 137.

Burbidge, G. R., Burbidge, E. M., and Hoyle, F. 1967, Ap. J., **14,** 1219.

Burbidge, G. R., Burbidge, E. M., Hoyle, F., and Lynds, C. R. 1966, Nature, **210,** 774.

Burbidge, G. R., Burbidge, E. M., and Sandage, A. R. 1963, Rev. Mod. Phys., 35, 947.

Burbidge, G. R., and Hoyle, F. 1956, Nuovo Cimento, 4, 558

—— 1966, Scientific American, December.

Burbidge, G. R., Strittmatter, P. A., and Sargent, A. 1966, in preparation.

Cameron, A. G. W. 1962, Nature, 194, 963.

—— 1965, Nature, 207, 1140.

Chandrasekhar, S. 1964a, Phys. Rev. Lett., 12, 114, 437E.

—— 1964b, Ap. J., 140, 417.

—— 1965, Phys. Rev. Lett., 14, 241; Ap. J., 142, 1488, 1519.

Clark, B. G., and Hogg, D. E. 1966, Ap. J., 145, 21.

Clarke, M. E. 1964, M.N.R.A.S., 127, 405.

Clarke, M. E., Bolton, J. G., and Shimmins, A. J. 1966, Austr. J. Phys., 19, 375.

Cohen, M. H. 1965, Nature, 205, 277.

Cohen, M. H., Gundermann, E. J., Hardebeck, H. E., Harris, D. E., Salpeter, E. E., and Sharp, L. E. 1966, Science, 153, 744.

Cohen, M. H., Gundermann, E. J., Hardebeck, H. E., and Sharp, L. E. 1967, Ap. J., 147, 449

Colgate, S. A. 1966, preprint.

Colgate, S. A., and Cameron, A. G. W. 1963, Nature, 200, 870.

Colgate, S. A., and White, R. H. 1966, Ap. J., 143, 626.

Conway, R. G., Kellermann, K. O., and Long, R. J. 1963, M.N.R.A.S., 125, 261.

Day, G. A., Shimmins, A. J., Ekers, R. D., and Cole, D. J. 1966, Austr. J. Phys., 19, 35.

Dent, W. A. 1965, Science, 148, 1458.

—— 1966, Ap. J., 144, 843.

Dent, W. A., and Haddock, F. T. 1965, Nature, 205, 487.

—— 1966, Ap. J., 144, 568.

Dibai, E. A., and Pronik, V. I. 1964, Astron. Tsirk. No. 286.

Dibai, E. A., and Yesipov, V. F. 1967a, Astron. Zh., 44, 33.

—— 1967b, Astron. Tsirk., no. 403.

Divan, L. 1965, Ann. d'Ap., 28, 70.

Edge, D. O., Shakeshaft, J. R., McAdam, W. B., Baldwin, J. E., and Archer, S. 1959, M.N.R.A.S., 67, 37.

Ekers, R. D., and Bolton, J. G. 1965, Austr. J. Phys., 18, 669.

Ekspong, A. G., Yandagni, N. K., and Bonnevier, B. 1966, Phys. Rev. Lett., 16, E564(c).

Epstein, E. 1965, Ap. J., 142, 1282, 1285.

Epstein, E., Oliver, J. P., and Schorn, R. A. 1966, Ap. J., 145, 367.

Faulkner, J., Gunn, J. C., and Peterson, B. 1966, Nature, 211, 502.

Felten, J. E., and Morrison, P. M. 1966, Ap. J., 146, 686.

Field, G. B. 1964, Ap. J., 140, 1434.

—— 1965, Science, 150, 78.

Field, G. B., Solomon, P. M., and Wampler, E. J. 1966, Ap. J., 145, 351.

Ford, W. Kent, and Rubin, V. C. 1966, Ap. J., **145**, 357.

Fowler, W. A. 1964, Rev. Mod. Phys., **36**, 545, 1104(E).

———— 1965, Proc. Ann. Sci. Conf. Belfer Grad. School, Yeshiva University, New York: Academic Press.

———— 1966, Ap. J., **144**, 180.

Fowler, W. A., and Hoyle, F. 1965, Ap. J. Suppl., **9**, 201.

Ginzburg, V. L. 1961, Astr. Zh., **38**, 380; Soviet Astron., **5**, 282.

———— 1964, Soviet Phys. Doklady, **9**, 329.

Ginzburg, V. L., and Ozernoy, L. M. 1964, Zh. Theor. Phys., **47**, 1030; JETP **20**, 489.

———— 1966, Ap. J., **144**, 599.

Gold, T., Axford, I., and Ray, E. C. 1965, Quasi-Stellar Sources and Gravitational Collapse, Chicago: University of Chicago Press, p. 93.

Goldsmith, D. W., and Kinman, T. D. 1965, Ap. J., **142**, 1693.

Gower, J. F. R., Scott, P. F., and Wills, D. 1966, Mem. R. A. S., in press.

Greenstein, J. L., and Matthews, M. 1957, Ap. J., **126**, 14.

———— 1963, Nature, **197**, 1041.

Greenstein, J. L., and Schmidt, M. 1964, Ap. J., **140**, 1.

———— 1967, Ap. J., **148**, L 13.

Griffin, R. F. 1963, Astron. J., **68**, 421.

Gunn, J. E., and Peterson, B. A. 1965, Ap. J., **142**, 1633.

Haro, G. 1956, Bol. Obs. Tonantzintla y Tacubaya, Vol. 2, No. 14, p. 8.

Hazard, C., Gulkis, S., and Bray, A. D. 1966, Nature, **210**, 888.

———— 1967, in press.

Hazard, C., Mackey, M. B., and Nicholson, W. 1964, Nature, **202**, 227.

Hazard, C., Mackey, M. B., and Shimmins, A. J. 1963, Nature, **197**, 1037.

Heeschen, D. S. 1966, Ap. J., **146**, 517.

Hewish, A., Scott, P. F., and Wills, D. 1964, Nature, **203**, 1214.

Hiltner, W. A., Cowley, A. P., and Schild, R. E. 1966, P.A.S.P., **78**, 464.

von Hoerner, S. 1966, Ap. J., **144**, 483.

Hoyle, F., and Burbidge, G. R. 1966a, Ap. J., **144**, 534.

———— 1966b, Nature, **210**, 1346.

———— 1966c, Nature, **212**, 1334.

Hoyle, F., Burbidge, G. R., and Sargent, W. L. W. 1966, Nature, **209**, 751.

Hoyle, F., and Fowler, W. A. 1963a, M.N.R.A.S., **125**, 169.

———— 1963b, Nature, **197**, 533.

———— 1967, Nature, **213**, 373.

Hoyle, F., Fowler, W. A., Burbidge, G. R., and Burbidge, E. M. 1964, Ap. J., **139**, 909.

Hoyle, F., and Narlikar, J. V. 1964, Proc. Roy. Soc., **277**, 1; **278**, 465.

———— 1966, Proc. Roy. Soc., **290**, 143, 162.

Hoyle, F., Narlikar, J. V., and Wheeler, J. A. 1964, Nature, **203**, 914.

Humason, M. L., Mayall, N. U., and Sandage, A. R. 1956, Astron. J., **61**, 97, Appendix B.

Humason, M. L., and Zwicky, F. 1947, Ap. J., **105,** 85.
Jeffreys, W. H. 1964, Astron. J., **69,** 255.
Johnson, H. L. 1964, Ap. J., **139,** 1022.
Johnson, H. L., and Low, F. E. 1965, Ap. J., **141,** 336.
de Jong, M. 1965, Ap. J., **142,** 1333.
———— 1966, Ap. J., **144,** 553.
Kafka, P. 1967, Nature, **213,** 346.
Kardashev, N. S. 1964, Astr. Zh., **41,** 807; Soviet Astron., **8,** 643.
———— 1966, Proceedings of the Byurakan Conference.
Kardashev, N. S., and Komberg, B. V. 1966, Astr. Tsirk. No. 357.
Kellermann, K., and Pauliny-Toth, I. K. 1966, Ap. J., **146,** 621.
Kinman, T. D. 1965, Ap. J., **142,** 1241.
———— 1966, Ap. J., **144,** 1232.
Kinman, T. D., Bolton, J. G., Clarke, R. W., and Sandage, A. R. 1967, Ap. J.,
    147, 848.
Kinman, T. D., and Burbidge, E. M. 1967, Ap. J., **148,** May.
Kinman, T. D., Lamla, E., and Wirtanen, C. A. 1966, Ap. J., **146,** 964.
Koehler, C., and Robinson, B. J. 1966, Ap. J., **146,** 488.
Layzer, D. 1965, Ap. J., **141,** 837.
LeRoux, E. 1961, Ann. d'Ap., **24,** 71.
Longair, M. S. 1965, M.N.R.A.S., **129,** 419.
———— 1966, Nature, **211,** 949.
Low, F. E. 1965, Ap. J., **142,** 1287.
Luyten, W. J. 1963, Pub. Obs. Minn., **3,** No. 13.
Luyten, W. J., and Smith, J. A. 1966, Ap. J., **145,** 366
Lynds, C. R. 1965, private communication.
———— 1967a, Ap. J., **147,** 396.
———— 1967b, Ap. J., **147,** 837.
Lynds, C. R., Hill, S. J., Heere, K., and Stockton, A. N. 1966, Ap. J., **144,** 1244.
Lynds, C. R., and Stockton, A. N. 1966, Ap. J., **144,** 446.
Lynds, C. R., Stockton, A. N., and Livingston, W. L. 1965, Ap. J., **142,** 1667.
Lynds, C. R., and Villere, G. 1965, Ap. J., **142,** 1296.
Maltby, P., Matthews, T. A., and Moffet, A. T. 1963, Ap. J., **137,** 153.
Maltby, P., and Moffet, A. T. 1962, Ap J. Supp., **7,** 141.
———— 1965a, Ap. J., **142,** 409.
———— 1965b, Science, October 1, p. 63.
Matthews, T. A., Morgan, W. W., and Schmidt, M. 1964, Ap. J., **140,** 35.
Matthews, T. A., and Sandage, A. R. 1963, Ap. J., **138,** 30.
McCrea, W. H. 1964, M. N. R. A. S., **128,** 336.
———— 1966, P. A. S. P., **78,** 49; Ap. J., **144,** 516.
McVittie, G. C. 1965, Ap. J., **142,** 1637.
Mills, B. Y., Slee, O. B., and Hill, E. 1958, Austr. J. Phys., **11,** 360.
Moffet, A. T. 1964, Science, **146,** 764.
———— 1965, Ap. J., **141.** 1580.

———— 1966, Ann. Rev. Astron. and Astrophys., **4,** 145.

Münch, G. 1948, Ap. J., **108,** 116.

* Ne'eman, Y. 1965, Ap. J., **141,** 1303.

Noerdlinger, P. 1966, Ap. J., **143,** 1004.

Noerdlinger, P., Jokipii, J., and Woltjer, L. 1966, Ap. J., **146,** 523.

Novikov, I. D. 1965, reported by V. A. Ambartsumian in Structure and Evolution of Galaxies (13th Solvay Congress), p. 172; JETP, March 1966; also Soviet Astronomy, **41,** No. 6, 1964.

Oke, J. B. 1963, Nature, **197,** 1040.

———— 1965, Ap. J., **141,** 6.

———— 1966, Ap. J., **145,** 668.

Oppenheimer, J. R. 1966, Pub. del Comitato Nazionale per le Manifestazioni Celebrative del IV Centenario della Nascita di Galileo Galilei Vol. 2, Tomo 3, (Firenze, G. Barbèra, Editore) p. 102.

Osterbrock, D. E. 1963, J. Planet. Space Sci., **11,** 621.

Osterbrock, D. E., and Parker, R. A. R. 1965, Ap. J., **141,** 892.

———— 1966, Ap. J., **143,** 268.

Ozernoy, L. M. 1966a, Astr. J. U.S.S.R., **43,** 300.

———— 1966b, Soviet Phys. Doklady, **10,** 581.

Pacholczyk, A. G., and Wisniewski, W. Z. 1967, Ap. J., **147,** 394.

Pacini, F. 1966, Nature, **209,** 389.

Palmer, H. P., Rowson, B., Anderson, B., Donaldson, W., Miley, G. K., Gent, H., Adgie, R. L., Slee, O. B., and Crowther, J. H. 1967, Nature, **213,** 789.

Pauliny-Toth, I. I. K., Wade, C. M., and Heeschen, D. S. 1966, Ap. J. Suppl., **13,** 65.

Pengelly, R. M. 1964, M.N.R.A.S., **127,** 145.

Penston, M. V., and Robinson, G. M. R. 1967, Nature, **213,** 375.

Piddington, J. H. 1964, M.N.R.A.S., **128,** 345.

———— 1966, M. N. R. A. S., **133,** 163.

Pilkington, J. D. H., and Scott, P. F. 1965, Mem. R. A. S., **69,** 183.

Price, R. M., and Milne, D. K. 1965, Austr. J. Phys., **18,** 329.

Read, R. B. 1963, Ap. J., **138,** 1.

Rees, M. J. 1966, Nature, **211,** 468.

Rees, M., and Sciama, D. W. 1965a, Nature, **208,** 371.

———— 1965b, Nature, **207,** 740.

———— 1966, Ap. J., **145,** 6.

———— 1967, Nature, **213,** 374.

Roeder, R. C., and Mitchell, G. F. 1966, Nature, **212,** 165.

Roxburgh, I. 1965, Nature, **207,** 363.

Ryle, M., and Neville, A. 1963, M.N.R.A.S., **125,** 9.

Ryle, M., and Sandage, A. R. 1964, Ap. J., **139,** 419.

Ryle, M., and Scheuer, P. A. G. 1955, Proc. Roy. Soc. A, **230,** 448.

Sandage, A. R. 1961, Ap. J., **133,** 355.

———— 1964, Ap. J., **139,** 416.

————— 1965, Ap. J., **141**, 1560.
————— 1966a, Ap. J., **146**, 13.
————— 1966b, IAU Circ. No. 1961.
————— 1966c, Ap. J., **144**, 1234.
————— 1966d, Pub. del Comitato Nazionale per le Manifestazioni Celebrative del IV Centenario della Nascita di Galileo Galilei Vol. 2, Tomo 3 (Firenze, G. Barbèra, Editore) p. 104.
————— 1966e, High-Energy Astrophysics (Varenna Lectures) New York: Academic Press, p. 25.
Sandage, A. R., and Luyten, W. 1967, Ap. J., in press.
Sandage, A. R., and Miller, W. C. 1966, Ap. J., **144**, 1240.
Sandage, A. R., and Véron, P. 1965, Ap. J., **142**, 412.
Sandage, A. R., Véron, P., and Wyndham, J. D. 1965, Ap. J., **142**, 1306.
Sandage, A. R., Westphal, J. A., and Strittmatter, P. A. 1966, Ap. J., **146**, 322.
Sandage, A. R., and Wyndham, J. D. 1965, Ap. J., **141**, 328.
Saslaw, W. C. 1966, Nature, **211**, 729.
Scheuer, P. A. G. 1965, Nature, **207**, 963.
Scheuer, P. A. G., and Wills, D. 1966, Ap. J., **143**, 274.
Schmidt, M. 1963, Nature, **197**, 1040.
————— 1964, paper read at Second Texas Conference on Relativistic Astrophysics, Austin, December 1964.
————— 1965, Ap. J., **141**, 1295.
————— 1966, Ap. J., **144**, 443.
Schmidt, M., and Matthews, T. 1964, Ap. J., **139**, 781.
Sciama, D. W. 1963, M.N.R.A.S., **126**, 195.
————— 1965, Science Progress, **53**, 1.
Sciama, D. W., and Rees, M. J. 1966a, Nature, **211**, 1283.
————— 1966b, Nature, **212**, 1001.
Sciama, D. W., and Saslaw, W. C. 1966, Nature, **210**, 348.
Scott, P. F., and Ryle, M. 1961, M.N.R.A.S., **122**, 381.
Seaton, M. J. 1954, M. N. R. A. S., **114**, 154.
Seaton, M. J., and Osterbrock, D. E. 1957, Ap. J., **125**, 66.
Setti, G., and Woltjer, L. 1966, Ap. J., **144**, 838.
Sharov, A. S., and Efremov, Y. U. 1963, Int. Bull. on Var. Stars, No. 23, Com. 27, IAU.
Shklovsky, I. S. 1961, Astr. Zh., **37**, 945; Soviet Astron., **4**, 885.
————— 1964, Astr. Zh., **41**, 801; Soviet Astron., **8**, 638, 1965; 1964, Astron. Circ. No. 303.
————— 1965, Astr. Zh., **42**, 893.
————— 1966, Proceedings of Byurakan Symposium.
Sholomitsky, G. B. 1965, Int. Bull. Var. Stars, Com. 27, IAU, No. 83.
Slish, V. I. 1963, Nature, **199**, 682.
Smith, H. J., and Hoffleit, D. 1961, A. S. P., **73**, 292.
————— 1963, Nature, **198**, 650; Smith, Dallas Symp. volume, p. 227.

Spitzer, L., and Saslaw, W. C. 1966, Ap. J., **143**, 400.

Stein, W. 1967, Ap. J., in press.

Stockton, A. N., and Lynds, C. R. 1966, Ap. J., **144**, 451.

Stothers, R. 1966, M. N. R. A. S., **132**, 217.

Strittmatter, P. A. 1966, unpublished.

Strittmatter, P. A., and Burbidge, G. R. 1967, Ap. J., **143**, 13.

Strittmatter, P. A., Faulkner, J., and Walmsley, M. 1966, Nature, **212**, 1441.

Sturrock, P. A. 1965, Nature, **208**, 861.

——— 1966, Nature, **211**, 697.

Terrell, J. 1964, Science, **145**, 918.

——— 1967, Ap. J., **147**, 827.

Tooper, R. F. 1966, Ap. J., **143**, 465.

Ulam, S. M., and Walden, W. E. 1964, Nature, **201**, 1202.

Van den Bergh, S. 1966, Ap. J., **144**, 866.

Véron, P. 1966, Nature, **211**, 724; Ann. d'Ap., **29**, 231.

Wade, C. M. 1966, Phys. Rev. Letters, **17**, 1061.

Wagoner, R. V. 1965, Phys. Rev. Lett., **16**, V503(c).

Wagoner, R. V. (1967a), Nature, **214**, 766.

——— (1967b), preprint.

Wampler, E. J. 1967, Ap. J., **147**, 1.

Wampler, E. J., and Oke, J. B., 1967, Ap. J., in press.

Williams, I. P. 1965, Phys. Letters, **14**, 19.

Williams, P. J. S. 1963, Nature, **200**, 56.

——— 1966, Nature, **210**, 285.

Wills, D. 1966, Observatory, **86**, 245.

Woltjer, L. 1964, Nature, **201**, 807.

——— 1966a, Structure and Evolution of Galaxies (13th Solvay Congress), New York: Wiley, p. 30.

——— 1966b, Ap. J., **146**, 597.

——— 1967, paper read at Third Texas Conf. on relativistic Astrophysics, New York, January

Wyndham, J. D. 1965, Astron. J., **70**, 384.

——— 1966a, Ap. J., **144**, 459.

——— 1966b, preprint.

Zapolsky, H. S. 1966, Science, **153**, 635.

Zeldovich, Ya. B., Okun, L., and Pikelner, S. B. 1965, Phys. Letters, **17**, 164.

Zwicky, F. 1965, Ap. J., **142**, 1293.

NAME INDEX

SUBJECT INDEX